DK Illustrated Dictionary of
Religion

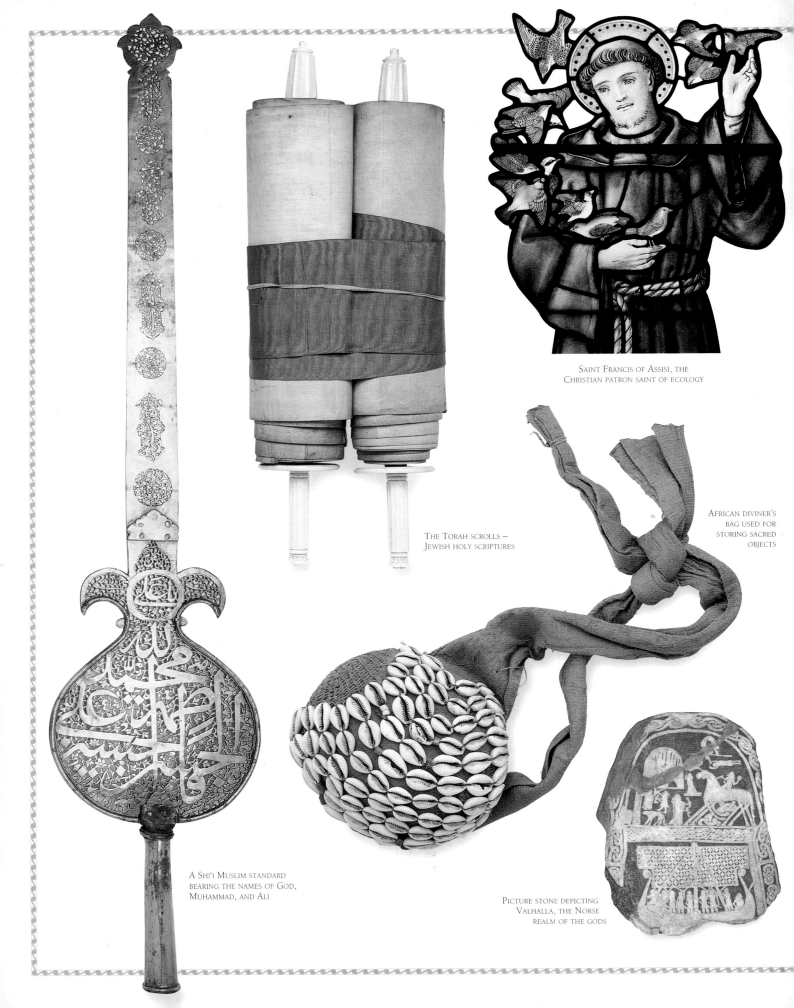

SAINT FRANCIS OF ASSISI, THE
CHRISTIAN PATRON SAINT OF ECOLOGY

THE TORAH SCROLLS —
JEWISH HOLY SCRIPTURES

AFRICAN DIVINER'S
BAG USED FOR
STORING SACRED
OBJECTS

A SHI'I MUSLIM STANDARD
BEARING THE NAMES OF GOD,
MUHAMMAD, AND ALI

PICTURE STONE DEPICTING
VALHALLA, THE NORSE
REALM OF THE GODS

DK Illustrated Dictionary of
Religion

Rituals, beliefs, and practices
from around the world

Sikh prayer beads

Written by Philip Wilkinson
Consultants: Department of Theology and Religious Studies,
Roehampton Institute, London

LONDON • NEW YORK • MUNICH • MELBOURNE • DELHI
www.dk.com

BISHOP'S MITRE

A DORLING KINDERSLEY BOOK

CONSULTANTS (DEPARTMENT OF THEOLOGY AND
RELIGIOUS STUDIES, ROEHAMPTON INSTITUTE, LONDON)
Dr Simonetta Calderini, Mr David Hill, Dr John Jarick,
Mr Brook Pearson, Professor Stanley Porter,
Dr Yvonne Sherwood, Mr Nick Swann,
Dr Lynn Thomas, Mr David Tombs

FROM BATH SPA UNIVERSITY COLLEGE
Dr Brian Bocking, Denise Cush

FROM THE UNIVERSITY OF READING
Dr Stephen Hunt, Nikki Lightly

Produced for Dorling Kindersley by
PAGEOne, Cairn House, Elgiva Lane, Chesham,
Buckinghamshire HP5 2JD

EDITORIAL DIRECTOR Helen Parker
ART DIRECTOR Bob Gordon
EDITORS Michael Spilling, Sophie Williams, Marion Dent
DESIGNER Suzanne Tuhrim

FOR DORLING KINDERSLEY
MANAGING EDITOR Jayne Parsons
MANAGING ART EDITOR Gill Shaw
DTP DESIGNER Nomazwe Madonko
PRODUCTION Josie Alabaster
PICTURE RESEARCH Amanda Russell, Frances Vargo
DK PICTURE LIBRARY Sally Hamilton
JACKET DESIGN Dean Price

First American edition, 1999
First American paperback edition, 2006
06 07 08 09 9 8 7 6

DK Publishing, Inc.
375 Hudson Street
New York, NY 10014

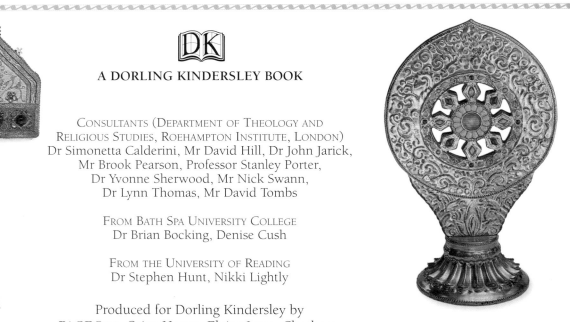

THE EIGHT-SPOKED WHEEL IS A SYMBOL
OF THE BUDDHIST EIGHTFOLD PATH

ANCIENT EGYPTIAN
CHILD PRIEST

MUSLIM PRAYER MAT WITH COMPASS,
SHOWING THE WAY TO MECCA

ISBN: 0-7566-2018-X

Colour reproduction by Colourscan. Singapore
Printed and bound in Hong Kong

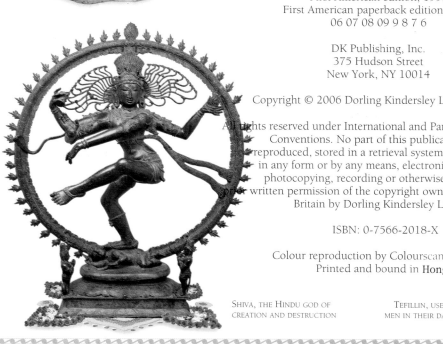

SHIVA, THE HINDU GOD OF
CREATION AND DESTRUCTION

TEFILLIN, USED BY JEWISH
MEN IN THEIR DAILY PRAYERS

CONTENTS

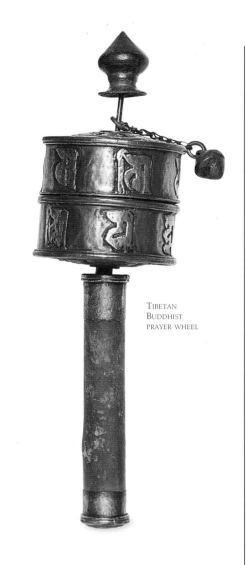

TIBETAN
BUDDHIST
PRAYER WHEEL

INTRODUCTION

Religion influences nearly everything in our daily lives, from buildings, the foods we eat, and the books we read to the rituals of marriage and death, and the customs of courtroom and government — it shapes our beliefs, moral codes, and national identities. Both individuals and nations describe themselves in religious terms — Hindu or Muslim, Shinto or Buddhist, Christian or Jew.

VARIETY AND UNITY

Every religion is different, with its own beliefs and rituals, art, dress and festivals. However, it is also surprising how many of the myths, deities, and moral codes from different parts of the world show striking resemblances. This book explores these diverse patterns in the faiths of the world. It examines the great global faiths, religions that have a large following, generally spread all over the world. It also looks at ancient belief systems as well as religions with a smaller, or more localized membership, and some of the religious movements of recent centuries.

JAPANESE CHILD CELEBRATING
RELIGIOUS FESTIVAL

PRESENT TO FUTURE

It seems that people will always find ways of adapting their beliefs to modern life. Religion provides people with hope for the future, and comforts them in times of despair. It is also a focus for charitable work, a source of inspiration for art, and a social center to many. Religious conflict worldwide has caused pain and death, but religion has also been the basis for many peace movements.

WHAT IS RELIGION?

A religion is a set of beliefs and practices, often associated with a supernatural power that shapes or directs human life and death, or a commitment to ideas that provide coherence for one's existence. Adherence to a religion implies a belief in a divine force, as well as offering moral guidance for believers. Religions also bind people into communities with common goals and values. There are many religions in the world. Some are practiced within specific geographical areas, but five – Hinduism, Buddhism, Judaism, Christianity, and Islam – have spread throughout the world and have millions of followers.

THE ORIGINS OF RELIGION

People have always asked difficult questions about the nature of life and the universe. How did the world begin? Can we explain good and evil? What happens to us when we die? Religion may have begun as one of the ways of answering some of these questions. Some religions, such as Hinduism, are founded on ancient myths that tell of powerful creator gods and forces of destruction. Early humankind worshiped these gods in an attempt to win their favor, because they believed gods controlled the forces of nature. Other religions, such as Christianity, Islam, and Buddhism, developed because of the work of important spiritual leaders or prophets. Jesus, Muhammad, the Buddha, and the Jewish prophets of the Bible were all spiritual leaders who, in their different ways, inspired their followers and stimulated the spread of religious movements that are still alive today.

BELIEF IN GODS?

Most religions are founded on a belief in one or several gods and goddesses. Judaism, Christianity, and Islam are known as monotheistic religions, because they believe in and worship a single, all-powerful, creator God. Interestingly, these religions all developed in the Middle East and share many rituals, festivals, narratives, and myths. For example, the Hebrew Bible became a major part of the Christian Bible, while Jesus, the founder of Christianity, is also considered a prophet by Muslims. Several religions are polytheistic, believing in many gods, whereby each god controls one aspect of nature or human activity. Gods who are closely linked to human life are often the most popular, with deities of fertility, agriculture, and hunting regularly worshiped. While Hinduism can also be described as a polytheistic faith, the hundreds of Hindu gods and goddesses are said to be aspects of one absolute force, known as Brahman. Some religions are non-theistic and do not believe in gods. Buddhism and Jainism, for example, do not include a belief in a supreme creator or god. Buddhists follow the Buddha, whom they regard as a teacher rather than a deity, while Jains follow spiritual teachers called Tirthankaras.

The Hindu god Vishnu is portrayed here as a unifying entity that contains all the forces in the universe, including the other Hindu gods.

Christians believe that Jesus of Nazareth was the Son of God, whereas Muslims see him as one of a number of prophets.

RELIGIOUS COMMITMENT

Religion is practiced in almost every human community. Even in places where a specific religion has been banned, people have continued to worship secretly, often at great personal risk. Why should this be? Religion offers people a meaning in life beyond mundane reality, providing transcendent explanations for life's more mysterious occurrences. People who are not spiritual sometimes see religion as an illusory escapism from reality, a way of turning one's back on a dismal world. But religious people are likely to reply that it is a way of explaining the wonder of existence in a manner that science cannot. Religions offer their followers ways toward understanding the vastness and complexity of the universe. Importantly, religion also creates a sense of belonging to a wider community with shared beliefs. Religion can provide social organization and moral guidance, reinforcing social stability and security. Organized religion provides ways of marking the key stages in life, including birth, marriage, and death.

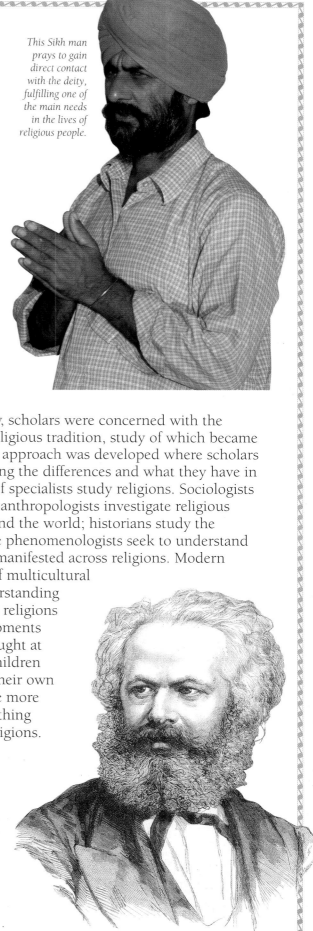

This Sikh man prays to gain direct contact with the deity, fulfilling one of the main needs in the lives of religious people.

STUDYING RELIGION

For thousands of years, people have studied religion, discussing the ideas of prophets and religious leaders and writing down their interpretations. Initially, scholars were concerned with the religious beliefs and practices of their own religious tradition, study of which became known as theology. Later, a more comparative approach was developed where scholars began to study the world's religions, noting the differences and what they have in common. Today, many different types of specialists study religions. Sociologists research the role of religion in society; anthropologists investigate religious practices, rituals, and behaviour around the world; historians study the influence of religion on events; while phenomenologists seek to understand the symbols, doctrines, and rituals manifested across religions. Modern communications and the growth of multicultural societies have led to greater understanding among academics of the world's religions than ever before. These developments influence the way religion is taught at school. Whereas in the past, children would only study their own faith, today they are more likely to learn something about a variety of religions.

The 19th-century German political thinker Karl Marx saw religion as a way of disguising the causes of human misery. Marx said: "Religion is the sigh of the oppressed creature, the heart of a heartless world, the spirit of unspiritual conditions. It is the opium of the people."

MYTH AND DOCTRINE

The diverse religions of the world share one key feature. They all aim toward a spiritual goal, whether this be union with a supreme God or gods, or the realization of a higher spiritual state (such as the Buddhist striving for nirvana). However, approaches vary enormously. In most religions, a body of ideas and teachings called doctrines has been assembled. Doctrines often reflect basic notions about creation, the universe, God (or gods), and human conduct. Often illustrated by myths and narratives, they embrace key issues of belief and practice, influencing behavior and religious laws and ethics.

This Native American kachina doll represents the spirit of a dead person who can act as a messenger between humans and the gods.

NARRATIVES IN COMMON

Most religions preserve tales and myths that encapsulate their most basic beliefs. While some of these have been passed on orally, in many faiths they have been written down in sacred texts. Some texts – such as the Qur'an for Muslims and Bible for Jews – are regarded as revelations and are considered to be the word of God. Many religions share creation myths in which a creator god brings the earth and heavens into being, and, in many versions, creates the first man and woman. Other religions, such as Buddhism, have no such myths. Certain themes and stories also recur, such as the tale of the great flood, which is mentioned in the *Epic of Gilgamesh,* an ancient Mesopotamian text – the oldest of all written narratives. In the Hebrew Bible it is the story of Noah. Another common theme is the idea that a messiah, savior, or prophet will return to announce a new religious age. Many Christians look forward to the second coming of Jesus; Hinduism contains the notion of a forthcoming avatar of the god Vishnu; and many Muslims speak of al-Mahdi, the hidden Imam who will appear at the end of time. These beliefs illustrate how religions, however different in doctrine, often share notions about the origin of the universe (cosmogony) and expectations for the future (eschatology).

Many cultures have flood stories, from Native American and ancient Mesopotamian myths to the story of Noah in the Hebrew Bible. Noah preserved a male and female of each animal species on his ark.

The medieval Christian view of hell as a place of torment for the damned is vividly portrayed in this 12th-century French manuscript illustration. Many modern Christians believe in hell, but interpret it as a state of absence of God rather than a place of physical torture.

REWARD AND PUNISHMENT

Religion tries to make sense of the universe and the human condition, providing accounts of time, human nature, and human destiny. Many faiths have formulated the idea of heaven, a place where God or gods dwell, and where the souls of the faithful go after death. In religions that postulate a heaven, there may also be a hell or underworld – a place of torment or a state of absence – to which the souls of the unworthy are consigned. Christianity, Islam, and Judaism see evil as a fall from grace – the fall of Satan, originally an angel, is mirrored by that of Adam, the first man. Other faiths see evil as the result of the activities of spirits or, as in Zoroastrianism, the outcome of conflicts between opposing deities. Alternatively, the soul may attain a state of perfection. In Hinduism and Buddhism, believers aim to reach a state in which they are freed from the repeating cycle of death and rebirth. Such beliefs provide motivation for people to live a religious and moral life.

ETHICS AND LAW

Believers aim to follow their faith's moral code, or ethics, as closely as possible. Apart from including instructions about religious observance and ritual, religions teach people to respect each other and help those in need. Moral codes have inspired organizations such as the Christian Red Cross, Muslim Red Crescent, and Habitat for Humanity. While charity is important to many believers, not doing harm to others is at the heart of the Jain belief system. Many religions inform every aspect of daily life, from laws regarding marriage and divorce to the details of choice and preparation of food and the way children are raised and educated. Shari'a (Islamic law) provides a legal foundation for every aspect of life from diet to marriage to economics and politics, while for Buddhists, the dharma (teachings of the Buddha) offers guidance on how to live a religious life.

This Hindu lives the life of an ascetic.

For Buddhists, helping others also brings merit to the helper; this man – who is giving alms to a group of Buddhist monks – is also improving his own chances of a favorable rebirth.

EMOTIONAL DIMENSIONS

Faiths such as Jainism and Buddhism encourage their followers to explore their inner consciousness, hoping eventually to reach beyond the self to a state of enlightened being. Other religions, such as Judaism and Christianity, emphasize the worshiper's relationship with, or experience of, God. Some people dedicate their lives to their faith by becoming monks or ascetics in the hope of gaining a direct experience of God. Such dedication is often accompanied by a very intense religious experience. Ascetic practice, extended prayer, or the prolonged chanting of mantras can lead to mystical experiences, divine visitations, encounters with saints and spirits, or in the case of Jains and Buddhists, glimpses of a higher state of consciousness.

SACRED PLACES AND RITUAL

An Orthodox Jewish man prays at the Western Wall, Jerusalem, one of the most sacred places in Judaism.

Worship – most often an expression of devotion to a deity or religious teacher – lies at the heart of most religions. Offerings and sacrifices, singing and chanting, preaching a sermon, or reading from a sacred text are all forms of worship. Prayer may also form part of worship. Prayers can range from the expression of devotion to God, asking for guidance or favors from a deity, to chanting in order to achieve a state of higher spiritual consciousness. In most religions, acts of worship and prayer can take place in public – in a temple, church, or other sacred place, or in private – for example, at a home shrine. In either case, the faithful observe the correct forms, often adopting a special posture, or carrying out rituals before they pray or begin to worship. These rituals may be designed to purify the worshiper in preparation, or to help them to concentrate on the act of worship.

Mountains are believed to be sacred. Mount Fuji, Japan's highest mountain, has been sacred for thousands of years. It has many shrines to which followers of Shinto make numerous pilgrimages in honor of Sengen-Sama, the goddess of the rising sun.

SACRED PLACES

Sacred places can be sites of worship and pilgrimage. For Muslims, Mecca is a sacred city that is linked to the founding and development of Islam. Other places, such as the Roman Catholic shrine at Lourdes in France, are the site of miraculous healings. Many places, such as the Ganges River in India, play a key role in ancient Hindu myth.

RELIGIOUS INSTITUTIONS

Some religions have a highly organized formal structure. Often, this includes a hierarchy of leadership through which instructions are passed down. This is seen clearly in Roman Catholic Christianity, with its Pope, bishops, and priests; other faiths, such as Shi'a Islam, have similar institutions. Even when there is not such a clear hierarchy, there may still be leaders – such as elders or senior priests – who provide guidance on everything from ritual to daily conduct. Organized religion is essentially social. Institutions enable people to worship together, creating groups to cater to special interests and needs, and helping foster shared values, beliefs, and a sense of community.

RITUAL

All religions involve ritual – repeated, ceremonial actions that are always carried out in a set way. Virtually all religious events, from regular worship to once-in-a-lifetime pilgrimages, include some kind of ritual. Ritual usually involves some specific bodily action, such as kneeling in prayer, walking around a temple, anointing the statue of a god, performing a dance, or sitting in a special position while meditating. The most familiar types of ritual, such as prayer, are linked to regular forms of worship, often on set days such as Saturdays for Jews and Fridays for Muslims. Rituals of worship generally take place in a religious building, and are led by an official such as a rabbi or imam. Rites of passage mark periods of transition at key stages in life. Such rites are held soon after birth, at puberty or when the person becomes a member of the religion, at marriage, and after death. Festival rituals are held at important points in the religious calendar. They may occur on dates associated with the faith's founder, prophets, and other key figures. Other types of ritual – especially important in primal religions – include healing ceremonies, rites that bring protection for the individual and community, exorcisms, and rituals that help the holy man see into the future.

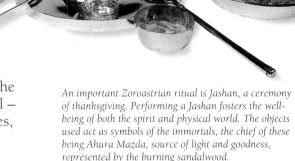

An important Zoroastrian ritual is Jashan, a ceremony of thanksgiving. Performing a Jashan fosters the well-being of both the spirit and physical world. The objects used act as symbols of the immortals, the chief of these being Ahura Mazda, source of light and goodness, represented by the burning sandalwood.

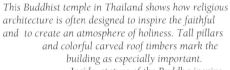
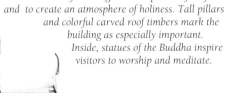

This Buddhist temple in Thailand shows how religious architecture is often designed to inspire the faithful and to create an atmosphere of holiness. Tall pillars and colorful carved roof timbers mark the building as especially important. Inside, statues of the Buddha inspire visitors to worship and meditate.

SACRED OBJECTS AND ICONS

Items that are regularly used for worship soon gain a sacred quality of their own. In many faiths, the highest skills and the most precious materials are used to make objects used in sacred ceremonies, ranging from chalices to synagogue and temple decorations. The vessels used in rituals might be made of silver or gold. Such rich decoration is designed to inspire worshipers in their devotion. Religious buildings, whether Christian cathedrals or Hindu temples, are adorned with beautiful carvings. However, in some religions – such as Islam and Protestant Christianity – there has been a reaction against excessive ornamentation, which is thought to distract the faithful from the recipient of devotion.

Icons – small paintings of Jesus or one of the saints – are used as a focus for devotion and prayer. Icons like this Black Madonna from the Roman Catholic monastery of Jasra Gora, Poland, are said to act as channels for the blessing of God.

RELIGION AND SOCIETY

Religion explores the human relationship with the divine and helps deal with the mysteries of death. Consequently, religion remains an essential part of the fabric of human culture. Religion has also provided inspiration for some of the world's great art. Grand cathedrals and Buddhist stupas, Orthodox Christian icons, Islamic calligraphy, and Greek statues – the impact of religion is all around us, in our streets and on the walls of our art galleries. Religion influences every aspect of human society from social institutions and politics to music and food. Few other forces have played such a significant role in human development.

CLASSIFICATION OF RELIGION

Many religions can be classified according to the part of the world in which they originated. Indian religions, including Hinduism, Buddhism, and Jainism, share the idea that existence consists of a continuous cycle of birth, death, and rebirth, from which the religious person tries to break free. Chinese and Japanese religions share a common belief in revering the spirits of dead ancestors. Among the major monotheistic religions – Judaism, Christianity, and Islam – a belief in one God, the concept of revelation and the role played in it by prophets, and sacred texts are characteristics in common. The primal religions of the world believe that spirits inhabit many aspects of nature and use religious rituals for such functions as promoting fertility.

Deities of farming and fertility, such as the African goddess Orisha Oko, are prominent in primal religions.

Before the invention of printing, manuscripts of sacred texts, like this eighth-century page from the Gospel of St. Matthew, were precious. Meticulous copying of scriptures as an act of devotion was very popular amongst Muslims, Jews, and Christians. Even today's printed texts are regarded with special respect and reverence by their users.

LEVELS OF RELIGION

Religious belief and activity can be practiced on a number of levels. A person may say daily prayers, meditate, or perform regular acts of worship alone, allowing space for the individual's experience of the holy. However, for many people, religious practice is a social activity shared with the family, tribe, or local congregation. These gatherings – and the religious activities that sustain them – allow people to support each other, explore their faith, and celebrate special times together. On a much larger scale, religion can be practiced on a national level. This often includes official scriptures and national celebrations, where an entire people identifies with a particular faith.

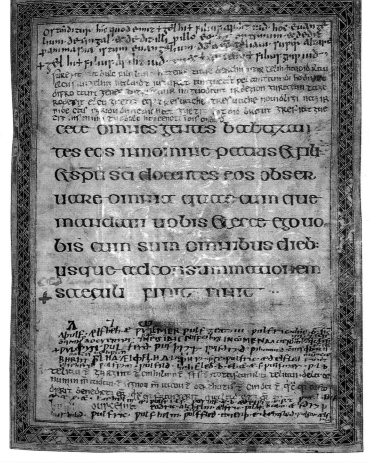

The Crusades were a series of wars during the Middle Ages in which Christian soldiers fought against other faiths. The wars were authorized by the Pope, initially in order to gain control of the holy city of Jerusalem.

RELIGION AND CONFLICT

When a religion is identified closely with a nation or group, conflicts can sometimes arise. Religious intolerance, often mixed with political and territorial issues, has been the cause of many conflicts throughout history. This can take the form of persecution, where followers of one faith are punished for belonging to a different religion from the dominant group. Religious conflicts can escalate into full-scale wars. Misguided missionary zeal – where one group believes its idea is an absolute for all others – has often led to forced conversions, conquests, and bloodshed.

The Dalai Lama, Tenzin Gyatso, regards compassion as Buddhism's highest ideal. In 1989 he won the Nobel Peace Prize.

PEACEMAKING

Although religion is often blamed for causing conflicts, most sacred texts, and most religious leaders and their followers, teach the value of understanding, compassion, and respect for others. With the right leadership, religion can foster understanding and help resolve differences. There have been a number of examples in recent history of religious leaders who have used their faith to increase understanding and tolerance. Archbishop Desmond Tutu was one of the most ardent campaigners against the racist apartheid system in South Africa. The Dalai Lama, exiled from his native Tibet, leads Tibetans by the example of his compassion. Many other less famous people work for peace in the world's trouble spots and contribute to the work of charities and aid agencies in healing the damage caused by war. Although they are not famous as individuals, their example shows how religion can make a real difference – in people's everyday existence as well as in their spiritual lives.

GLOBAL RELIGION

The media often report a decline in religious belief and observance, especially in developed countries. Western society is said to be increasingly secular and dominated by material values. Despite this trend in the West, many Christian churches report increased attendance, and faiths such as Islam and Buddhism are expanding. Religious devotion is an implicit part of many people's feelings about topics not normally associated with religion, from sport to political ideologies and popular icons like Elvis Presley and Princess Diana. People still look beyond modern science to explain the human condition and humanity's place in the universe, seeking religious solutions to spiritual problems.

Despite differences, most religions strive for a world in which people of every faith will be able to live side by side in peace and mutual respect.

ANCIENT RELIGIONS

We know much about ancient religion from the early civilizations of the Mediterranean and Middle East, and from the Norse and Celtic cultures of northern Europe. All of these peoples worshiped many gods, most of whom controlled a particular part of the universe, such as the moon, stars, oceans, or mountains, or an area of human life, such as love, war, or farming.

GODS AND GODDESSES

Most ancient peoples worshiped their gods because they needed reliability and feared chaos. They sacrificed to the corn goddess to make the crops grow, or worshiped the god of war so that they would be successful in battle. Praying to specific gods gave other benefits. For instance, priests of the star and moon deities in ancient Mesopotamia became the first astronomers and mathematicians when they figured out the moon's phases and the movements of the stars.

AFTERLIFE

Early religions showed people how to cope with death. Many of the ancient faiths taught that people were judged on their earthly deeds and that this judgment affected their place in the next world. The Egyptians took this concept furthest, mummifying the bodies of their deceased and developing an elaborate cult of the dead.

EGYPTIAN MUMMY

ANCIENT EGYPT

EGYPTIAN CIVILIZATION LASTED from *c*.3000 BCE to the first century BCE. Over this long period, the people developed a complex religion, with many different gods. This began with the idea that every living thing had a spirit, so gods often developed as deified versions of local features. As a result, certain gods were associated with particular places. In Memphis, Ptah was said to be the creator, but in Heliopolis Ra-Atum was the supreme god. Over time, some deities gained national importance. For example, the rulers of the underworld, Isis and Osiris, and the sun god, took many forms and influenced every aspect of Egyptian life.

EXTENT OF ANCIENT EGYPTIAN CIVILIZATION

ANCIENT EGYPT
The ancient Egyptians settled along the banks of the **Nile** River, from the delta (Lower Egypt) to modern Aswan in the south (Upper Egypt). The river provided water for irrigation, and the fertile black mud created during floods helped grow plentiful crops.

THE NILE
Egyptian life was dictated by the Nile, the main water source. The god of the Nile flood was Hapy, called "Master of the river bringing vegetation," a reference to the fertile Nile mud. Portrayed as a human figure with aquatic plants on his head, Hapy had large breasts and a fat belly, both symbols of fertility. No temples were dedicated to him.

CREATION
According to one myth, the creator of the world was the sun god Ra-Atum. The priests of Heliopolis told how Ra-Atum emerged from the chaos and gave himself human shape. He then sneezed into the space around him, and from this action he created the air god Shu and the moisture goddess Tefnut, the ancestors of the other gods.

Scarab, symbol of the rising sun

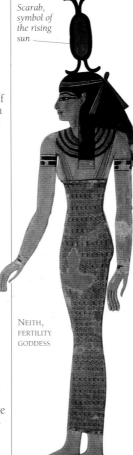

NEITH, FERTILITY GODDESS

ANIMAL GODS
Many Egyptian gods took the form of animals. There was a huge variety – from the gentle cow goddess Hathor, who protected women in childbirth, to fearsome deities like the crocodile god Sobek, a source of the **pharaoh**'s power, and the scorpion goddess Serket, repeller of evil. Even the sun god could take animal form, either as the scarab beetle Khepri or the hawk Ra-Harakhty. One of the most popular animal deities was Bastet, the goddess of childbirth and sexual love, often portrayed as a cat.

Bastet was first portrayed as a lioness, but later as a cat.

BASTET, GODDESS OF CHILDBIRTH AND SEXUAL LOVE

FERTILITY AND LIFE
The people of the **Nile** Delta worshiped the fertility goddess, Neith, as their creator. She rose from the Nile River and spat into its waters. Her spittle turned into Apep, serpent god of the underworld. Neith was also said to have invented the process of childbirth, bringing the other gods, the human race, and animals into existence.

DEATH AND AFTERLIFE
The Egyptians believed that the souls of the dead went to an underworld region called Duat. To enter Duat, the dead had to pass a test in front of ranks of assessor gods in Osiris's throne room to prove that they had led a good life.

OSIRIS
The supreme god Osiris and his wife Isis ruled Duat. It was said that he was the first **pharaoh** and had taught humans the arts of agriculture and civilization. His son Horus, the falcon-headed sky god whose eyes were the moon and the sun, guided souls to Duat.

DEATH
When Egyptians died, their bodies were mummified, to preserve them so that they could be used in the next world. Rich Egyptians were also buried with valuable possessions, which they would be able to use in Duat.

SALVATION
The way to Duat was perilous, so Egyptians learned spells from a text called *The Book of the Dead,* to protect them on their way. When they arrived, their hearts, or conscience, were weighed, to determine whether they had lived a good life.

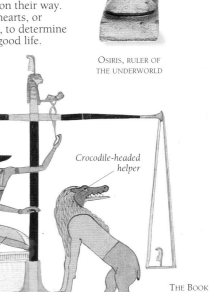

Regal headdress depicts Osiris as a king.

OSIRIS, RULER OF THE UNDERWORLD

Scales for weighing human hearts

Crocodile-headed helper

Anubis, jackal-headed god of embalming

THE BOOK OF THE DEAD

PYRAMIDS

The **pharaohs**, or **kings**, of Egypt's Old Kingdom (c.2700–2200 BCE) and Middle Kingdom (c.2000–1800 BCE) were buried in massive stone pyramids, meant to help achieve eternal life. At the heart of each pyramid was a burial chamber that contained a pharaoh's beautifully decorated coffin and possessions. The overall complex included a mortuary temple where burial rites were performed. The pyramid's shape recalled the mound on which the sun god stood at the time of **creation**.

THE GREAT PYRAMID

TEMPLE WORSHIP

All over Egypt temples were erected to the different gods. People believed that the god actually lived in his temple. Priests made regular offerings of food. During offering ceremonies, the priests burned incense and scattered holy water to keep the temple pure.

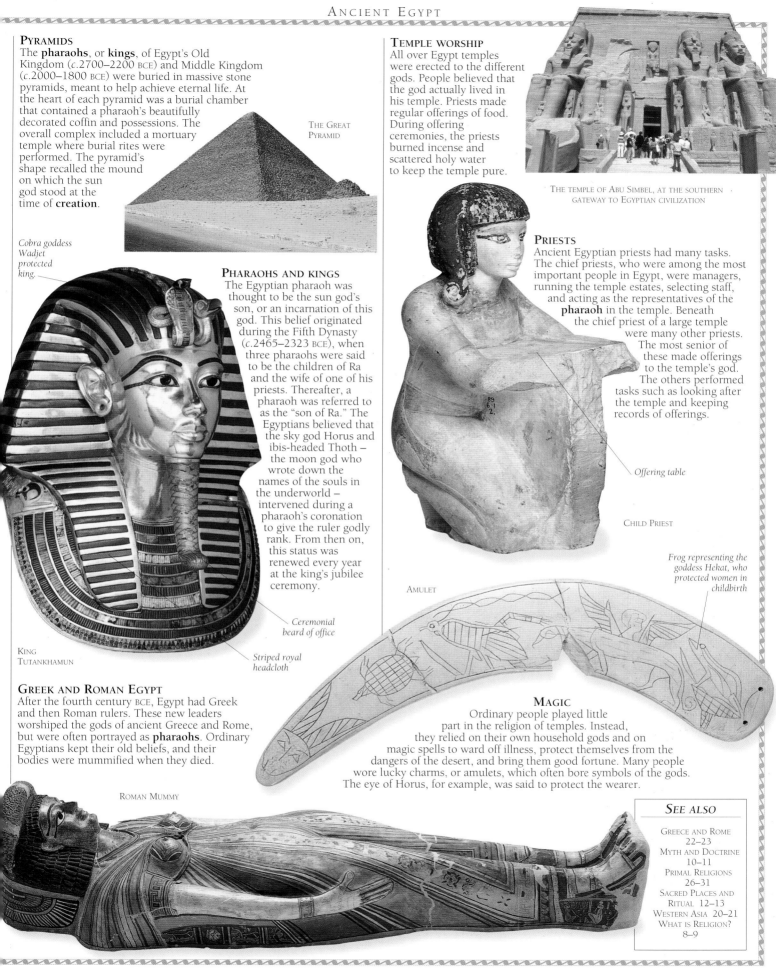

THE TEMPLE OF ABU SIMBEL, AT THE SOUTHERN GATEWAY TO EGYPTIAN CIVILIZATION

PRIESTS

Ancient Egyptian priests had many tasks. The chief priests, who were among the most important people in Egypt, were managers, running the temple estates, selecting staff, and acting as the representatives of the **pharaoh** in the temple. Beneath the chief priest of a large temple were many other priests. The most senior of these made offerings to the temple's god. The others performed tasks such as looking after the temple and keeping records of offerings.

Offering table

CHILD PRIEST

Cobra goddess Wadjet protected king.

PHARAOHS AND KINGS

The Egyptian pharaoh was thought to be the sun god's son, or an incarnation of this god. This belief originated during the Fifth Dynasty (c.2465–2323 BCE), when three pharaohs were said to be the children of Ra and the wife of one of his priests. Thereafter, a pharaoh was referred to as the "son of Ra." The Egyptians believed that the sky god Horus and ibis-headed Thoth – the moon god who wrote down the names of the souls in the underworld – intervened during a pharaoh's coronation to give the ruler godly rank. From then on, this status was renewed every year at the king's jubilee ceremony.

Ceremonial beard of office

KING TUTANKHAMUN

Striped royal headcloth

Frog representing the goddess Hekat, who protected women in childbirth

AMULET

GREEK AND ROMAN EGYPT

After the fourth century BCE, Egypt had Greek and then Roman rulers. These new leaders worshiped the gods of ancient Greece and Rome, but were often portrayed as **pharaohs**. Ordinary Egyptians kept their old beliefs, and their bodies were mummified when they died.

MAGIC

Ordinary people played little part in the religion of temples. Instead, they relied on their own household gods and on magic spells to ward off illness, protect themselves from the dangers of the desert, and bring them good fortune. Many people wore lucky charms, or amulets, which often bore symbols of the gods. The eye of Horus, for example, was said to protect the wearer.

ROMAN MUMMY

WESTERN ASIA

SOME OF THE FIRST GREAT CIVILIZATIONS arose in Western Asia. Surviving remains of temples, sculptures, and clay writing tablets tell us about their religions. Especially prominent were deities who controlled the cosmos, such as the sun and moon. People also thought that the gods controlled the weather and with it, the changing seasons, freak conditions, and ultimately the ripening of crops and food supply. Offerings at the temple were a part of life, and priests, as mediators to the gods, were very powerful people.

WESTERN ASIA
The three separate areas of Western Asia – the eastern Mediterranean, Mesopotamia (between the Tigris and Euphrates Rivers, including Assyria, Sumeria, and Babylonia), and Persia (modern Iran) – produced many different religious traditions.

WESTERN ASIA

MESOPOTAMIA

Evidence from *c.*2600 to 330 BCE shows that the Sumerians, Babylonians, and Assyrians of Mesopotamia worshiped many gods, most of whom were born from a primeval sea before they created the earth and its inhabitants. Higher deities, like Utu the sun god, ruled over parts of the cosmos. Others, such as Ninmah the goddess of birth, controlled key areas of human life.

FIGURE OF A RAM FROM UR

UR
One of the most important cities in the area was Ur, by the Euphrates River, which was the center of the Mesopotamian empire around 2100 BCE. At the city's heart were several temples, including the great **ziggurat**, sacred to the city's patron deity, Nanna the moon god. His symbol was a crescent moon.

TIAMAT   TIAMAT
The goddess Tiamat was the saltwater ocean and represented the chaos before creation. The other Mesopotamian deities were created when she mingled with her consort Apsu, the god of fresh water. For a while the gods lived in peace. Eventually, there was a war and Tiamat was killed by her son, Marduk. One half of her body became the sky, the other half the earth.

ISHTAR   ISHTAR
The goddess Ishtar, also called Inanna, was worshipped throughout Western Asia. In Assyria she was a war goddess, but in Mesopotamia she was goddess of love and fertility. She visited the underworld annually. The arrival of winter and the death of vegetation reflected her absence.

CANAANITES

When the ancient Canaanite city of Ugarit was excavated in the 1920s, clay tablets were found. These revealed struggles between the gods, which seemed to explain the changing seasons.

EL
The Canaanite creator god, El, was known as father of the gods and the first humans. He lived at the source of all the rivers.

ASHERAT
Fertility goddess Asherat, **El**'s wife, was mother of 70 other deities. Known as Astarte, in ancient Greece she became Aphrodite, and in Mesopotamia, **Ishtar**.

ASHERAT, GODDESS OF FERTILITY

BAAL
The name Baal means "lord," and was the title given to the local god in many Western Asiatic cities. His best known form is Baal-Hadad, the Canaanite god of thunder and fertility. Baal fought the water monster Yam, and his victory showed that he had control over the life-giving rains.

MOT
Baal's enemy Mot was the god of death and was associated with sterility and drought. According to legend, the two gods fought bitterly, and the thunder god seemed to be defeated. Miraculously, Baal came back to life just as the rains returned after the dry season.

BAAL, GOD OF THUNDER

NEBUCHADNEZZAR

In the seventh century BCE, the city of Babylon was rebuilt by King Nebuchadnezzar and became the capital of a revived Babylonian empire. There were sacred buildings all over the city. Temples were built to the major gods, including the creator god Marduk and the great goddess **Ishtar**. Each of the city's gates was dedicated to a deity. The city walls bore religious symbols, such as dragons representing Marduk, bulls for the weather god Adad, and lions, symbols of Ishtar.

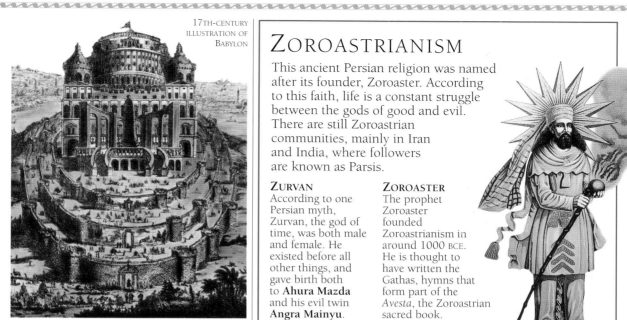

17TH-CENTURY ILLUSTRATION OF BABYLON

ZIGGURAT

The major Mesopotamian temples were built in the form of ziggurats – large stepped towers, some as tall as 150 ft (45 m), made from mud bricks. At the top was a small shrine, which people saw as a god's dwelling place. Stairways ran up the sides of the tower. The Mesopotamians thought of these as steps up to heaven.

TREE OF LIFE

The ancient Persians made an intoxicating drink from the sap of the haoma tree, or tree of life, which was said to have come from paradise. They believed this drink brought them health and fertility, even making them immortal. Later, **Zoroastrian** priests adopted the practice of drinking haoma.

TREE OF LIFE

Decoration from the wall of the throne room of Nebuchadnezzar

GILGAMESH

This epic poem is the world's oldest work of literature, dating back to c.2000 BCE. It tells how the people of Uruk in Mesopotamia asked the gods to do something about the tyrannical Gilgamesh, their king who was later deified. After many adventures, Gilgamesh wept when his friend Enkidu was killed. This moved him to seek the secret of immortality. His ancestor Utnapishtim, the only human to be granted immortality, told Gilgamesh to visit the underworld and to retrieve a magic plant. Gilgamesh found the plant, but a snake stole it before he could return to earth.

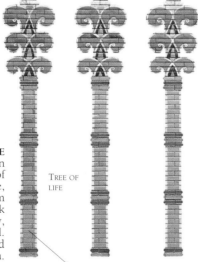

STATUE OF THE HERO GILGAMESH

BABYLONIAN FLOOD

Utnapishtim told **Gilgamesh** that he became immortal after the gods sent a flood to kill all people. Advised by the god Enki, Utnapishtim built a boat to save himself and his family. This story is very similar to the story of **Noah** in Judaism.

ZOROASTRIANISM

This ancient Persian religion was named after its founder, Zoroaster. According to this faith, life is a constant struggle between the gods of good and evil. There are still Zoroastrian communities, mainly in Iran and India, where followers are known as Parsis.

ZURVAN

According to one Persian myth, Zurvan, the god of time, was both male and female. He existed before all other things, and gave birth both to **Ahura Mazda** and his evil twin **Angra Mainyu**.

ZOROASTER

The prophet Zoroaster founded Zoroastrianism in around 1000 BCE. He is thought to have written the Gathas, hymns that form part of the *Avesta*, the Zoroastrian sacred book.

ZOROASTER

AHURA MAZDA

Sky god Ahura Mazda, or Wise Lord, was said to be the source of all good in the world. Zoroastrian priests taught that he would win his war with **Angra Mainyu**, so the universe would become wholly good.

Wings spread to protect the world

AHURA MAZDA

ANGRA MAINYU

ANGRA MAINYU

God of darkness, death, and evil, Angra Mainyu created dangerous storms, plagues, and monsters during the struggle with **Ahura Mazda**, his twin. The Zoroastrians taught that Angra Mainyu was necessary because we can understand good only if evil is also present.

PHOENICIANS

The Phoenicians were seafaring people who were based along the eastern Mediterranean coast. They shared the gods of the **Canaanites**, including **El**, **Baal**, and **Asherat**. However, they also imported deities from other peoples with whom they traded, especially those from ancient Egypt. Some of their temple statues look like the Egyptian deities Isis and Hathor.

SEE ALSO

NOAH 76

ANCIENT EGYPT 18–19
MYTH AND DOCTRINE 10–11
PRIMAL RELIGIONS 26–31
SACRED PLACES AND RITUAL 12–13

GREECE AND ROME

THE ANCIENT GREEKS AND ROMANS had many gods and goddesses, who took human form and controlled different aspects of life. They saw the gods as behaving like mortal men and women – the deities had their own distinct characters, their own loves, and their own conflicts. People worshiped a specific deity when they needed his or her help. For example, a Greek woman who was expecting a baby might make offerings to Artemis, the goddess of childbirth, while a Roman emperor about to go into battle might promise to build a temple to Mars, the god of war.

THE MEDITERRANEAN
From 1600 to 300 BCE, the ancient Greeks traded all around the Aegean Sea and set up colonies in Italy. Their religious beliefs were established by the time the Romans had created an empire. Rome assimilated Greek culture, building temples in this area and beyond.

ITALY
ADRIATIC SEA
• Rome
AEGEAN SEA
• Athens
MEDITERRANEAN SEA

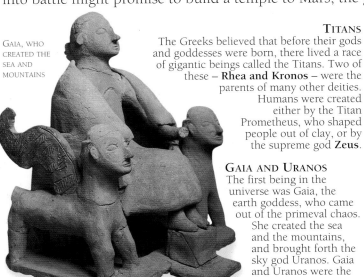

GAIA, WHO CREATED THE SEA AND MOUNTAINS

TITANS
The Greeks believed that before their gods and goddesses were born, there lived a race of gigantic beings called the Titans. Two of these – **Rhea and Kronos** – were the parents of many other deities. Humans were created either by the Titan Prometheus, who shaped people out of clay, or by the supreme god **Zeus**.

GAIA AND URANOS
The first being in the universe was Gaia, the earth goddess, who came out of the primeval chaos. She created the sea and the mountains, and brought forth the sky god Uranos. Gaia and Uranos were the parents of the **Titans**.

RHEA AND KRONOS
The **Titans** Rhea and Kronos were the parents of the **Olympian** gods. Fearful of being overthrown, Kronos even tried to destroy his own children by swallowing them. But Rhea hid her youngest child, **Zeus**, and later Kronos regurgitated the others.

ZEUS
After a battle with the **Titans**, Zeus became ruler of the gods. His special kingdom was the sky, giving the sea and the underworld to Poseidon and Hades, his brothers. Using thunderbolts, Zeus punished his enemies and dispensed justice. He had many wives and lovers.

ZEUS

OLYMPIANS
Zeus and the other 12 most important gods and goddesses were said to live on top of Mount Olympus, the highest mountain in Greece. Each deity represented at least one aspect of life. For example, Aphrodite was goddess of love, Hephaistos was god of craftsmanship, and Ares was god of war.

Aegeus, king of Athens, consults the Delphic oracle.

ODYSSEUS BLINDS THE CYCLOPS.

MINOAN SNAKE GODDESS

MINOANS AND MYCENAEANS
Between 2000 and 1450 BCE, the Minoans created a great civilization on the island of Crete. The Mycenaeans from mainland Greece invaded Crete and took over Minoan customs and religion. Deity worship was important to both peoples. Minoan religion also involved symbols such as double-headed axes and snakes and bulls, which may have been signs of fertility.

VASE PAINTING OF THE ORACLE AT DELPHI

ORACLE
Ordinary people went to the shrine of an oracle to ask a god or goddess for advice. The deity would reply, usually through the voice of a priest or priestess, sometimes through odd sounds. The most famous oracle was at Delphi.

WORSHIP
The Greeks believed that if a deity's power was acknowledged, then that god or goddess would be kind to them. They did this by offering sacrifices in front of the temple and pouring libations (wine) to that deity.

FESTIVALS
Another form of worship included holding religious festivals. Often a festival had a solemn procession, followed by a large sacrifice. Festivals also included athletic contests, such as the first Olympics in honor of **Zeus**, and competitions between poets, choirs, and dramatic performers to celebrate other gods.

GREEK HEROES
Heroes like Odysseus, protagonist of Homer's poem *The Odyssey*, play a large part in Greek mythology. It is from the works of such writers that we know so much about Greek beliefs. Heroic deeds of strength and cunning fascinated the Greeks. Stories of the mortals' relationships with the gods showed how their lives were interlinked.

ROMAN RELIGION

Religion was part of everyday life for the Romans. Everyone would appeal to the gods to help them with their problems. Most Roman houses, and even workshops, had their own shrine, with statues of ancestors and household gods, such as Lares or Penates (gods of homes and larders respectively). Here, the head of the family performed simple daily rituals. The Romans also built large temples to the classical gods in all their towns and cities.

ROMAN PANTHEON

The Romans borrowed most of their gods and goddesses from the ancient Greeks, but gave them different names. The Greek goddess of love, Aphrodite, became Venus, while Ares became **Mars**. The Romans also had some native gods, such as the two-faced god Janus, the creator god of entrances.

Staff for casting thunderbolts

JUPITER

JUPITER

The king of the Roman gods – and the equivalent of the supreme Greek god **Zeus** – was Jupiter. The Romans worshiped Jupiter as the protector of their state and defender of justice. They built one of their greatest temples to him, the temple of Jupiter Optimus Maximus in Rome.

MARS

The Roman war god and god of farming, Mars was much more important to the militaristic Romans than his equivalent, Ares, was to the Greeks. The Romans valued his virtues of strength and bravery. They invented their own myths about him, including the story that he was the father of **Remus and Romulus**, the founders of Rome. His main festivals were held in March, which was named after him.

WORSHIP

Temple-based worship was similar to that of ancient Greece, with offerings and animal sacrifices performed on an altar in front of the temple, and libations poured into the fire that burned on the altar. An **emperor** might go much further, by building an entire temple in order to ensure a particular god's favor. Some gods became fashionable for coping with specific problems – Asclepius, the god of healing, was worshiped in times of plagues and epidemics. At home, ordinary Romans would make offerings at their household shrines.

Bronze cymbals

MUSICAL INSTRUMENTS USED IN TEMPLE CEREMONIES

Bronze flute

EMPERORS

After Rome became an empire, the Romans usually referred to an emperor as "son of a god." Many emperors were declared to be gods by the Roman Senate after they died. Some of their rulers, such as Caligula (CE 12–41) and Domitian (CE 51–96), actually claimed to be gods while they were still alive.

ROMULUS AND REMUS

The twins Romulus and Remus were the sons of a princess from the town of Alba Longa. They were abandoned soon after they were born, near the Tiber River, but a she-wolf rescued them. They decided to build a city at the place where the wolf found them. This site was later called Rome.

VIRGIL

The poet Virgil (70–19 BCE) wrote a famous epic, *The Aeneid,* about the life of the hero Aeneas, son of King Anchises and the goddess Venus, and of **Romulus and Remus'** ancestor. Virgil wanted to show how Rome's early rulers had divine ancestry, thereby linking the later **emperors** with the gods.

EMPEROR CALIGULA

ETRUSCAN RELIGION

The Etruscans ruled northern Italy before the Romans and were influenced by the Greeks. Their gods were similar to Roman and Greek deities – Tin was like **Jupiter** or **Zeus**, Turan like Venus or Aphrodite, Menvra like Minerva or Athene. The Etruscans believed that they could contact their gods through nature, and that phenomena such as lightning and eclipses were the actual "voices" of the gods.

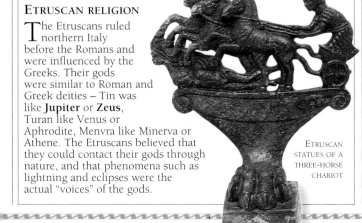

ETRUSCAN STATUES OF A THREE-HORSE CHARIOT

MITHRAISM

One Roman cult especially popular with the army was that of Mithras, the protector god. The origins of Mithras are unknown, but by the 2nd century CE, the Romans worshiped him in shrines, where there was an image of the war god killing a bull. Devotees believed that the ritual slaying of a bull would make them become immortal.

MITHRAS, PROTECTOR GOD OF SOLDIERS

Mithras slaying the bull

SEE ALSO

MYTH AND DOCTRINE
10–11
NORSE AND CELTIC
24–25
PRIMAL RELIGIONS
26–31
SACRED PLACES AND
RITUAL 12–13

NORSE AND CELTIC

AMONG THE ANCIENT SOCIETIES OF NORTHERN EUROPE, the Norse and Celtic peoples gave supreme importance to warfare. Warrior gods are widespread – in fact, all the Norse gods are warriors. In Norse and Celtic areas, the passing of seasons and their effect on agriculture were vital to survival, so people held regular seasonal festivals to promote the fertility of the soil and a good supply of food. The Norse and Celts worshiped by making offerings and sacrifices. Both believed that their religious leaders could foretell the future by carrying out special rituals.

THE NORSE AND CELTS
The peoples of northern and western Europe held a rich variety of religious beliefs. The Nordic regions (Denmark, Sweden, Finland, and Norway) shared one group of similar deities and beliefs, while the **Celtic** lands (Ireland, Britain, and northern France) produced a quite different set.

Asgard, home of the gods

YGGDRASIL, THE TREE OF LIFE

Midgard

Norns lived in the tree's roots.

NORSE CREATION
A group of creator gods, Odin, Vili, and Ve, fought the cruel **giant** Ymir, killed him, and used his body to create the world. Ymir's teeth became rocks, his flesh was made into the earth, and his blood was turned into the rivers and seas. Above the earth, the gods placed Ymir's vast skull, which became the sky, and clouds were made from his brains. The gods then made the first people, the man Ask and the woman Embla, from a pair of logs they found on the seashore. They became the parents of the human race.

YGGDRASIL
A giant ash tree called Yggdrasil, or the Tree of Life, linked together the entire Norse cosmos. High up in the branches was Asgard, the home of the gods. Lower down, Midgard – the earth inhabited by humans – was connected to Asgard by the bridge Bifröst. Beneath the earth, among the tree's roots, were a series of realms where the dead, the **giants**, and the Norns, who controlled the fate of humans, had their dwellings.

HEL
The Norse underworld, or Hel, was deep down in the roots of **Yggdrasil**, a region ruled by a goddess, also called Hel. She had the face and upper body of a beautiful woman, but her lower half was formed by a decomposing corpse. Hel led the dead (who silently served her), and an army of monsters.

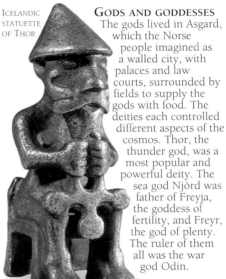

ICELANDIC STATUETTE OF THOR

GODS AND GODDESSES
The gods lived in Asgard, which the Norse people imagined as a walled city, with palaces and law courts, surrounded by fields to supply the gods with food. The deities each controlled different aspects of the cosmos. Thor, the thunder god, was a most popular and powerful deity. The sea god Njörd was father of Freyja, the goddess of fertility, and Freyr, the god of plenty. The ruler of them all was the war god Odin.

GIANTS
The Norse people believed that the universe began as ice and fire. The first giant, Ymir, was created where the two systems came together. From Ymir's sweat, two other giants were born. They became parents of a race of giants, who lived everywhere – in the mountains, the sea, and the clouds. They waged war on the gods but, eventually, the supreme god Odin gave the giants a land of their own – called Jotunheim – found at the roots of **Yggdrasil**.

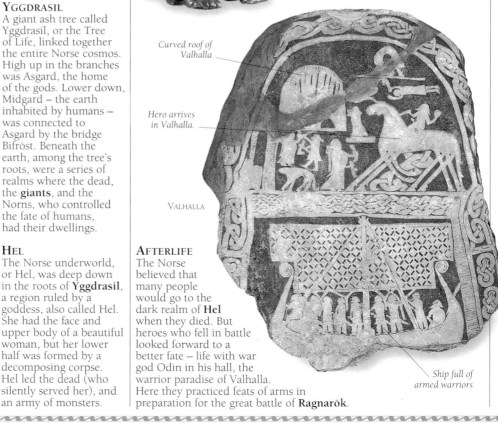

Curved roof of Valhalla

Hero arrives in Valhalla.

VALHALLA

Ship full of armed warriors

AFTERLIFE
The Norse believed that many people would go to the dark realm of **Hel** when they died. But heroes who fell in battle looked forward to a better fate – life with war god Odin in his hall, the warrior paradise of Valhalla. Here they practiced feats of arms in preparation for the great battle of **Ragnarök**.

CELTIC RELIGION

The Celtic peoples had numerous gods, many of whom controlled fertility, plentiful crops, food, and the seasons. Each year they held seasonal festivals – Beltaine, a spring festival in May, Lugnasad in August, Oimelc in February, and Samhain, the new year feast, in November. Although the Celts left no extensive written records, we know about their religion from the writings of the Romans, who conquered them.

TRIPLE MOTHER GODDESS

Three was a sacred number for the Celts, and many myths mention groups of three deities. Often, the mother goddess in particular is shown as three women. They often carry items to do with raising a child or, as here, foods such as bread, fruit, and fish.

ENGLISH STONE RELIEF OF TRIPLE MOTHER GODDESS

SUCELLUS

The god of spring, called Sucellus, was also known as the king of the gods. He was especially important because people relied on plants and trees for their food supply. Sucellus carried a large, long-handled hammer with which he hit the earth, waking up the vegetation and making it spring to life. His hammer may also be a symbol of the god's authority, like a king's scepter.

Stag, with horns similar to those of Cernunnos

EPONA AND HER HORSE

EPONA

Goddess of the horse, Epona was also connected with fertility and water. She remained popular into the Roman period, when Celtic cavalry soldiers worshiped her. The Romans even allowed an official festival.

CERNUNNOS

One of the most ancient Celtic gods was Cernunnos, The Horned One. He was depicted with the antlers of a stag and was seen as the lord of the beasts. He is often shown with animals, especially snakes and stags, sometimes feeding them. This suggests that Cernunnos was a god of plenty, who could tame wild creatures by offering them food. Consequently, he was one of the most powerful of the Celtic gods.

Ram-headed serpent

CERNUNNOS

LUGH

Called the "Bright One," Lugh was the Celtic sun god. He was highly skilled in the arts and crafts, and made a magical boat called the "Wavesweeper."

GOLDEN BOAT

TARANIS

The Celtic thunder god was called Taranis, a figure similar to the Roman god **Jupiter**. The Celts believed that thunder was caused by the sound of the rumbling wheels of Taranis's chariot, while lightning came from sparks made by the horses' hooves.

BELANUS

The Celts had several gods of fire and light, shown by the word Bel, or Shining, in their names. One of them, Belanus was also said to have healing powers. The Roman conquerors of the Celtic world therefore saw him as similar to Apollo, a god of light who could heal both men and immortals.

OAK LEAVES, USED FOR HEALING

DRUIDS

Celtic religious leaders, called druids, were highly trained, learning their craft by word of mouth over many years. Druids controlled the religious life of the Celts, presided at sacrifices, gave advice about religious questions, and predicted when was the best time to sow crops or put herds to pasture. They also had knowledge of herbs and healing, and acted as judges in disputes.

Horse carved into the hillside

UFFINGTON WHITE HORSE

SACRED PLACES

The Celts often worshiped in special places – by a tree, lake, spring, or on a hillside associated with their gods. Often, chalk figures cut into hills marked sacred places.

TRICKSTERS

The trickster part-god, part-giant Loki and his son, Fenrir the wolf, were two of the gods' enemies. Like all tricksters, Loki could change his shape and played practical jokes on the gods. At **Ragnarök**, Loki led dead souls and the **giants**.

FENRIR THE WOLF

RAGNARÖK

According to Norse myths, a time would come when the gods would fight their enemies, the **giants**, in a final battle called Ragnarök – the twilight of the gods. In this great conflict most of the original gods, including Odin and Thor, would be destroyed. Some of the gods would remain to rule over a new age in which evil would be banished. Two people would also survive, to become the parents of a new human race.

SEE ALSO

JUPITER 23

GREECE AND ROME 22–23
MYTH AND DOCTRINE 10–11
PRIMAL RELIGIONS 26–31
SACRED PLACES AND RITUALS 12–13
WHAT IS RELIGION? 8–9

PRIMAL RELIGIONS

From Africa to Australia, small groups of indigenous people still practice their own "primal" religions. Because these groups are widely dispersed around the world, the faiths they follow vary greatly. However, most primal religions have one element in common – a belief that the world is full of spirits that have a vital influence on life.

SPIRITS AND RITUALS

Most primal religions have a creator spirit – often a sky god – as well as a range of nature spirits and local deities. When people die, they are said to live on in the spirit world. The followers of primal religions believe that the spirits affect their lives in many ways, from bringing disasters such as diseases, storms, and forest fires to healing the sick. Humans come into contact with the spirit world through dreams and visions, and also through special rituals, often performed by a shaman or medicine man.

SHAMAN'S MEDICINE BAG

A WORLD OF RELIGIONS

No one is sure how many people follow primal religions. This is because they are mostly practiced among groups who live traditional lifestyles, often in isolated parts of the globe. Primal religions play a vital part in the lives of people all over the world, including Australian Aborigines, people in rural South America, African tribes, and the inhabitants of Pacific Islands.

THE SPIRIT WORLD

This mask is seen to embody a female, nurturing spirit.

FROM THE ISLANDS OF THE PACIFIC to the frozen tundra of North America, live small groups of indigenous people, who follow traditional lifestyles. Many of these people have their own "primal" religions, so called because they existed long before today's major world religions – Judaism, Islam, Christianity, Buddhism, and Hinduism. Many primal religions have now, however, been displaced or diluted by such faiths. Beliefs and ideas differ from one people or geographical area to the next, but many primal religions have certain basic aspects in common. Above all, they believe in the existence of a number of active spirits, who have great influence over human life and with whom contact can be made through rituals. Specialized priests or shamans are often chosen to conduct these rituals because it is believed that they can communicate with the spirit world.

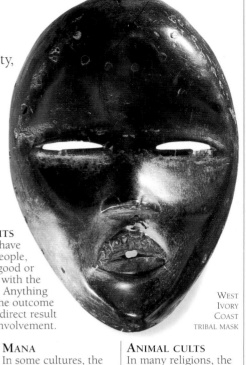

WEST IVORY COAST TRIBAL MASK

GOOD AND EVIL
In primal religions, difficulties or problems are often said to be caused by evil, mischievous, or displeased **spirits**. People seek to reduce the influence of these spirits by performing rituals that will please them or send them away. These rituals are usually performed by a shaman or **medicine man** – someone who is skilled in communicating with the tribal spirit world.

SPIRITS
Many things – people, animals, or places – have spirits. These spirits are more powerful than people, and can work in different ways, for either good or evil. Much primal religion is concerned with the human relationship with the spirit world. Anything that affects a person's daily life, whether the outcome is good or bad, is believed to be a direct result of the spirits' involvement.

ANCESTORS
People honor the **spirits** of their dead ancestors in the hope that they will pass their prayers on to higher spirits. Ancestor spirits are often seen as protectors or guides in their own right.

This voice disguiser is used in rituals to create a bond between the living and their ancestors.

NIGERIAN VOICE DISGUISER

MANA
In some cultures, the power of the **spirits** is known as mana. This power is viewed in different ways in different primal religions. It may be passed from the **gods** through a line of **ancestors** to the people. Alternatively, it may be present as a good or evil force in any being that has a spirit.

ANIMAL CULTS
In many religions, the **gods and goddesses** take animal form, with various creatures ruling certain parts of creation. Sky gods often take the form of birds, especially birds of prey such as the eagle. Sea creatures, from whales to seals, rule the oceans.

ULURU, ABORIGINAL SACRED SITE

ANIMISM
The idea that all things have a spirit is known as animism. This is a vital part of many primal religions. Animals, plants, and inanimate objects can have a spirit. **Spirits** may dwell in specific places, such as trees, streams, or mountains, and on other planes of existence, such as in the heavens or the underworld. All of these spirits have their own special power over the world. They are able to influence everything from the weather to the actions of an individual person. Respecting the spirits and pleasing them is therefore a vital part of animistic religion.

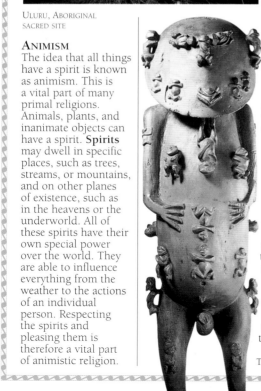

TANGAROA, GOD OF THE SEA

HIGH GOD
In many cultures, one deity stands out above all others. This figure, which may be male or female, is usually the Creator. It may also be a remote figure, who has withdrawn to heaven after creating the world. In some cultures, the deity communicates with people via the lesser gods, urging them to avoid evil.

GODS AND GODDESSES
Beneath the **High God** are many other deities that control different aspects of life. They usually reflect the lives and concerns of the people, and range from weather and agricultural gods to gods of the arts.

Carving representing a raven

NATIVE AMERICAN TOTEM POLE

TOTEMISM
A totem is an object that represents the ancestor of a group or a people. A totem might be an animal, in which case the people will avoid hunting and eating that creature and will revere it. North American totem poles depict **ancestors** and the **spirits** associated with them.

CONTACTING THE SPIRIT WORLD

In primal religions, great emphasis is placed on the importance of spirits and how they influence all aspects of daily life. Followers must make contact with these spirits to request their help, and to control or defeat them. Two of the most common ways of contacting the spirit world are through the use of a shaman and through spirit possession.

SHAMANISM

This practice is common in parts of Africa, Asia, and North America. Shamans, who are usually men, engage in rituals, often involving dance and drumming, to enter a state in which they can travel into the spirit world. They use knowledge gained from the **spirits** to heal people, to predict the future, to resolve disputes, or even to ward off natural disasters. Shamans are highly respected: Their journeys to the spirit world are thought to be very dangerous.

MODERN-DAY SHAMAN

MAGIC

One way of using spiritual powers to control the world is through magic. This may take two broad forms. Contagious magic involves the belief that performing an action on one thing will affect something that has been close by. Burning a hair from a person's head may therefore cause that person harm. Imitative magic involves performing an action on a similar object, such as a doll that resembles a particular person.

NATIVE AMERICAN SHAMAN SPIRIT HELPER

WITCHCRAFT

People in many traditional societies believe that certain individuals possess an evil power that may be used to harm others by performing acts called witchcraft. Problems and calamities that are otherwise unexplainable, such as sudden deaths or accidents, are often said to be the result of witchcraft.

SPIRIT POSSESSION

This type of contact with the **spirits** is common in Africa, and involves a person being physically taken over by a spirit. This may be a painful process, during which the possessed person may become crazed or ill. In this case, he or she will seek to be exorcised. Possession may also give the person a more positive contact with the spirit world, leading to ecstatic **visions**.

Magpie tail feather

White eagle feather

SHAMAN'S HEADDRESS, REPRESENTING A GUARDIAN SPIRIT

BAG USED BY UGANDAN DIVINER TO STORE SACRED OBJECTS

DREAMS AND VISIONS

People believe that vivid or unusual dreams, or visions, contain messages from the **spirits**, and will ask a shaman to interpret them. In some cultures, hallucinatory substances are used to encourage dreams and visions.

HALLUCINATORY MUSHROOMS

DIVINATION

Gaining hidden information through spiritual means is known as divination, which plays an important role in primal religion. The future may be predicted by examining a natural object and interpreting it. Alternatively, a shaman may enter into a trance to make contact with the spirit world, and use the knowledge he gains to give advice or foretell future events.

Cowrie shells are often used to symbolize fertility.

SEE ALSO

MEDICINE MAN 30
OMENS 30
PRIEST 30
VOODOO 31

SACRED PLACES AND RITUALS 12–13

RITUALS AND PRACTICE

THE PRACTICE OF PRIMAL RELIGIONS is dominated by spirits, whose closeness to daily life is felt at all times. In traditional societies, rituals are used as a way of keeping the spirits happy, so that they look favorably on the people. Rituals may be performed to help individuals through the different stages of life; functions such as healing the sick or easing people through times of stress or difficulty may also be accompanied by the performance of special rites. In each case, elaborate equipment, such as masks, costumes, and musical instruments, is used, in order to bring the participants closer to the realm of the spirits.

PRIEST MAKING AN OFFERING TO THE SPIRITS

MEDICINE MAN
In primal religions, illnesses are seen as being influenced by **spirits**. In order to get rid of sickness, the assistance of someone who is able to communicate with the spirit world is required. This is often the medicine man. He organizes religious practice and rituals, and may also take on many other roles – **shaman**, adviser, and **priest**. He is usually a healer who knows the curative powers of the local herbs and who may use rituals to gain the aid of the spirits to cure the sick.

PRIEST
The main task of the priest is to look after the relationship between the community and the world of the **spirits**. This is achieved by supervising rituals and taking care of shrines and sacred places. These jobs may be done by a priest or by the medicine man.

NATIVE AMERICAN MEDICINE MAN'S MASK

Strands of horsehair used as decoration

MASKS
Masks are commonly used in ceremonies and are believed to be extremely powerful. **Shamans** may wear masks during rituals when a spirit is being called: The person wearing the mask is often said to "become" the spirit, so strong is the possession. Some masks are worn on top of the head to prevent their powerful gaze from being directed at onlookers.

YORUBAN GELEDE MASK

MYTHS
In primal religions, myths tell of the creation of the cosmos and the lives of the **gods and goddesses**. They explain concepts such as the seasons and the phases of the moon to people who have, until recently, been cut off from scientific explanations. They offer instructions about morality and the meaning of life, and also provide reasons for the social order. Myths therefore provide a complete picture of everything that matters in primal societies, and they are frequently recited or acted out in rituals.

MEXICAN WALL HANGING, DEPICTING WORLD CREATION

AMULET USED IN HEALING RITUALS

Charms used to ward off evil

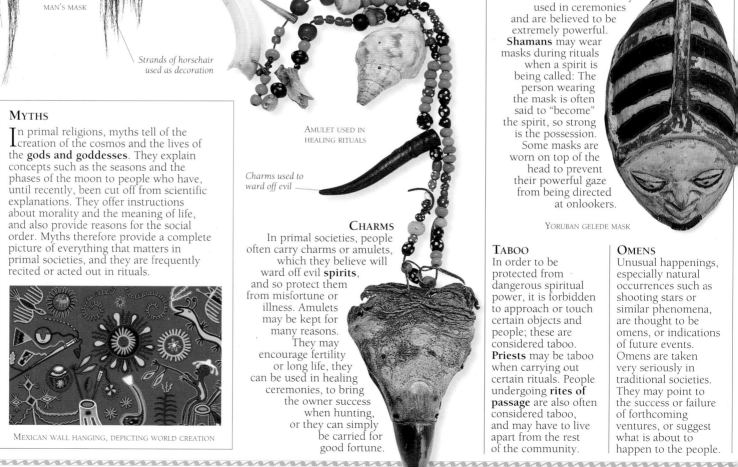

CHARMS
In primal societies, people often carry charms or amulets, which they believe will ward off evil **spirits**, and so protect them from misfortune or illness. Amulets may be kept for many reasons. They may encourage fertility or long life, they can be used in healing ceremonies, to bring the owner success when hunting, or they can simply be carried for good fortune.

TABOO
In order to be protected from dangerous spiritual power, it is forbidden to approach or touch certain objects and people; these are considered taboo. **Priests** may be taboo when carrying out certain rituals. People undergoing **rites of passage** are also often considered taboo, and may have to live apart from the rest of the community.

OMENS
Unusual happenings, especially natural occurrences such as shooting stars or similar phenomena, are thought to be omens, or indications of future events. Omens are taken very seriously in traditional societies. They may point to the success or failure of forthcoming ventures, or suggest what is about to happen to the people.

RITES AND RITUALS

Religious rites and rituals help keep traditional societies in touch with the spirit world, strengthening the people's relationship with the spirits. Some are held at the same time each year, others when there is a specific problem that needs the help of the spirits.

IROQUOIS MASK, USED IN NEW YEAR AND PROTECTION RITUALS

PROTECTION RITUALS
Certain rituals may be performed at times of stress or at important moments for the people, and these provide the followers with a sense of security. For example, when a group's supply of food is affected, whether just before harvest or when the men are about to go hunting, a ritual may be performed to persuade the gods to look favorably on the people.

UGANDAN CIRCUMCISION DANCE, USED TO INITIATE BOYS INTO MANHOOD

A MALANGGAN, USED IN MELANESIAN DEATH RITUALS

PEACE RITUALS
During special ceremonies, particularly in Native American societies, tobacco was often smoked in a sacred pipe, called a calumet, to mark the end of fighting. The ritual presentation of a calumet to another tribe also ensured that peace would be upheld, since war could not be waged against the recipient.

Tobacco held in metal bowl

NATIVE AMERICAN PEACE PIPE

NEW YEAR RITUALS
The start of a year is an important time. New Year rituals typically involve discarding the old and beginning afresh, for example, by putting out and relighting the village fires.

OFFERINGS
One way of pleasing the **spirits** and encouraging them to help people on earth is to make offerings. A common form of offering is food, which may be left at a shrine or shared with the spirits during a communal meal.

RITES OF PASSAGE
Particular rites, called rites of passage, occur at key points in a person's life, notably birth, coming of age, and marriage. The person undergoing the rite is often made to live apart from the rest of the people, during which time he or she is given instruction and prepared for the next stage in life. They return to society in a ceremony that may be like a symbolic rebirth.

COMMUNAL RITUALS
Some rituals bring together an entire community in celebration. Such rituals are valued because they enhance the sense of togetherness shared by the people. Many rituals involve a cross-section of the community, for example, when groups of young people are communally initiated into adulthood.

KENYAN TRIBESPEOPLE CELEBRATE AN INITIATION RITUAL.

DEATH RITUALS
When people die, they join their **ancestors** in the spirit world. Most peoples have special rituals to help them on their way or to please the ancestors, so that the spirit of the deceased gets a good welcome.

RITES OF ORDEAL
Sometimes, individuals undergo extreme pain or discomfort during rites. The hope is that the **spirits** will see the individual's ordeal and end any pain or crisis endured by the rest of the people.

SACRIFICE
In some societies, sacrifices are offered to the gods. People kill a valued animal such as a sheep or goat and offer it at the shrine. A personal possession may also be given as a sacrifice.

VOODOO
The popular religion of Haiti, called Voodoo, is a mixture of African religion (brought to the West Indies by slaves) and Christian elements. The voodoo deities, called loa, may be either ancestor spirits or spirits of the natural world. They fall into two broad groups, the helpful rada and the destructive petro. During ceremonies, there occurs a form of spirit possession, in which a person's body may be taken over by the loa.

VOODOO DOLL

HEAD-HUNTING
In certain warrior cultures, it was traditionally thought that taking an enemy's head brought benefits such as fertility, status, or prosperity to the warrior's tribe. However, a warrior who had taken a head was considered unclean and dangerous, and had to undergo a ritual purification ceremony. In some cultures, head-hunting once formed part of an important life-cycle ritual. In parts of Nigeria, for instance, a man was only allowed to marry if he had beheaded an enemy.

HUMAN SKULLS IN MALAYSIA

Keeping skulls on display is believed to bring beneficial results to the tribe of the headhunter.

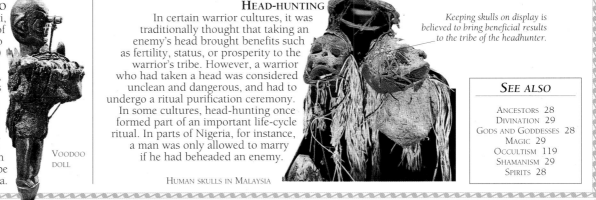

SEE ALSO

HINDUISM

With its roots dating back over thousands of years, Hinduism is one of the oldest of all religions. Hindus hold many diverse beliefs, but are all dedicated to the idea that our life on earth is part of an eternal cycle of births, deaths, and rebirths. Every person is reborn, or reincarnated, each time they die. Only by living a good life, however, can a person be reborn well, and therefore eventually achieve release from this cycle.

WAYS OF LIFE

SYMBOL OF HINDUISM

Today, there are more than 745 million Hindus in the world, the majority of whom live on the Indian subcontinent – and these numbers are still growing, mainly because of India's steadily increasing population. Many Hindus are vegetarian because of their belief in reincarnation and their view that all living beings are part of the same spirit. They therefore believe that animals and humans alike should be treated with respect and reverence. By living a peaceful life, studying the ancient texts of Hinduism, praying, and meditating, Hindus aim eventually to find oneness with Brahman or God.

DEITIES AND WORSHIP

There are hundreds of Hindu gods and goddesses, but two gods – Vishnu, the protector, and Shiva, the destroyer – stand out as the most popular and have many temples dedicated to them alone. In addition, many Hindus have a shrine in their own home, where they can perform daily acts of worship to the god of their choice. These rituals of home prayer, together with a rich and varied calendar of festivals, form the core of worship for many Hindus.

THREE GODS IN ONE

HINDUISM HAS GROWN and developed over the last 4,000 years, during which time it has spread across India and to many other parts of the world. As a result, Hinduism has great variety. There is no founder or single set of beliefs, but there are many gods. The faith has been described as being like a great river into which many different tributaries flow, the waters continually changing. But within this diversity, there is also unity, in which all the gods – and all of creation – are part of a universal absolute being, called Brahman. Of the many gods and goddesses, three principal figures stand out – Brahma (the Creator), Shiva (the Destroyer), and Vishnu (the Protector).

THE TRIMURTI

VEDIC GODS

Around 2000 BCE, India was invaded by Aryan people from the steppes of Central Asia. They brought with them a series of hymns, the Vedas, which were later written down. The Vedic gods are the earliest known Indian deities.

AGNI, GOD OF FIRE

SURYA
The Vedic sun god, Surya, is linked with **Agni** and **Vayu**. Like many early gods, their stories helped to explain to people once-mysterious forces, such as the sun and wind.

AGNI
The fire god, Agni was one of the most popular of the Vedic deities. By acting as a mediator between gods and humans, he played a vital part in religious rituals, which often involved burning a sacrifice to the gods.

INDRA
MOUNTED ON
AN ELEPHANT

INDRA
The warrior leader Indra led the Vedic gods in battles against the evil demons, the Asuras and Rakshasas. Strong and brave, he was also a great eater and drinker – qualities that appealed to the early Aryan people.

VAYU
The Vedic god of air and wind, Vayu, is often linked with **Indra** and his chariot. In later Hindu scriptures, Vayu is involved in conflicts with **Vishnu**.

VARUNA
All-knowing and all-seeing, Varuna, god of the sky and water, was the king of the Vedic gods. He had the power to punish sins, and to win his favor one had to lead a virtuous life.

BRAHMAN
To Hindus, Brahman is the ultimate reality. This unknowable force is the origin of all creation: pure being, pure delight, and pure intelligence.

TRIMURTI
Just over 2,000 years ago, three gods, who were known as the trimurti or triad, emerged as the most important – **Brahma**, **Vishnu**, and **Shiva**.

BRAHMA
Born from a lotus flower that grew from **Vishnu**'s navel, Brahma is the Creator god who creates the universe anew in each world cycle. Although he is a major member of the **Trimurti**, he is not often worshiped independently today. As Vishnu and Shiva represent opposite forces, Brahma represents the balance between them.

AVATARS OF VISHNU

When the world is under threat from evil, Vishnu appears in one of his avatars, or incarnations, to protect it. Hindu myths select ten avatars – from countless many – as being of special importance and power. These avatars also ensure that good thrives in the world.

VARAHA

MATSYA
The fish avatar, Matsya, like **Gilgamesh** and **Noah**, saved the first man, Manu, from the great flood. Since Manu had rescued the fish from an enemy, Matsya advised him that, to be safe, he should build a boat and fill it with all living things.

MATSYA

KURMA
The tortoise avatar, Kurma, helped to create the world by supporting the sacred Mount Mandara on his back. The gods used Mount Mandara to churn the Ocean of Milk and recover the elixir that had been lost during the flood.

VARAHA
The boar avatar, Varaha, was the third of the animal avatars. When the earth was plunged into the sea, Varaha used his tusk to raise up the earth – seen as a beautiful woman – to keep it from being drowned in the cosmic ocean.

KURMA

VISHNU RESTS ON THE SERPENT ANANTA.

VISHNU
Known as the Protector, Vishnu represents the binding force that holds together the universe and makes light and life possible. The cult of Vishnu is very popular, especially in the form of two of his avatars – **Krishna** and **Rama**. He embodies divine love and controls human fate. Vishnu is recognizable by his dark blue color and also by his four arms, which suggest that he can reach into all four corners of the universe.

GARUDA

GARUDA
The heavenly eagle Garuda is **Vishnu**'s steed. When Vishnu rides the eagle across the skies, Garuda becomes a symbol of the sun and is often linked with the fire god, **Agni**.

SHIVA
Known as the Destroyer, Shiva takes away life so that it can be recreated. Many opposites are combined in his fearsome figure – he is awe-inspiring and mild, the source of both creation and destruction, active yet thoughtful, and fertile but also chaste.

Shiva's vertical third eye

Shiva beats drum to summon up a new creation.

SHIVA

Flame of destruction symbolizes rebirth.

Flaming halo symbolizes the cosmos.

BHAIRAVA
The destructive aspect of **Shiva** is known as Bhairava, the "joyous devourer." As a figure of death, he is depicted with white skin – a symbol of the ashes of the cremation ground.

NARASIMHA
The half-man, half-lion avatar, Narasimha, fought Hiranyakashipu, an evil demon whom **Brahma** had made invulnerable to blows from the weapons of gods or men. Narasimha defeated the demon, and disemboweled him.

NARASIMHA

VAMANA
The dwarf avatar, Vamana, asked the demon Bali for as much land as he could cover in three steps. Bali agreed, and Vamana transformed himself into a giant, winning back the world from the demon.

VAMANA

PARASHURAMA
The avatar known as "**Rama** with the axe" wiped out the entire warrior class 21 times, because they threatened to take over the world. He also used his axe to kill the hundred-armed Arjuna, as well as his own mother.

PARASHURAMA

RAMA
The lord Rama – the seventh and one of the most popular avatars – is the hero of the *Ramayana*, one of the great Hindu epic poems. Rama defeated demon-king **Ravana**, the ruler of Sri Lanka, who had abducted his wife, **Sita**.

RAMA

BUDDHA

BUDDHA
The founder of Buddhism is seen as the ninth avatar of **Vishnu**. It was said that **Buddha** came to earth to end animal sacrifices. It was also said that he misled sinners, so that they could not avoid punishment.

KRISHNA
Worshiped as a god in his own right, Krishna is a popular avatar, and is famous for killing the demon king Kamsa. Many other stories are told about his qualities as soldier, lover, and ruler.

KRISHNA

KALKI
Vishnu's final avatar, Kalki, has not yet appeared on earth. He is expected as a warrior on a white horse, and he will destroy all evil. This will enable good to prosper – to begin a new Golden Age.

KALKI

LINGAM AND YONI
Shiva is most closely associated with sexuality. One of his symbols is the lingam, or male sexual organ. Lingam statues sit in the middle of Shiva's temples to symbolize the earth's center. They are accompanied by their female counterpart – the yoni.

NANDIN BULL
Shiva's mount is a milk white bull, Nandin, who is a powerful symbol of the god's fertility and strength. In temples, a recumbent statue of Nandin often appears near the entrance to the shrine, looking toward the **lingam**.

GODS AND GODDESSES

HINDUISM HAS HUNDREDS of gods and goddesses. The ones shown in this book are a selection of the greatest deities, figures whose images are seen in temples all over India and who are widely revered and recognized. There are also lesser gods and goddesses who are worshiped in particular regions of India, where they are said to be local incarnations of the great gods. This variety of gods and goddesses may be confusing to non-Hindus, but Hindus learn about the deities from an early age, listen to stories about them, and see images of many of them in their homes. Each statue or portrait has its own special attributes – such as the elephant head of Ganesh and the blue skin of Vishnu – which make them easy to recognize.

DURGA

DEVI
The name Devi means "the Goddess." All of the Hindu goddesses are, in one sense, different aspects of Devi. Devi has caring incarnations such as **Parvati**, and violent ones such as **Durga** and **Kali**, who demand living sacrifices from their devotees. Although Devi was not recognized as a major deity until much later, worship of the mother goddess probably has ancient roots in pre-Vedic India.

VILLAGE GODDESSES
In addition to the great goddesses who are recognized all over India, most villages and regions worship their own local goddesses. There are thousands of village goddesses, many of whom have a tribal origin, founded on the idea of an earth goddess associated with farming and fertility. Village goddesses are often also called Mata or Amma, both of which mean "mother."

SHAKTI
Each of the principal gods has both a male and a female side. The female aspect of the gods is known as the "shakti." Therefore, each of the three gods of the Hindu **trimurti** has a female counterpart – **Sarasvati** is the consort of **Brahma**, and **Lakshmi** is the wife of **Vishnu**. Shiva's consort can take many forms, including the benign **Parvati** and the fearsome **Durga**.

LAKSHMI, GODDESS OF WEALTH

Skull necklace, a symbol of reincarnation

Sword for beheading demons

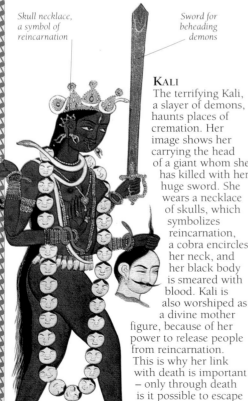

KALI
The terrifying Kali, a slayer of demons, haunts places of cremation. Her image shows her carrying the head of a giant whom she has killed with her huge sword. She wears a necklace of skulls, which symbolizes reincarnation, a cobra encircles her neck, and her black body is smeared with blood. Kali is also worshiped as a divine mother figure, because of her power to release people from reincarnation. This is why her link with death is important – only through death is it possible to escape the endless cycle of rebirth.

WRATHFUL KALI

PARVATI
The most important of the gentle, modest, and benign forms of **Shiva**'s wife is Parvati. She is the ideal partner for the god, because her active, caring character complements Shiva's more detached nature. Stories about Parvati tell of her birth from the sacred Himalayan mountain range and her determination to lure the ascetic Shiva into marriage.

LAKSHMI
Vishnu's wife Lakshmi is the goddess of wealth and good fortune. In two of her four arms, she carries a lotus blossom (symbol of the soul) and a coin (to denote blessings and wealth). As the consort of the Protector, she embodies the active side of creation: Vishnu stands for the idea of creation, Lakshmi represents the creative process itself.

DURGA
The goddess Durga is portrayed carrying weapons and riding a lion or tiger. A figure of violence, she protects the good and destroys evil. Her main festival occurs at harvesttime, symbolizing her continuing link with fertility.

SARASVATI
The goddess of the arts, Sarasvati is often shown holding a book and a vina (a musical instrument), or sitting meditating on a lotus flower. As the wife of the Creator **Brahma**, she is said to be able to create whatever comes into Brahma's thoughts. She also invented Sanskrit, the language of the Hindu scriptures. Sarasvati has a spring festival dedicated to her, called Vasant Panchami. On this day, people gather to worship her by playing music.

Lotus flower

SARASVATI, GODDESS OF POETRY AND MUSIC

GANESH, GOD OF GOOD LUCK

GANESH

The elephant-headed god Ganesh, the son of **Shiva** and **Parvati**, is popular with many Hindus. As the god of good luck, people pray to him to remove any obstacles they might face, especially before new undertakings such as moving, marriage, or exams.

HANUMAN

The monkey god Hanuman is known for his strength, his bravery, and his devotion to **Rama**. The great Hindu epic poem, the *Ramayana*, tells how he helped Rama to rescue his abducted wife Sita. His exploits included fighting demons and organizing the building of a bridge linking India and Sri Lanka, where Sita was imprisoned.

YAMA

The Hindu god of death is called Yama, similar to **Osiris** in ancient Egypt. Yama rides a buffalo, and carries a mace and a noose, which he uses to catch his victims. He rules over the land of the dead, and is accompanied by his two dogs, each with four eyes. The soul of a dying person has to hurry past the dogs guarding the entrance to Yama's kingdom. Yamaduta, Yama's messenger, guides souls on their journey.

Flaming wheel of fire, a symbol of Vishnu

HANUMAN, THE MONKEY GOD

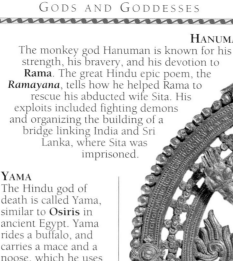

RAMA WITH HIS BOW DEFEATS THE DEMONS.

The gold city of Lanka (now Sri Lanka)

Krishna's skin is blue, the color of the sea and sky.

Flute is a symbol of cowherds, with whom Krishna spent part of his youth.

KRISHNA, THE EIGHTH AVATAR OF VISHNU

KARTIKEYYA

The son of **Shiva**, called Kumara, Skanda, Subrahmanya, or Kartikeyya, is the god of war. In one story of his birth, he was born from the Ganges River, and is known as Ganga-ja, or "born from the Ganges." In another, he started life as six children, made from six sparks from Shiva's eyes. **Parvati** hugged her sons so tightly they turned into one six-headed child.

KRISHNA

The eighth **avatar** of the god **Vishnu**, Krishna is worshiped as a god in his own right. Krishna had a happy childhood, and is often worshiped as a child who brings joy to his devotees. He is seen as a handsome youth, and his love for his consort Radha reflects the devotion his followers feel toward him. In the *Bhagavad Gita* (part of the *Mahabharata* epic), Krishna is the supreme lord, who speaks of the need to lose desire in order to realize **moksha**.

RAMA

The lord Rama, hero of the *Ramayana* and the seventh **avatar** of **Vishnu**, is a much more human figure than **Krishna**. Rama weeps when his father dies, and he shows deep emotion when he has to part with his mother and go into exile. But his honesty and rectitude make him a hero, and he is worshiped by many Hindus.

BELIEFS AND WRITINGS

ALTHOUGH THERE IS NO SINGLE essential belief that makes a person a Hindu, and no single sacred text, certain central beliefs are shared by most Hindus. These include the notion of samsara – the cycle of death and rebirth. Above all, Hindus strive to attain moksha, or liberation from this cycle. There are various paths to moksha, including those listed in the *Bhagavad Gita*: *jnana marga* – the path of wisdom, by which one lives a life of meditation; *karma marga* – the path of action, by which one performs one's assigned duty; and *bhakti marga* – the path of devotion, where one is dedicated to God. Each path requires letting go of the self, the senses, and other worldly matters.

MOKSHA

Hindus hope to achieve moksha, or release from the cycle of rebirth. When a person attains moksha – for example, by following the path, or *marga*, of devotion, insight, and action – he or she becomes united with **Brahman**. Opinions differ as to what happens when moksha is reached – some Hindu writings describe it in impersonal terms, as the blending of the soul with Brahman, others as a closeness to God.

SADHUS (HOLY MEN) ON THE WAY TO ACHIEVING MOKSHA.

SAMSARA
Hindus believe that we are caught in **samsara** – an endless cycle of death and rebirth. After death, we are born again, and the nature of the rebirth depends on our spiritual state when we died.

KARMA
Karma refers to both action and the law of cause and effect that rules life and rebirth. If our actions are good, we shall acquire good karma, a good life, and a favorable rebirth; bad actions have the opposite effect.

WHEEL OF LIFE, REPRESENTING SAMSARA

BRAHMAN
In their pursuit of liberation from **samsara**, Hindus hope to become one with **Brahman**, the ultimate reality. Brahman consists of mind and spirit only – all physical substance is unreal.

ATMAN
The eternal soul, or atman, is a person's essential self. The atman in the person is parallel with **Brahman** within the universe. Their union achieves **moksha**. The jivatman, or mind, is concerned with the everyday world and is distinct from atman.

KAMA, OR SENSUAL PLEASURE, IS ONE OF THE FOUR AIMS OF HINDU LIFE.

Radha

Krishna

DHARMA
A person's **dharma** is his or her moral duty. This varies with a person's social position or **jati** (caste), and the stage in life that he or she has reached. It is also influenced by the universal dharma to which everyone is subject. Hindu scriptures state that each person should follow his or her dharma, not that of another. **Gurus** and philosophies may help in a quest for dharma.

MAYA
The word maya was used in the **Vedas** to describe the creative energy of the gods. The world was said to be made by this creative energy. In later Hindu writings, maya acquired a more negative meaning. The later philosophers, like **Shankara**, described maya as the illusion that prevents us from seeing that the world is an aspect of **Brahman**.

FOUR AIMS OF LIFE
Hinduism singles out four aims of human life. It is acceptable to pursue the first two – pleasure (*kama*) and prosperity (*artha*) – provided there is no conflict with the third aim – moral duty, or **dharma**. The ultimate aim is enlightenment, or **moksha**.

AHIMSA
Nonviolence and respect for all living things is known as **ahimsa**. It is important in Hinduism because doing violence to life also harms the person who commits violence. This will result in bad **karma** and may lead to an unfavorable rebirth.

FAMOUS TEACHERS

There is a long tradition of Hindu teachers, who have guided individuals toward moksha or passed on their teachings to the wider community. Many teachers are associated with specific sacred writings, such as commentaries on the Upanishads.

SHANKARA
The greatest philosopher of Hinduism, Shankara (788–820) insisted on the authority of scripture and on the identity of the soul with **Brahman**.

RAMAKRISHNA
Sri Ramakrishna (1836–1886) said God is present in every religion; other faiths offer paths to the truth that are as valid as Hinduism for their followers.

GANDHI
Mohandas Gandhi (1869–1948) campaigned all his life against oppression and discrimination. He protested against British rule in India, but his belief in **ahimsa** led him to use only non violent methods of opposition. He is widely revered as a great teacher, demonstrating through his life how Indians could live free from the problems caused by class and caste.

MOHANDAS GANDHI

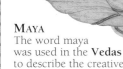

SACRED TEXTS

Hinduism has no single sacred book, but rather many texts from the 12th century BCE onward, written in the ancient Sanskrit language. Some of these works are known as *shruti*, or "revealed" texts. Shruti texts are said to have always existed, and are believed to have been written by divinely inspired prophets. *Smriti*, or "remembered" literature, is also said to have been divinely inspired.

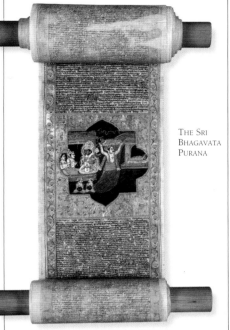

THE SRI BHAGAVATA PURANA

PURANAS

The Puranas (CE 250–1700) are a vast body of complex narratives that include stories about the gods, conduct of the different social castes, and the celebration of festivals. These *smriti* writings also contain much information about Hindu mythology. Each text conventionally focuses on a member of the Hindu **trimurti**.

VEDAS

The *Vedas,* meaning "knowledge," consist of four *samhitas*, or collections, of ancient *shruti* texts, composed before 1000 BCE but written down later. The four Vedas are the **Rig Veda***, Yajur Veda, Sama Veda,* and *Atharva Veda.* Each of the Vedas has a Brahmana (explanatory text), Aranyaka (magical formulas), and **Upanishad** (teaching) added to it.

RIG VEDA

This is the oldest and most sacred of the four Vedas, dating from *c.*1200 BCE. Its ten books contain more than 1,000 hymns addressed to deities. The *Rig Veda* is used mainly in temple rituals that include chanting and prayers.

UPANISHADS

The title "Upanishads" comes from Sanskrit, meaning "to sit nearby," since these are texts that were based on teachers' lessons to their followers. They reveal Hinduism's mystical side and introduce the idea of **Brahman** and its relationship with **atman**.

LAWS OF MANU

The mythical Manu was said to be the first man, and also a great law giver. Written in CE 300, the *Laws of Manu* are *smriti* texts offering instruction on the Hindu's moral and social duties, such as teachings about the conduct of the different social classes.

MAHABHARATA

The longest poem ever written, the *Mahabharata* (*c*.300 BCE–CE 300) tells of a war between the families of Pandu and his brother Dhritarashtra. The poem tells a story about the conflict of good and evil and of the difficulty in knowing one's **dharma**. It includes episodes that cover all aspects of life, from love to war.

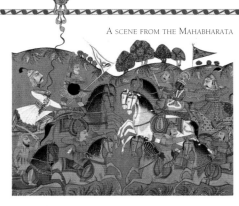

A SCENE FROM THE MAHABHARATA

The warrior Arjuna

Krishna, driving the chariot

SCENE FROM THE BHAGAVAD GITA

RAMAYANA

This great epic Sanskrit poem, probably written between 200 BCE and CE 200, tells of Rama's love for Sita, her abduction by the demon Ravana, and her rescue. For 2,000 years, poetry, drama, and temple ritual have celebrated this popular story.

A SCENE FROM THE RAMAYANA

LAKSHMAN

Rama's brother, Lakshman, was a devoted companion during Rama's search for **Sita**, his abducted wife. With the help of the **monkey army**, Lakshman and Rama battled to win her back.

SITA

The name Sita means "furrow," and refers to her birth from the soil plowed by her father, King Janaka. When she became **Rama**'s wife, she proved herself to be an ideal consort – devoted, pure, and faithful. After her abduction by **Ravana**, Rama was forced to send Sita into exile.

RAVANA

The demon Ravana was ruler of the island of Sri Lanka. He was an evil monster, with ten heads and twenty arms. He was so strong that no god could kill him.

MONKEY ARMY

The monkey god **Hanuman**, along with an army of monkeys provided by the monkey king Sugriva helped **Rama** to fight **Ravana**. The monkeys did this because Rama had once helped their king when he was dethroned by his half-brother.

BHAGAVAD GITA

The sixth book of the *Mahabharata*, this is the best known of the great Sanskrit texts. It takes the form of a dialogue between prince Arjuna and his charioteer **Krishna**. During this discussion, **Vishnu** teaches Arjuna the three paths to **moksha**.

LIFE AND SOCIETY

THE SCRIPTURES PORTRAY Hindu society as a harmonious whole, where every part functions for the good of all. Each of the four varnas, or social classes, plays its assigned part. It is, for example, the duty of the warrior class to protect the people by fighting their enemies, an activity inappropriate for other classes. Today, social barriers are breaking down, and it is becoming possible for people of one class to perform jobs normally done by members of another.

SAMSKARAS
The key stages in a person's life – birth, coming of age, marriage, and death – are marked by rites of passage, or samskaras. These sacred rituals are designed to guide the person into the next stage of existence.

SAMSKARA OF BIRTH

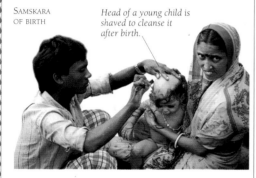

Head of a young child is shaved to cleanse it after birth.

UPANAYANA
In a coming-of-age ceremony to mark his spiritual birth, a high-caste boy is given a sacred thread to wear for the rest of his life. He studies the scriptures and is taught the Gayatri, from the **Rig Veda**.

JATI
Every Hindu is born into one of thousands of jatis, or social castes. Caste is linked to the idea of **samsara** (rebirth) and **karma** (cause and effect). Hindus are assumed to be born into particular castes as a result of past karma. Traditionally, the caste of a family determines its members' jobs, their marriage partners, and even with whom they eat. For example, there are castes for specific professions, such as potters and leather workers. Today these social barriers are slowly breaking down.

BIRTH
When a Hindu is born, the baby is ritually washed, and the sacred syllable, "om," is written with honey on the tongue. Another important ritual is the naming ceremony, or namkaran.

HINDU WEDDING CEREMONY

UNTOUCHABLES
Members of the lowest social level, beyond the caste system altogether, were formerly called untouchables, now called Dalits, or the oppressed. Traditionally, they were banished from normal social life. Today, education helps make it possible for Dalits to rise in society.

MARRIAGE
Hindu weddings may last for up to 12 days, with feasting, dancing, and religious rituals. The central ritual traditionally occurs at night. The couple walks around a sacred fire and takes seven steps – each symbolizing one aspect of their life together.

DEATH
Hindus are usually cremated, traditionally on an open pyre lit by the deceased's eldest son. The bones should be thrown into water, ideally the **Ganges River**, to purify them and release the person's spirit.

FUNERAL PROCESSION

ASHRAMAS
Traditionally, Hindus recognize four ashramas, or stages of life. The first is the period of education, when a person studies the **Vedas** and prepares for a useful role in society. During the second, a person marries and brings up a family. The third ashrama is at retirement, when one gives up work and material possessions to adopt a more spiritual lifestyle. Finally, in the fourth ashrama, a Hindu gives up all social life and concentrates on a religious quest.

A STUDENT IN THE FIRST ASHRAMA

VARNAS

Hinduism classifies all members of society into one of four broad groups, or classes, called varnas. According to the *Purusa-sukta*, one of the hymns of the *Rig Veda*, the four varnas came into being at the creation of the world, when a primeval being called Purusha was sacrificed. Purusha's mouth, arms, legs, and feet became the four different varnas.

BRAHMINS
The priestly class, or Brahmins, are the highest of the four varnas. Said to come from the mouth of Purusha, the Brahmins chant the sacred scriptures – a skill that was especially important in early Hinduism when all knowledge of the scriptures was by word of mouth.

BRAHMIN OFFICIATING AT TEMPLE CEREMONY

KSHATRIYAS
The second class – the Kshatriyas – are warriors and rulers. Springing from the arms of Purusha, they use this part of their body to protect their people and fight for them.

VAISHYAS
Merchants and farmers make up the Vaishyas, the third varna. They grew from the legs of Purusha, which is fitting for people who need to travel, but also perform skilled tasks.

SHUDRAS
The fourth class, the Shudras, are the laborers, who are said to have come from the feet of Purusha. Just as the feet serve the body, the Shudras perform the menial jobs.

HOLY MEN AND WOMEN

One route toward moksha is to become a sadhu – an ascetic holy man or woman. Sadhus renounce all possessions, wear as few clothes as possible, dwell away from society, and obtain their food by begging. Laypeople revere and respect sadhus, support them, and look to them for religious advice.

Shiva devotees are recognizable from marks across the forehead.

SHIVA DEVOTEE

SADHU AND SANNYASIN

Sadhus and Sannyasins, who have reached the final **ashramas**, practice many ascetic disciplines. One of the duties of a sadhu is to undergo ritual disciplines, such as fasting or practicing **yoga** postures. These disciplines, which an ascetic may sometimes do for long periods, are said to create *tapas*, or heat. This influences the inner being of the sadhu and brings him or her closer to **moksha**.

SHIVA DEVOTEES

Some **sadhus** devote their lives to **Shiva**, a god who gave up everything to lead an ascetic life. Like Shiva, devotees cover themselves with ashes and let their hair become matted. They wear white lines of ash and a red mark on their foreheads, to recall Shiva's third eye of enlightenment and to signify their rejection of society.

GURU

Spiritual teachers are called gurus. A guru must be learned in the scriptures, free from desire and deceit, and spiritually fulfilled. Gurus can teach the **sacred texts** to high-caste youths. Hindus ask a guru's advice at important points in their life, such as marriage or a new job. Many gurus set up religious communities called ashrams where they teach devotees.

SACRED COW

SACRED COW

Krishna is often depicted as a cowherd. The cow is an ancient symbol of mother earth and of the earth's fertility, and is sacred in Hinduism – even the act of feeding a cow is seen as a kind of worship. This reverence for the cow reflects Hindu respect for all animals. Most Hindus are vegetarian.

PRACTICING YOGA MEDITATION

The padma asana, *or lotus position, with legs crossed and palms facing outward*

TANTRIC HINDUISM

This branch of Hinduism is based on texts called the Tantras. Tantric Hinduism stresses Shakti, the female energy of the Mother Goddess, and sees the human body as a mirror of the cosmos. Tantric Hindus try to achieve liberation through spiritual power, or siddhi.

YANTRAS

Tantric Hindus use yantras – diagrams drawn on the ground, on stone, or on cloth – to form a focus for meditation. The most powerful of all yantras is the Sri Yantra, an image of the entire cosmos. The interpenetrating triangles at the center stand for **Shiva** and **Shakti**, the masculine and feminine energies.

CHAKRAS

According to Tantric Hinduism, a system of wheels, or centers, of power exists in the body. These wheels, called chakras, act as centers of energy that flow up and down the body. Each chakra corresponds to a specific organ of the body, and to an aspect of life – from the basic will to live to our highest consciousness.

YANTRA

YOGA

A complete system of philosophy, yoga involves both physical and mental disciplines to help the practitioner achieve **moksha**. Yoga helps the mind master concentration and efficient meditation and encourages attitudes such as nonviolence and self-discipline, correct posture and breathing. The ultimate goal is to reach a level of higher consciousness as a prelude to moksha.

FESTIVALS AND WORSHIP

A HOME SHRINE DEPICTING
THE GOD VISHNU

FOR MANY HINDUS, the center of religious life is the home, with its own shrine where family members may worship daily. During the year, major festivals are devoted to specific gods or goddesses, which provide extra opportunities to honor Hindu deities. Temple worship is also important. Hindu temples are some of the most beautiful and ornately decorated of all religious buildings – fitting homes for the gods and goddesses who dwell there. Hindus do not have to attend the temple, unlike people of other faiths. Another important part of Hindu worship is to go on a pilgrimage.

HINDU TEMPLES

The sacred chamber is ornately decorated with Hindu gods and goddesses.

Hindu temples vary in design. At the temple's heart is a shrine or sacred chamber, called the *garbhagriha*, that houses the image of the god to whom the temple is dedicated. The shrine has a spire-shaped roof that acts both as a link between heaven and earth, and symbolizes Mount Meru, the home of the gods. A temple also includes at least one *mandapa*, or outer hall, containing shrines to other deities.

MINAKSHI TEMPLE, MADURAI

WATER
One important feature of Hindu temples is the presence of water. Water is important in Hinduism for several reasons. Ritual cleanliness is vital, and priests bathe in running water before worship. Traditionally, rivers are the gods' dwelling places, so water in and around the temple helps make the place attractive to the deity who lives there.

SHRINES
Regular temple worship is not as important in Hinduism as in other faiths, so many Hindus worship at home. Hindu homes usually contain a shrine, which can vary in size from a small shelf with a statue of a god to a whole room. Here the family burns lights and incense, makes offerings, and prays. There are many shrines along the sacred **Ganges River**.

MURTIS
Each shrine contains a statue, or murti, of a god. More than just an image, a murti contains the essence of the deity it represents. Murtis are therefore treated with the greatest reverence and respect. Every morning in Hindu temples, the priests awaken, wash, dress, and garland the murtis.

PUJA
Worship, or **puja**, is based on service and offerings to the **murti**. The worshipers may wash the murti, touch its face and feet with a flower dipped in water, dress it, garland it with flowers, and anoint it with oils. They offer food to the deity, burn incense, and entertain it by singing hymns. Most important, devotees make eye contact with the murti in a ritual called **darshana**.

Used to sprinkle rosewater around the shrine in symbolic purification

ROSEWATER SPRINKLER

DARSHANA
The worshiper and god communicate in darshana, or "seeing," when they make eye contact. This usually takes place as the worshiper walks around the statue of the god in a clockwise direction. By paying homage to the god and looking at him, the worshiper hopes the deity will grant a request and bestow him or her with his grace and insight.

PRASADA
Offerings of food made by the priests to the **murti** – called prasada – include beautiful arrangements of cooked rice, ghee (clarified butter), fruit, and sugar. It is believed that the god takes the essence of the food while it is left in the presence of the murti. Priests collect the leftovers and distribute them to the worshipers. Consecrated by the god, this food is thought to be a great blessing.

PRASADA FRUIT

PRIESTS
It is the priests' job to tend and worship the **murtis** in their temple. The priests lead in prayers, chant to invoke the deity's presence, and act as go-betweens – linking worshipers to the deity, entering the central shrine, and making offerings on behalf of the worshipers. Priests are usually, but not always, members of the **Brahmin** class.

MANTRAS
Sacred Sanskrit chants called mantras – from the **Vedas** – are used in Hindu rituals. Hindus believe reciting them will put them in touch with God.

PILGRIMAGE

From a short journey on foot to visit a local hilltop shrine to an exhausting walk lasting many months, pilgrimages form an important part of Hindu worship. People go on pilgrimages to bathe in sacred rivers, to visit special sites in the Himalayas, to worship a deity by means of darshana, and, above all, to purify the soul and bring the pilgrim closer to God.

PILGRIM BATHING IN THE GANGES

GANGES RIVER
Rivers have always been seen as the special dwelling places of gods. Water is both cleansing and life-giving, so rivers are important sites of pilgrimage. The most sacred river is the Ganges, which is said to have flowed in heaven. The river is worshiped as the goddess Ganga.

VARANASI

SACRED SITES
Other places of pilgrimage include Mathura, **Krishna**'s birthplace in northern India; **Rama**'s capital city, Ayodhya; **Vishnu**'s Badrinath shrine in the Himalayan foothills; and the shrine to the Mother Goddess at the Minakshi temple, Madurai.

KUMBHA MELA
While this five-day religious fair is held frequently, the most important festival is held every 12 years at Allahabad. Millions attend the fair, which features stalls, sideshows, and acrobats, as well as processions of holy men and bathing in the sacred **Ganges River**.

VARANASI
The city of Varanasi, also called Benares, is on the **Ganges** River. It is India's most important place of pilgrimage and is said to be the home of **Shiva**. The city is also a center of Hindu scholarship. If a person dies at Varanasi and the ashes are thrown into the Ganges, they are purified and may achieve **moksha**.

KUMBHA MELA

DIWALI
All over India, Diwali, the autumn festival of lights, is celebrated. Lanterns are lit to symbolize the triumph of good over evil. The lights remind Hindus of the victories of good in their mythology, such as **Rama**'s return after defeating Ravana. **Lakshmi**, the goddess of good fortune, is worshiped at Diwali.

DIWALI

Children light candles for Diwali.

HOLI
Originally a fertility ceremony, the spring festival of Holi celebrates the Hindu New Year in March. It is a popular national celebration, especially in northern India. People build bonfires on which they roast special foods. They look into the flames of the fire because it is said that the most fertile land next year will lie in the direction of the flames. Other Holi customs, such as dancing, are also associated with fertility. Holi is a time when normal social barriers are ignored. Women may beat their menfolk, and members of different castes throw colored dyes at one another.

AT HOLI, BOYS RUB DYE IN EACH OTHER'S HAIR.

NAVARATRI
The festival of Navaratri, or nine nights, is held during September or October. Its main feature is worship of the goddess, often in the form of the warrior deity **Durga**. In some areas the festival is called Durga puja. Durga's image, seated on a lion, is worshiped, recalling the story of how the goddess, riding her lion, defeated the demon king Mahisha. Other goddesses are worshiped at Navaratri, especially **Sarasvati**.

DASSERA
Dassera is the day after **Navaratri**, when people celebrate **Rama**'s life, especially the rescue of his wife **Sita**. They worship shami trees in order to be reminded of an episode in the *Mahabharata*, when the sons of Pandu returned from exile and removed their weapons, which were hidden in these trees.

SHIVARATRI
At this national festival, held in March, people pay special honor to **Shiva**. During the day worshipers fast, then hold all-night vigils at Shiva's temples.

JANAMASHTAMI
This August festival celebrates the birthday of **Krishna**. A daytime fast is followed by **puja**, before the fast is broken in the evening.

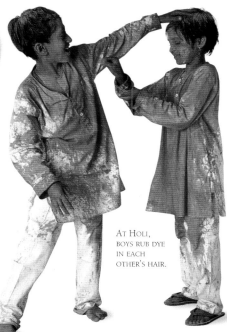

THE FESTIVAL OF NAVARATRI IS CELEBRATED WITH MUSIC.

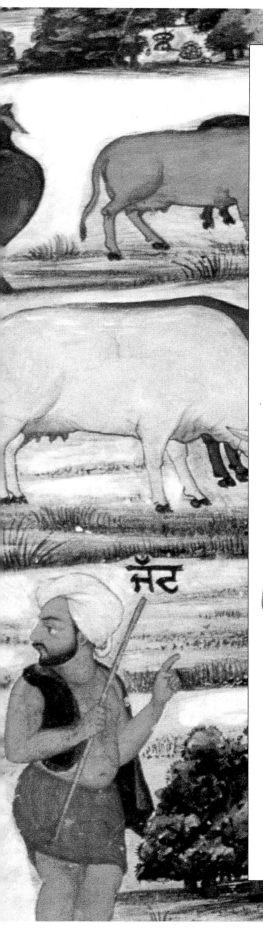

JAINISM AND SIKHISM

The two Indian religions of Jainism and Sikhism have few followers compared to the other Indian faiths, but are still influential. Jainism, with about 4 million followers, is concentrated mainly in northern and western India. Sikhism originated in the Punjab, where the majority of the world's 22 million Sikhs still live. Both faiths pursue freedom from the cycle of rebirth, but otherwise, their outlook is very different.

JAINISM

There is no supreme creator god in Jainism. Instead, Jains take their guidance from a series of teachers, or jinas. One of the most important doctrines of these teachers is that of nonviolence, or ahimsa. This has proved one of the most significant and influential ideas in modern Indian thought.

JAIN TIRTHANKARA, A SPIRITUAL TEACHER

SIKHISM

Sikhs believe in one God. They are a minority in mainly Hindu India, and have often experienced persecution as a result of their beliefs. Sikhs therefore have a strong sense of community and uphold the right to bear arms to defend themselves and their people. They strive to understand the ways of others and to care for anyone who is in need of help.

JAIN HISTORY AND BELIEFS

THE JAIN RELIGION EMERGED IN INDIA between the seventh and fifth centuries BCE, although Jains consider their faith to be eternal, and periodically renewed. Jains are followers of a Jina, or conqueror, one of a series of religious leaders who have cast off all worldly concerns and achieved the highest level of knowledge. Jinas, also called Tirthankaras, show their followers how to achieve liberation from the cycle of reincarnation by attaining the Three Jewels – right knowledge, faith, and conduct. Correct conduct means abandoning violence, greed, and deceit, being chaste, and taking a series of vows.

TIRTHANKARA ALTAR

TIRTHANKARAS

Jains believe that time is infinite, made up of many cosmic cycles stretching back millions of years. Each cycle contains periods of improvement and of decline, when faith and human behavior reach a low point. During times of decline, a great leader and teacher called a Tirthankara – a pathmaker or maker of a ford across the ocean of **rebirth** – appears. He will revive the religion and show people how to behave and achieve liberation.

MAHAVIRA'S BIRTH AT THE HANDS OF THE GOD INDRA

THE SAMAVASARANA OF MAHAVIRA

SAMAVASARANA

When a **Tirthankara**, or savior-teacher, delivers his first sermon, he uses a structure called a samavasarana. The Tirthankara sits on a platform in the center, and the listeners gather in a circle around him and contemplate his words.

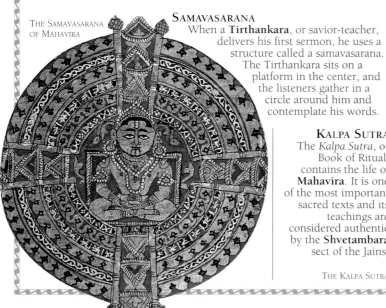

MAHAVIRA

The 24th **Tirthankara** of the current time cycle, Mahavira was born during the sixth century BCE. He was a prince, but at the age of 28 he gave up his comfortable life to become an ascetic and seek liberation from the cycle of **rebirth**. He taught a doctrine of nonviolence and spiritual equality. At age 42, he achieved full enlightenment and taught for 30 years until his death. His community of followers spread Jainism in Mahavira's native Bihar in northeastern India and beyond.

KALPA SUTRA

The *Kalpa Sutra*, or Book of Ritual, contains the life of **Mahavira**. It is one of the most important sacred texts and its teachings are considered authentic by the **Shvetambara** sect of the Jains.

THE KALPA SUTRA

AHIMSA

The Jain ideal of non-violence and respect for all life is called **ahimsa**. It is a key Jain belief, reinforcing nonattachment to worldly things. As in Hinduism, ahimsa is also important because Jains believe that as a result of **karma**, violence has a harmful effect on both the victim and the person who commits it.

ANEKANTAVADA

For Jains, reality is characterized by change and impermanence. According to the Jain philosophy of anekantavada, there is no single reality and there are many perspectives on the truth. This is illustrated by a story about a group of blind men touching an elephant: One touched its trunk and thought it was a snake, another grasped its tail and thought it was a rope.

JAMBUDVIPA, INNER CONTINENT OF THE JAIN UNIVERSE

LOKA

Jains see the loka, or cosmos, as revealing how all things depend on each other. At its heart is a series of concentric realms centering on Jambudvipa, the inner continent where mortal life exists. At the center of Jambudvipa is the sacred mountain, Mount Meru. The outer circles are realms of the senses, where no religious life exists. Below these lie the eight levels of hell.

FIVE SUPREME BEINGS

Jains revere five classes of being, which reflect most closely the religious life to which Jains aspire. Devout Jains follow a daily ritual of invoking the five supreme beings, bowing to the four points of the compass as they do so.

ARHATS

Also known as a **Tirthankara** or **Jina** (great teacher), an arhat is the first supreme being, a teacher who lays the foundations for the liberation of others, and can do so without the guidance of another teacher. His image is at the center of the siddhachakra.

Siddha

Monk

Arhat

ACHARYAS

Spiritual teachers known as acharyas make up the third level of supreme beings. Each acharya leads an entire order of monks or nuns. The image of the acharya is in the east of the siddhachakra.

UPADHYAYAS

The fourth level of supreme beings consists of the upadhyayas – teaching monks who pass on their knowledge of the scriptures to other monks and nuns. The image of the upadhyaya is in the south of the siddhachakra.

A SIDDHACHAKRA DEPICTS THE FIVE SUPREME BEINGS OF JAINISM.

Acharya

Upadhyaya

SIDDHAS

The second supreme being is the siddha, the Jain equivalent of a **saint**. A siddha is a soul who has achieved liberation through the guidance of a teacher, and who lives in a state of bliss at the top of the cosmos.

MONKS

The rest of the Jain monks occupy the fifth level of supreme beings. The monk's image is placed in the west of the siddhachakra. The **Digambara** believe that only males can attain liberation.

ASCETICISM

Ideally, Jains seek to live an ascetic life, denying themselves worldly comforts and pleasures and joining one of the monastic orders. To become a monk, novices must be physically and morally fit and take the **Five Great Vows**. New monks and nuns are expected to join with two or three others to live a life of increasingly rigorous discipline, wandering between **temples** and meditating.

DIGAMBARA

The sect of the Digambara, or "skyclad", believes that a monk should give up all possessions, including clothes. They believe that clothes inspire worldly notions of modesty and that a person who washes clothes is open to the risk of doing violence. Digambara monks go completely naked and carry only a peacock feather whisk – to sweep away insects from their path so that these creatures are not killed.

A "SKYCLAD" DIGAMBARA MONK

SHVETAMBARA NUNS

LIFE CYCLE

Jains, like the followers of other Indian religions, believe that human souls are continually being reborn, and that the way people live affects this rebirth. The ideal is to avoid worldly attachments, rid our souls of the harmful substance called karma, and achieve liberation.

JIVA

The universe contains an infinite number of souls, or jivas. Jivas exist eternally and have no material substance of their own. Their natural state is one of bliss and knowledge of the self. However, jivas become associated with the material world because of the effects of **karma**.

KARMA

As a result of worldly actions, a substance called karma becomes attached to the **jiva**, clothing it in a material body. Karma weighs down the soul, making liberation impossible and entangling the soul in the cycle of **rebirth**.

MOKSHA, THE RELEASE OF THE SPIRIT

REBIRTH

According to its **karma**, a soul can be reborn in any form – as a human, an animal, or even a plant. Only by ridding itself of its karma can a soul achieve liberation.

RENUNCIATION

To avoid the further accumulation of **karma**, people should adopt a way of life that renounces, or gives up, worldly ways. This is why **asceticism** is so important in Jainism. Through discipline, a person's soul can rid itself of karma that has already accumulated.

MOKSHA

When the soul achieves moksha, or liberation, it is freed from **karma** and the cycle of **rebirth**, and regains its natural lightness. The soul floats to the top of the universe where it dwells in bliss.

TATTVARTHA SUTRA

Written by Umasvati, who lived sometime between 150 and 350 CE, this text summarizes Jain doctrine in 350 Sanskrit sentences. Later medieval writers composed commentaries on the text, which explore many aspects of Jainism.

SHVETAMBARA

When a man becomes a Shvetambara, or white-clad monk, he is given three pieces of cloth to wear, a staff, a begging bowl, and a wool whisk. Like the **Digambara**, these monks must beg for food. For eight months each year, they wander the countryside, visiting **temples** and places of pilgrimage. In the rainy season, they are given instruction and meet their leaders. Women may become Shvetambara nuns.

LIFE AND WORSHIP

THE JAIN WAY OF LIFE is dominated by the need to achieve a favorable rebirth, or, better still, to attain liberation from the cycle of birth and rebirth altogether. For some, this means becoming a member of a monastic order. Laypeople also try to follow as closely as possible the austere lifestyle of the monk, chiefly by avoiding violence and pursuing a career, such as trade or banking, which does not involve doing harm to life. Laypeople also help monks and nuns by giving them food, water, and any other items that they are allowed to accept. Regular worship is also important, and devout people worship every day.

Mask to prevent
inhaling insects

JAIN MONK

Brush to sweep
insects out of harm's way

THREE JEWELS
Jains begin their journey on the path to salvation by achieving the Three Jewels. The first – right knowledge – comes from learning the creed of the Jain faith. Right faith – the second Jewel – is acquired as a result of belief in the creed. The third of the Three Jewels – right conduct – means following the correct code of behavior, according to a series of vows taken by both lay people and members of religious orders.

FIVE GREAT VOWS
Monks and nuns take a series of vows that determine their way of life. First and most important of these are the Five Great Vows – **ahimsa**, or nonviolence; satya – telling the truth; asteya – not stealing and not taking what has not been given; brahmacharya – chastity; and aparigraha – renouncing possessions. A sixth vow – of not eating after dark – was later added to the list.

ANUVRATAS
Laypeople are not expected to achieve the **asceticism** of Jain **monks** or nuns, but take a series of less strict vows called Anuvratas. These reflect the **Five Great Vows** – laypeople are expected to be vegetarian, to be truthful, to be faithful in marriage, not to become too attached to possessions, and to avoid violence in their work by following one of the approved Jain professions.

FESTIVALS

With the exception of the most important Jain festival – the eight-day Paryusana – festivals normally last for one day only. They are occasions not only for celebration and special temple services, but also for fasting, followed by feasting and the confession of sins. Jains also fast at the time of the full moon.

PARYUSANA
This festival is held at the Jain year-end in August. During this time laypeople attempt to live like members of the monastic orders. They confess their sins, seek reconciliation with enemies and relatives, and spend time fasting. On the last day, everyone joins in the fast and attends the temple for confession.

KARTTIKA-PURNIMA
This event marks the end of the rainy season when **monks** and nuns go back to a life of wandering. Karttika-Purnima includes a Car Festival – a wooden vehicle, with the image of a Jina, proceeds through the streets.

FESTIVE SWEETS AND CANDLE FOR DIWALI

INSTALLATION OF MAHAVIRA FOR THE FESTIVAL OF MAHAVIRA-JAYANTI

VIRA-NIRVANA
This festival, celebrated in November, marks the time when **Mahavira** died and attained **Nirvana**. A 24-hour fast is followed by a special service in the temple. The festival is at the same time as the Hindu **Diwali**, a public holiday in India that Jains also celebrate.

MAHAVIRA-JAYANTI
Most Jain festivals commemorate key events in the lives of the **Tirthankaras**. The birth of **Mahavira** is celebrated at this festival, in which a rich couple take the roles of the weather god, **Indra**, and his queen, the sky goddess Indrani, and make a large donation to the temple. The image of Mahavira is anointed, there are special chants, and flower petals are scattered over the image. Mahavira's life is read aloud in the temple before people return home to enjoy a lavish meal.

SAMAYIKA
Samayika meditation prescribes that Jains meditate daily for 48 minutes (or one-thirtieth) of every day. The meditation begins with a prayer of forgiveness. The aim of subsequent meditation is to achieve peace of mind, in which a person can concentrate fully on the teachings of the faith. The ritual includes a prayer asking for friendship with all living things, pleasure in virtue, and compassion for suffering.

STATUE DEPICTING MEDITATION

PILGRIMAGE
There are many places in India, like Mount Abu in Rajasthan, Mount Ginar in Saurashtra, and Shatrunjaya in Gujarat, which are sacred to the Jains. Most of these sites are associated with the **Tirthankaras** or other supreme beings. Some sites mark where they achieved liberation. Jains make pilgrimages to the temples and monuments at these sacred places.

SALLEKHANA
Ritual self-starvation, or sallekhana, was traditionally regarded as the ideal way of dying for pious Jains. This religious suicide, which must be supervised by a religious teacher, showed the person's complete detachment from worldly things. It is ideally a passionless death, where life is given up voluntarily without clinging. It is seldom practiced by modern Jains.

WORSHIP

Laypeople can worship at home or at the temple. For some Jains, the main aim of worship is to concentrate on the image of one of the Tirthankaras, in order to advance their spiritual progress and help them follow the Tirthankara toward liberation. Other Jains do not believe in images, and worship in plain halls.

BADRIDAS TEMPLE COMPLEX, SITAMBAR, CALCUTTA

TEMPLE
The layout of Jain temples is similar to **Hindu temples**. They have a central chamber, often topped by a tall tower, which is surrounded by outer rooms and includes an entrance hall. At the heart of the temple is the shrine, which contains the image of the **Tirthankara** to whom the temple is dedicated. Temples are highly ornate, in imitation of the heavenly halls of the Tirthankaras.

The Jain conception of the universe, loka-akasha, is formed with rice grains.

JAIN WORSHIPER RECITES THE PANCA-NAMASKARA MANTRA.

PANCA-NAMASKARA MANTRA
When approaching the image of a **Tirthankara**, Jains recite this special **mantra**. The words of the mantra pay homage to the five orders of Supreme Beings – the **Tirthankaras**, the souls that have achieved liberation, the spiritual leaders, the teaching monks, and the other monks. When the mantra is completed, the person is ready to perform an act of worship.

LORD BAHUBALI
Bahubali was a prince and a warrior. During a battle with his half-brother, who had threatened to kill him, Bahubali defeated his sibling, but would not put him to death. Consequently, he gave up his worldly possessions and lived a life of meditation and contemplation. The **Digambara** believe that Bahubali was the first person in this age to achieve liberation. There is a massive statue of him at Shravana Belgola in southern India – the site of a ceremony of worship and pilgrimage every 12 years.

PUJA
This ritual involves anointing and decorating the statue of the **Tirthankara**. The worshiper first washes the statue with water, milk, and five nectars. Then the statue is marked in 14 places with saffron and decorated with flowers and jewels. Worshipers sing verses in praise of the Tirthankara and leave an offering.

LORD BAHUBALI

Flowers are used in temple ritual.

PUJA

EIGHT SUBSTANCES
In the central chamber of the **temple**, eight substances are placed that are symbolic of the spiritual path toward liberation – water, sandalwood, flowers, incense, a lamp, rice, candy, and fruit. All eight substances may be left as offerings at the temple during worship, or **puja**.

DEITIES
Although Jainism recognizes no creator or supreme god, Jains revere certain deities associated with the **Tirthankaras**. They ask for their help when facing problems in their everyday lives. These gods and goddesses are lesser beings compared to Tirthankaras and **siddhas**, and their statues are placed in the outer concourses of temples. Ambika, the mother goddess, is a popular deity associated with fertility and childbirth.

THE MOTHER GODDESS AMBIKA

HOME SHRINES
Many Jains have shrines in their own homes. Home shrines were especially popular during periods when Jains were persecuted and the building of temples was forbidden. They are still widely popular today. The shrines are usually wooden structures, elaborately adorned with carvings of gods and goddesses, like smaller versions of the stone shrines at the heart of every Jain temple. Devout Jains can perform their daily worship at such shrines, the men dressing in clean clothes without stitching.

HOME SHRINE

DARSHAN
The simplest form of worship – darshan – consists of making eye contact with the image of the **Tirthankara**. The worshiper recites a **mantra** while looking at the image. When worshipers perform darshan, they believe themselves to be face to face with the Tirthankara.

SIKH HISTORY AND IDEAS

SIKHISM WAS FOUNDED IN THE PUNJAB, northern India, during the 16th century CE, by Guru Nanak. Guru Nanak respected the Hindu and Islamic faiths then prevailing in India, but believed that their rituals concealed the truth about God. Sikhism is a faith that stresses the individual's relationship with God. A Sikh believes in one God, and follows the Ten Gurus, from Guru Nanak to Guru Gobind Singh, who revealed the truth about the deity. The Sikh scripture, the Adi Granth or Guru Granth Sahib, is also described as a guru, as is the Sikh community, the Guru Panth. Sikhs therefore pursue unity with God through worship (reading the Guru Granth Sahib) and service to the community.

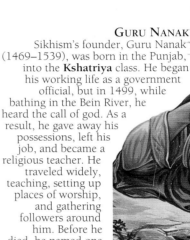

KHANDA
This Sikh symbol is framed by two swords, standing for spiritual and worldly power. At its center is a single double-edged sword, representing belief in one God. The circle, or **chakra**, symbolizes this one god, and the unity of the Sikh community.

THE KHANDA

FRESCO DEPICTING GURU NANAK'S LIFE

SAT GURU
A Sikh is one who follows the teachings of a guru (a teacher or guide), toward belief in the one God. According to Sikh faith, it was God alone who inspired the human gurus and the Sikh holy book the **Guru Granth Sahib**. It is for this reason that God is called the "Sat Guru," or "true guru."

SANTS
The Sants, a group of religious teachers who were active in northern India, were influenced by several different traditions, notably **Hinduism, Yoga**, and **Islam**. They played down the importance of the caste system (some of the Sants were themselves of a low caste), stressed the importance of faith over the performance of rituals, and concentrated on the individual's devotion to God. The Sants had a strong influence on the early Sikhs, especially on **Guru Nanak**.

GURU NANAK
Sikhism's founder, Guru Nanak (1469–1539), was born in the Punjab, into the **Kshatriya** class. He began his working life as a government official, but in 1499, while bathing in the Bein River, he heard the call of god. As a result, he gave away his possessions, left his job, and became a religious teacher. He traveled widely, teaching, setting up places of worship, and gathering followers around him. Before he died, he named one of these followers to be the next guru.

GURU NANAK

GURU NANAK, WITH TWO ATTENDANTS AND THE NINE FOLLOWING GURUS

TEN GURUS
Sikhism's Ten Gurus make up a successive and unbroken line. Each guru was chosen by his predecessor, and each possessed the same knowledge and insight into God. The Ten Gurus were leaders of their community, as well as being spiritual teachers and guides. They laid down the basic elements of Sikh doctrine, and wrote the words of most of the hymns that make up the **Guru Granth Sahib**.

GURU RAM DAS
The fourth guru, Ram Das (1534–1581) was the founder of Amritsar, the holiest city for Sikhs. He also wrote a hymn that is central to the Sikh marriage ceremony.

GURU ARJAN
The fifth guru, Arjan (1563–1606), was the son of his predecessor, **Guru Ram Das** (1534–1581). Guru Arjan collected the hymns of the previous Gurus and added many of his own to make up the **Guru Granth Sahib**. He also built the Harimandir, or Golden Temple, at Amritsar.

GURU GOBIND SINGH
After the execution of Guru Tegh Bahadur (1621–1675), his son, Gobind Singh (1666–1708), became the tenth and final human guru. Gobind Singh was second only to Guru Nanak in importance. He combined the virtues of saint and soldier, and he was the founder of the **Khalsa**.

The Panj piare, or "five beloved ones"

GURU GOBIND SINGH FOUNDS THE KHALSA

KHALSA
During the time of **Guru Gobind Singh**, the Sikhs suffered persecution, so Gobind Singh founded the Khalsa, a community of Sikhs who took vows of loyalty and were ready to use weapons to defend their faith. The Khalsa helped give Sikhs a strong identity.

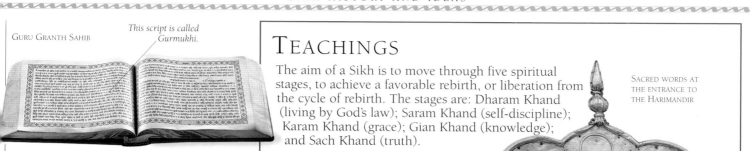

GURU GRANTH SAHIB

This script is called Gurmukhi.

TEACHINGS

The aim of a Sikh is to move through five spiritual stages, to achieve a favorable rebirth, or liberation from the cycle of rebirth. The stages are: Dharam Khand (living by God's law); Saram Khand (self-discipline); Karam Khand (grace); Gian Khand (knowledge); and Sach Khand (truth).

SACRED WORDS AT THE ENTRANCE TO THE HARIMANDIR

GURU GRANTH SAHIB

Guru Gobind Singh named no human successor. Instead, he said that the Sikh scripture was a guru. This sacred book, the Guru Granth Sahib, consists of a sequence of hymns and the music used in their performance. Its opening verses, called the Mul Mantra, begin with the phrase "Ek Onkar" ("God is one"), a sacred phrase written outside many **gurdwaras**.

DASAM GRANTH

Guru Gobind Singh wrote many poems in the Persian, Sanskrit, and Punjabi languages. During his lifetime, he would not allow any of these to be added to the **Guru Granth Sahib**. However, about 30 years after his death, his followers collected Guru Gobind Singh's poems in the Dasam Granth, Sikhism's second holy book. Some of these hymns are used in worship.

NAM

The Gurus use the word Nam ("name") to refer to God, specifically to God as revealed to the Sikhs, and especially to God's power. Meditating on the name and repeating it as a **mantra** are important Sikh spiritual exercises.

GURU NANAK TEACHES THE FAITHFUL.

NAMES FOR GOD

In addition to **Nam**, the Sikhs use several other names for God. In conversation, he is referred to as Vahiguru, which means "praise to the Guru." One of God's other names is Akal Purakh, or "the timeless one," stressing his eternal quality. The name Parmeshur has a similar meaning.

HAUMAI

Selfishness, a quality that blinds people to the presence and nature of God, is known as haumai. The Gurus taught that if people live their lives under the influence of haumai, valuing worldly success and possessions, they will never achieve liberation from the cycle of death and rebirth.

SHABAD

Guru Nanak saw shabad ("word") as the way in which God is revealed to the people. Shabad therefore refers primarily to God's word. The words of the sacred book, the **Guru Granth Sahib**, are also said to be shabad.

READING HYMNS FOM THE GURU GRANTH SAHIB

Metal holder

CHAURI

Yak tail hair

RAHIT-NAMA

The Sikh moral code, or Rahit Maryada, is recorded in volumes called Rahit-Namas. The code is based on the values of the **Khalsa**. It also lays down guidelines for the conduct of worship and ceremonies, and instructs Sikhs to guard against non-Sikh teachings. An important use of the Rahit Maryada is to ensure that Sikh practices are consistent. This is especially useful, since Sikhism has no hierarchy of **priests** to whom people can turn for instruction on ritual and worship.

CHAURI

The **Guru Granth Sahib** is reverently covered with cloths, and kept on a special throne. A sacred whisk, called the chauri, a symbol of kingship, is waved over the book when it is read.

KARMA

Sikhism relies on the idea of the moral law of karma. A person's actions in one life will affect his or her rebirth after death, and this is how karma is borne out. Unlike Hindu ascetics, for whom the ideal is to reach liberation from the cycle of rebirth by renouncing the world, Sikhs try to achieve liberation by living well in their everyday family lives. This involves serving the community and the **gurdwara**.

HUKAM

In order to overcome **haumai**, Sikhs are taught to live according to God's will, or hukam. Only by living in this way will they be able to achieve liberation or **mukti**.

MUKTI

Liberation from the cycle of death and rebirth is called mukti. When a person becomes one with God through knowledge of the truth, that is when mukti is attained.

RECENT SIKH HISTORY

There have been reform movements throughout Sikh history. Early in the 20th century, the Sikh Akali Dal party successfully campaigned for **gurdwaras** to be returned to Sikh control, from the Hindu priests who were in charge of them. Since 1945, before the independence of India, the Akali Dal party has also fought for a separate Punjabi state. In 1984, a leader of the independence movement, Sant Jarnail Singh Bhindranwale, fortified the Harimandir, but was defeated by the Indian army. Most Sikhs accept Indian rule, but hope that the country's central government will start to play a smaller role in Punjabi affairs.

A SIKH SEPARATIST

LIFE AND WORSHIP

THE SIKHS COME FROM THE PUNJAB, an area now split between India and Pakistan, which has often been the scene of invasions and religious disputes. They have therefore developed a way of life which helped them defend themselves in times of difficulty, gave them a sense of identity, and placed emphasis on caring for the whole community. This sense of identity makes many Sikhs stand out from other groups – for example, men let their hair grow and wear the turban. Their sense of caring does not stop with their own people – Sikhs are taught to help anyone who is needy, whatever their faith, and serving the community is seen as a way of growing nearer to God.

A SIKH BRIDE AND GROOM

Money gifts

NAMING CEREMONY
The baby is taken to the **gurdwara**, the Sikh temple, and laid on the floor next to the **Guru Granth Sahib**. An official opens the book at random, and a name is chosen from the text. Sikh names are often common to both boys and girls, so it is traditional to add the name Singh for a boy or Kaur for a girl to the chosen name.

AMRIT CEREMONY
At the age of 14, some boys and girls are initiated into the Sikh community in a rite which reenacts a ceremony that took place at the founding of the **Khalsa**. They drink amrit, a mixture of sugar and water, which is seen as the nectar of immortality. This is also sprinkled on their eyes and hair while they recite the Mul Mantra.

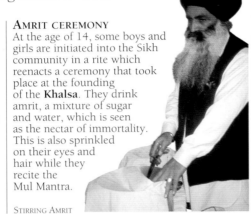

STIRRING AMRIT

MARRIAGE
Like other Sikh rituals, the marriage ceremony centers on the **Guru Granth Sahib**. The couple sits in front of the book, while the granthi explains the duties of married life to them. They then walk around the book, while the Lavan, a text about the soul's union with God by **Guru Ram Das**, is read aloud.

DEATH
When a Sikh dies, his or her body is washed, adorned with the **five Ks**, and carried in procession to the place of cremation. A close relative lights the funeral pyre, and the mourners sing special hymns and say prayers. There may be a mourning period of seven to ten days, with readings from the **Guru Granth Sahib**.

WORSHIP

Worship at the gurdwara involves singing hymns and listening to readings from the Guru Granth Sahib, which is also known as the Book, ritual sharing of sacred food, a congregational prayer called the Ardas, and a common meal, called a Langar. At the gurdwara, the Book is usually read by an official called a granthi, but all Sikhs may worship at home, reciting the texts and meditating on their meaning.

THE HARIMANDIR, OR "GOLDEN TEMPLE," AT AMRITSAR, PUNJAB

LANGAR
A shared vegetarian meal, or langar, is an important part of Sikh worship, and is served daily in large **gurdwaras**. To show that everyone is equal, all the diners sit on the floor, and members of all castes eat together.

MALA, SIKH PRAYER BEADS

Some Sikhs use prayer beads in their devotions.

GURDWARA
The word gurdwara means "place of God." At its heart is the prayer room, which contains a copy of the **Guru Granth Sahib**. Sikhs must remove their shoes and cover their heads before going into this room, and bow to the Book as they enter. Other, smaller rooms, such as a kitchen, and a place where children are taught, can also be found in the gurdwara.

AKHAND PATH
A continuous reading of the entire **Guru Granth Sahib** is called an akhand path. This takes 48 hours, and is undertaken on special occasions such as weddings or festivals.

KARAH PRASHAD
Sacred food called karah prashad, which is specially prepared in the **gurdwara** kitchen, is shared during worship. The food, which is sweet and warm, is made from flour, water, sugar, and ghee (clarified butter). Sharing karah prashad is a symbol of the unity and equality of all who attend the gurdwara.

NIT-NEM
Three times a day, Sikhs recite verses, known as Nit-nem ("daily rule"), from the scriptures. In the morning, they recite verses called the Japji, by **Guru Nanak**. At sunset, they sing nine hymns called the Rahiras. Finally, before going to sleep, they recite a group of hymns called the Sohila.

ARDAS
A formal prayer called the Ardas ("to ask for what you desire") ends most Sikh ceremonies. It is made up of three sections, which recall the lives of the **Ten Gurus**, request God's blessing, and ask for him to remember the needs of the community.

THE FIVE KS

The original members of the Khalsa wore five items of dress, all of which began with the letter K in the Punjabi language. Since then, adult Sikhs have worn the five Ks as a sign of moral strength and their belonging to the Sikh community.

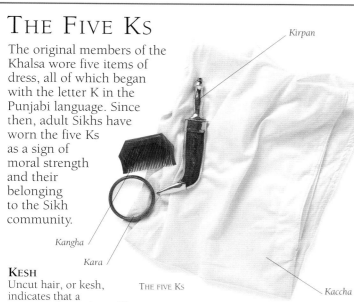

Kirpan

Kangha

Kara

THE FIVE KS

Kaccha

KESH
Uncut hair, or kesh, indicates that a person is devoted to God and accepts his will. Both head and body hair are left untrimmed, and the hair is tied up. Regular washing keeps the hair clean – Sikhs are expected to bathe every day.

KACCHA
Sikh men and women wear special knee-length shorts, called kaccha, as undergarments. Kaccha are symbols of moral strength, but they are also practical garments that allow freedom of movement.

KIRPAN
The short sword, or kirpan, shows that the Sikh is ready to defend the weak, and fight for what is right. Some Sikhs wear a miniature kirpan, or a comb with a piece of inlaid metal to represent the sword.

KANGHA
A special comb, called a kangha, keeps the Sikh's uncut hair neat. The comb, which is usually made of wood or ivory, is a symbol of cleanliness, purity, and self-discipline. The use of the comb is in marked contrast to the practice of many holy men of other faiths in India, who let their hair grow long and matted.

KARA
A steel bangle, or kara, is worn on the right wrist. Its circular shape is a symbol of unity, reminding the wearer both of the togetherness of the Sikh community and the unity of God with all things. Its steel reminds Sikhs that they should be strong under stress.

MEDITATION

SIKH MEDITATING

Nam simran, or meditation on God, is an essential part of Sikh worship. The focus is on the name of God, as this embodies his very essence. Meditation on his name brings God into the worshiper's very being without a priest's help.

KIRT KARNI
Guru Nanak taught that Sikhs should provide for themselves by following the ideal of kirt karni, earning an honest living. Any sort of work is acceptable, as long as it complies with this basic moral concept.

VAND CHAKNA
Sharing with others, vand chakna, is vital to the Sikh way of life. Worshipers at the **gurdwara** share the **karah prashad** and the communal meal. In everyday life, a Sikh should share his wealth with the poor.

TEACHING IS AN EXAMPLE OF KIRT KARNI

SEVA
Service to others, or seva, is a way of serving God. Traditionally, seva is seen as the act of maintaining the **gurdwara**. Today, however, seva also has a broader humanitarian sense: Sikhs are taught to help others, to give part of their income to the needy, to help the sick, and to be grateful to those who give the opportunity for seva. Reading the scriptures to give comfort to others is another form of seva. In addition to helping the needy, seva also helps the giver along the path to spiritual liberation.

HOLY DAYS

The first Sikh festivals began at the order of Guru Amar Das, who started a tradition of adapting Hindu festivals to Sikh themes. These festivals are now known as melas, or fairs. Today, the most important Sikh festivals are the gurpurbs, which celebrate the lives of the gurus.

CELEBRATING GURU NANAK'S BIRTHDAY

The Guru Granth Sahib is carried in a sacred procession.

SIKHS SHELLING PEAS DURING HOLA MOHALLA CELEBRATIONS

GURPURBS
Sikh festivals that commemorate key events in the life of a guru are called gurpurbs. These can be held in the place where the original event took place, and are marked by an **akhand path**, together with special sermons and readings about the guru. A **langar** will often take place at the conclusion of the festival.

MELAS
The melas, or fairs, are another type of Sikh festival. They include the spring celebration, Basant, and **Diwali**, which, for Sikhs, is a commemoration of Guru Hargobind's release from prison. Hola Mohalla, originally based on the Hindu **Holi**, is a mela associated with sports and Sikh military discipline.

BAISAKHI
Originally a Hindu harvest festival, Baisakhi is the commemoration of the Punjabi new year, and marks the harvesting of the spring crop. Baisakhi is also the anniversary of the founding of the **Khalsa**, and thus marks the birthday of Sikhism. New clothes are worn, and new flags are flown at **gurdwaras**.

BUDDHISM

Buddhists are followers of the Buddha, who showed people how to free themselves from the cycle of death and rebirth through achieving enlightenment. In so doing, he taught his disciples the Four Noble Truths and the Eightfold Path, which combines moral teaching with guidelines in meditation and concentration.

SYMBOL OF BUDDHISM,
WHEEL OF LAW

SPIRITUAL GUIDE

The Buddha was not a god, but a spiritual guide. Buddhists do not therefore see him the same way as followers of other faiths view their gods. Buddhist worship involves paying homage to the Buddha. A Buddhist may also follow another religion while living according to the Buddhist path. The most important goal for the Buddhist is to follow the Eightfold Path, which involves full understanding of the Buddhist truths, living well, and avoiding work that might harm others. In this way, Buddhists hope to achieve a favorable rebirth after death, or even to reach enlightenment, a state of spiritual purity which is completely free from wordly concerns and from the cycle of rebirth.

SPREAD OF BUDDHISM

Many Buddhists followed the example of their leader, becoming teachers and spreading the ideas of Buddhism throughout Asia and beyond. There are now more than 350 million Buddhists in the world. The faith is strong both in northern Asia (China, Tibet, and Japan) and in southern Asia (Sri Lanka, Cambodia, and Thailand). However, although most Buddhists still live in Asia, the religion has now spread worldwide.

THE BUDDHA

BORN AS SIDDHARTHA GAUTAMA, the Buddha lived in the fifth or sixth century BCE. Siddhartha was born into a high-ranking Indian family. He was expected to become the leader of his people, and seemed destined to live a life of privilege and luxury. However, Siddhartha gave up his riches to live a religious life, seeking "enlightenment" in order to free himself from the cycle of death and rebirth. The Buddha taught others how to live so that they too might attain enlightenment. The Buddhist religion is based on his life and teachings.

BIRTH OF THE BUDDHA

SIDDHARTHA GAUTAMA
Siddhartha Gautama was the son of a raja, or local leader, who formed part of the Shakya kingdom of northeastern India. He was a member of the **Kshatriya**, or Hindu warrior class. As a future ruler of his people, the young Siddhartha led a sheltered life of luxury. He was confined to the palace by Suddhodana, his father, and had no idea or experience of human suffering.

RENUNCIATION
Siddhartha lived as an ascetic for many years, hoping that by practicing a strict ascetic life and **yogic** discipline, he could free himself from **samsara**, or the cycle of death and rebirth. Weakened by deprivation, Siddhartha came to realize that the ascetic lifestyle would not give him the freedom he sought. Instead, he turned to **meditation** as a means of achieving **enlightenment**.

BIRTH OF THE BUDDHA
Many legends surround the birth of **Siddhartha**. According to one story, his mother, Queen Maya, dreamed that a white elephant entered her womb. Ten months later, Siddhartha was born from her right side, and immediately walked seven steps. The queen died soon afterward, having fulfilled her purpose in life. A sage prophesied that Siddhartha would become an enlightened being and a great teacher.

FOUR SIGHTS
Curious about the world beyond the palace, **Siddhartha** gained his father's permission to travel. The young man was shocked to encounter three different aspects of human suffering – old age, illness, and death. Deeply troubled, Siddhartha traveled for a fourth time and encountered a contented wandering ascetic, whose example inspired him to begin a new life as a seeker of truth and **enlightenment**.

ENLIGHTENMENT
After a long, deep **meditation** under a bodhi tree, **Siddhartha** reached a state where he was no longer affected by fears of suffering or death. He had become the "enlightened one," or the Buddha.

Excessive asceticism dimmed the natural luminosity of Siddhartha's skin.

SIDDHARTHA GAUTAMA, EMACIATED BY HIS ASCETIC LIFE

UNDER THE BODHI TREE

Disciple of the Buddha, one of the Sangha

FIRST SERMON
The Buddha preached his first sermon at **Varanasi**. He told his listeners to seek a "middle way," avoiding all extremes. He taught the **Four Noble Truths**, which describe the suffering of humankind, its causes, and the solution to this suffering. In mapping out the solution, Buddha preached the **Eightfold Path** that should be followed to achieve release from suffering.

THE FIRST SERMON

SANGHA
The first followers of the Buddha were known as the Sangha, the term still used for the community of Buddhist monks. Their symbol is the lotus flower; their work, to seek **enlightenment**.

PARINIRVANA
The Buddha died at the age of 80. By extinguishing his attachment to worldly things and fear of suffering, he achieved parinirvana, or final **nirvana**, and escaped the cycle of death and rebirth.

PARINIRVANA

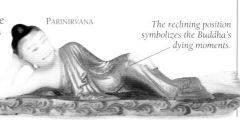

The reclining position symbolizes the Buddha's dying moments.

IMAGES OF THE BUDDHA

Images of the Buddha adorn every temple and sacred site. These are not intended to be realistic portraits, but employ a rich symbolism to indicate different aspects of the Buddha's character. Some 32 features symbolize various properties of Buddhahood. For example: the bump on the top of the head, or *usnisa*, indicates wisdom and spirituality, while a third eye symbolizes spiritual insight. Hand positions, or *mudra*, and posture, or *asana*, are also symbolic.

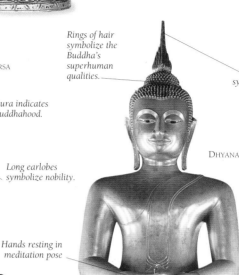

VITARKA

Thumb and forefinger form a circle.

VITARKA
In this **mudra**, the Buddha's thumb and forefinger form a circle, with the other fingers curving outward. This represents the turning of the Wheel of Law, and reminds Buddhists of the **first sermon**, when the Buddha outlined the basic principles of Buddhist doctrine, or **dharma**.

Rings of hair symbolize the Buddha's superhuman qualities.

Usnisa symbolizes wisdom.

BHUMISPARSA

BHUMISPARSA
This depiction shows the Buddha seated on the ground with the fingers of his right hand touching the earth. The **mudra** of bhumisparsa recalls the time during **Siddhartha's** long **meditation** under the bodhi tree when Mara, the personification of evil, tried to distract him by calling up tempests, demons, and various temptations. By touching the earth, Siddhartha asked nature to witness his resolve.

Aura indicates Buddhahood.

Long earlobes symbolize nobility.

DHYANA

Hands resting in meditation pose

ASANA
The Buddha is shown in many stylized poses, or asanas. The most common are sitting, standing, walking, and reclining. The first three are linked with the Buddha's life, while the fourth represents his death.

MUDRA
The hand positions, or mudras, on images of the Buddha have specific meanings that represent the Buddha's activities. These include teaching, offering protection, **meditation**, and calling for rain.

ABHAYA
When the Buddha's right hand is raised in the gesture of abhaya ("no fear"), this indicates that he is offering protection to his followers. Although sometimes seen on seated Buddhas, this gesture is more common on standing figures.

ABHAYA

DHYANA
Dhyana is the traditional pose of **meditation**. The positions of the fingers vary, but they are usually lined up with each other and the thumbs just touch. Often, the hands will rest on the lap with palms facing upward, right hand on top. Dhyana symbolizes the intense concentration that is required for a person to overcome the self and achieve **enlightenment**.

THE BUDDHA ON A FLYING HORSE

MIRACLES AND MYTHS

While the Buddha told his followers to beware of the power of miracles, many sacred texts describe miraculous occurrences performed by the Buddha. They include remarkable feats, such as calming storms and ending plagues, together with magical acts, like preaching in different places at the same time. It was said that the practice of **meditation** enabled him to develop special psychic powers.

JATAKA TALES
The Jatakas, or "birth stories," are a series of moral tales describing the Buddha's former 550 lives. The Buddha is depicted as a **bodhisattva**, someone who works over many lifetimes to guide others to **nirvana**. The tales recount many episodes of courage and self-sacrifice. The Buddha's previous incarnations took many forms, including animal, human, and divine. Many Jatakas are Buddhist versions of traditional folktales adapted to illustrate a Buddhist moral theme.

FIRST-CENTURY INDIAN SCULPTURE DEPICTING SCENES FROM THE JATAKA STORIES

SEE ALSO

BODHISATTVA 59
DHARMA 38, 62
FOUR NOBLE TRUTHS 60
KSHATRIYA 40
MEDITATION 62
NIRVANA 60
EIGHTFOLD PATH 61
SAMSARA 38, 60
VARANASI 43
YOGA 41

ORIGINS AND TEXTS

EARLY STONE CARVING DEPICTING THE BUDDHAPADA, OR BUDDHA'S FOOTPRINTS

THERE ARE TWO MAIN BRANCHES OF BUDDHISM, Theravada and Mahayana. Theravada Buddhism, which developed first, adheres strictly to the Buddha's original teachings through a defined set of scriptures, and is known as the "doctrine of the elders." Theravada practice focuses on enlightenment for the individual. Mahayana Buddhism developed later, during the first century BCE. It is more open to different ideas and approaches, using a wider set of scriptures, and emphasizes compassion and enlightenment for the sake of others. Consequently, the Mahayana school is known as the "greater vehicle," and Theravada as the "lesser vehicle."

BUDDHIST COUNCILS

During Buddhist history there have been several important councils to decide on key issues of doctrine. The first council was held at Rajgir after the death of the Buddha, where the content of the **Tipitaka** was decided. A second council, 100 years later, made decisions about monastic life. The last council was held in Rangoon in 1956, when a revised Pali Canon was agreed.

THERAVADA BUDDHISM

Theravada Buddhism is mainly practiced in the southern Asian countries of Sri Lanka, Burma, Cambodia, Laos, and Thailand. Theravada Buddhists reject the theory of **bodhisattvas**, following only the Buddha. They seek to become **arahats**, or saints, and believe that to attain **nirvana** it is essential to join a monastic order. The **Tipitaka** is the main scripture for Theravadan Buddhists.

THERAVADAN STATUE OF THE BUDDHA

MAURYAN EMPIRE

One of the most important events in the spread of Buddhism was the conversion of the emperor Asoka during the third century BCE. Asoka was ruler of the Mauryan dynasty, which governed most of India. After his conversion, Asoka aided the spread of Buddhism in India. Mahinda, his son, established the faith in Sri Lanka.

BUDDHAGHOSA

This fifth-century Indian philosopher became the greatest writer in the Theravadan tradition for revitalizing **Pali** Buddhist scholarship. His most famous work, the *Visuddhimagga* ("Path of Purification"), contains important commentaries on sacred texts and explanations for the practice of **meditation**. He also translated Sri Lankan Buddhist writings into **Pali**.

ARAHAT

An arahat is a Theravada Buddhist disciple who has fully absorbed the teachings of the Buddha, thereby reaching the end of the **Eightfold Path**. His mental and spiritual training is so refined that he has attained a rare level of perfection.

PALI

Originating in northern India, a language similar to Pali was spoken at the time of the early Buddhists. Consequently, it was used in Theravadan scriptures over literary languages like Sanskrit.

URN FOR CREMATED ARAHAT

TIPITAKA

The texts of the Tipitaka, or Pali Canon, were written down around 25 BCE. Tipitaka means "three baskets," a title that refers to the three divisions of the scriptures – *Vinaya* (discipline), *Sutta* (themes), and *Abhidhamma* (teachings).

VINAYA-PITAKA

These scriptures are concerned with monastic discipline, practice, and lifestyle; they also include instructions on living at peace, caring for the sick, giving to the poor, and teaching the lay community.

SUTTA-PITAKA

The teachings of the Buddha as related by his disciple Ananda are recorded in this text. Divided into five parts, the scripture contains a series of dialogues, illustrations, and parables linked by common moral and spiritual themes.

ABHIDHAMMA-PITAKA

The final part of the Tipitaka provides a systematic analysis of Buddhist ideas and notions of experience. The *Abhidhamma-pitaka* places special emphasis on describing and analyzing different mental states. It is considered an extremely important aid for **meditation** techniques.

DHAMMAPADA

This is the most famous section of the **Sutta-pitaka**. Its 423 verses provide practical advice and instruction on the path to a person's **enlightenment** and summarize many aspects of Buddhist teaching.

EIGHTEENTH-CENTURY CHINESE ILLUSTRATION OF SCENES FROM THE TIPITAKA

MAHAYANA
BUDDHIST
MONK PRAYING

MAHAYANA BUDDHISM

Buddhists who belong to the Mahayana school also follow the Buddha, but place special stress on scriptures that are not included in the **Tipitaka**. They believe that **enlightenment** is open to everyone, not just to **monks**. Mahayana Buddhists believe that **bodhisattvas** can provide an alternative source of inspiration, and through compassion help others toward enlightenment. They also believe that in the future, another Buddha will come and revive Buddhist teaching. Mahayana Buddhism is practiced chiefly in China, Tibet, Nepal, Vietnam, Korea, and Japan.

LIMESTONE CARVING OF A BUDDHIST
STUPA AT NAGARJUNAKONDA, INDIA

NAGARJUNA

Of the many Mahayana scholars who wrote commentaries on the **sutras**, the most famous was Nagarjuna, a second-century thinker who was said to have lived for 600 years. Nagarjuna was most famous for founding the **Madhyamaka**, or "Middle School," of Buddhist philosophy. There was also a second sage called Nagarjuna, a **tantric** yogi who lived in the eighth century.

THE BODHISATTVA
AVALOKITESHVARA

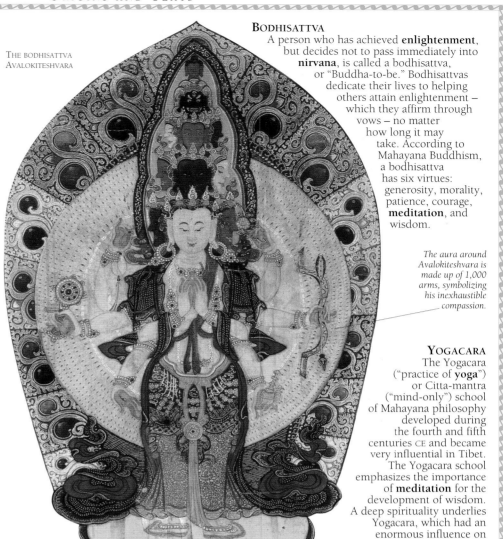

BODHISATTVA

A person who has achieved **enlightenment**, but decides not to pass immediately into **nirvana**, is called a bodhisattva, or "Buddha-to-be." Bodhisattvas dedicate their lives to helping others attain enlightenment – which they affirm through vows – no matter how long it may take. According to Mahayana Buddhism, a bodhisattva has six virtues: generosity, morality, patience, courage, **meditation**, and wisdom.

The aura around Avalokiteshvara is made up of 1,000 arms, symbolizing his inexhaustible compassion.

YOGACARA

The Yogacara ("practice of **yoga**") or Citta-mantra ("mind-only") school of Mahayana philosophy developed during the fourth and fifth centuries CE and became very influential in Tibet. The Yogacara school emphasizes the importance of **meditation** for the development of wisdom. A deep spirituality underlies Yogacara, which had an enormous influence on later Mahayana traditions.

ASANGA

The fourth-century Indian thinker Asanga was the founder of the **Yogacara** school. He wrote commentaries on the ideas of the Yogacara thinkers, drawing the various schools of thought together. Asanga taught that **meditation** played a key role in the quest for wisdom in helping to rid the mind of its preoccupations with everyday reality.

MADHYAMAKA

Founded by **Nagarjuna**, the Madhyamaka school taught that all physical things – from pots and furniture to mountains and even people – have no essential being or separate reality. The school believes in two realities: a mundane one, which is the reality we encounter every day, and an ultimate reality, where all is empty and equal.

The Buddha surounded by bodhisattvas

The bridge to heaven

A JAPANESE COPY OF
THE HEART SUTRA

MAHAYANA SUTRAS

As the religion has developed, Mahayana Buddhists have added their own sutras, or teachings, to those of the **Tipitaka**. These include the *Diamond Sutra* and *Heart Sutra,* which are concerned with the attainment of wisdom. The influential *Lotus Sutra* draws together all the threads of the Buddha's teachings and demonstrates that **enlightenment** can be attained by all people traveling a variety of paths.

SEE ALSO

EIGHTFOLD PATH 61
ENLIGHTENMENT 56
MEDITATION 62
MONKS AND NUNS 62
NIRVANA 60
TANTRIC BUDDHISM 65
YOGA 41

TEACHINGS

AFTER THE BUDDHA ACHIEVED ENLIGHTENMENT, he decided to forego immediately entering nirvana to teach others his vision. Buddha saw human suffering, as described in the Four Noble Truths, as the central problem of human existence. The solution to human suffering lay in living according to the precepts outlined in the Eightfold Path. These essential principles make up the core of the Buddha's dharma, or teaching. A number of additional teachings, notably the Five Precepts, were added later.

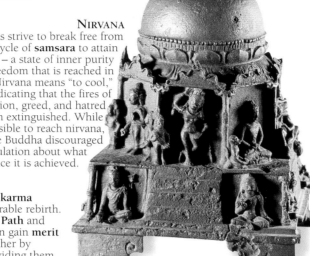

THIS NINTH-CENTURY STUPA OF A HIDDEN BUDDHA SYMBOLIZES NIRVANA.

SAMSARA
Like the other Indian religions, Buddhism views life as part of an endless cycle of birth, death, and rebirth, called **samsara**, or "endless wandering." All living things are part of this cycle, and cannot be released from it unless they attain **nirvana**.

REINCARNATION
By building up merit through good **karma** (actions), Buddhists hope for a favorable rebirth. Apart from following the **Eightfold Path** and the **Five Precepts**, lay Buddhists can gain **merit** by supporting their local monks, either by sponsoring their ordination, or providing them with food and clothing.

NIRVANA
Buddhists strive to break free from the cycle of **samsara** to attain nirvana – a state of inner purity and freedom that is reached in death. Nirvana means "to cool," indicating that the fires of delusion, greed, and hatred have been extinguished. While it is possible to reach nirvana, the Buddha discouraged speculation about what occurs once it is achieved.

KARMA
The sum of human actions, or karma, has a direct effect on the shape of future existence. Moral actions have consequences, and determine whether people are reborn in a better or worse reincarnation or achieve **nirvana**. If a person steals, for example, the victim loses his or her property; however, the thief is also affected, because such actions accumulate bad karma and make an unfavorable rebirth more likely. **Meritorious** actions, however, make a favorable rebirth possible.

FOUR NOBLE TRUTHS
A full understanding of the Four Noble Truths is an essential aim of Buddhist practice. The Four Noble Truths provide the basis for Buddhist teaching: Firstly, all existence involves suffering; the origin of suffering lies in desire and ignorance; by eliminating desire and ignorance, suffering can be destroyed; and finally, release from suffering can be achieved by following the **Eightfold Path**.

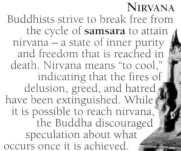

CARVING DEPICTING THE BUDDHA
TEACHING THE FOUR NOBLE TRUTHS

SKANDHAS
The Buddha taught that a person consists of five basic elements, or skandhas: physical body, sense perception, ideas, will, and consciousness. All of these elements are impermanent and changing, combining together to make a person. However, there is no "self" uniting the skandhas.

THREE MARKS OF EXISTENCE

Buddhism recognizes three features of existence, which combine to influence every aspect of both human life and the cosmic order. By achieving "right understanding" – the first part of the Eightfold Path – Buddhists can appreciate the Three Marks of Existence.

BUDDHIST NUN FLOATS IN A POOL
SEEKING ANATMAN.

ANICCA
The concept of anicca means that nothing is permanent. All things are in a constant state of change: The endless cycle of death and rebirth characterizes human existence.

DUKKHA
Suffering, or dukkha, is the second of the Three Marks. Dukkha and anicca are directly linked, since human striving for permanence results in suffering. All experience – whether happy or hurtful – involves suffering because of anicca.

ANATMAN
In direct opposition to the Hindu notion of **atman**, the concept of anatman means "no self." All of the elements, or **skandhas**, of a person are continuously changing; remove each skandha and no permanent self remains. For Buddhists, the notion of a permanent self is an illusion that leads to further suffering.

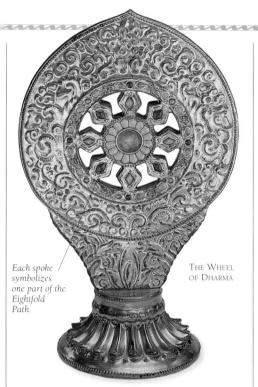

Each spoke symbolizes one part of the Eightfold Path.

THE WHEEL OF DHARMA

COSMOLOGY

In Buddhist cosmology, time is cyclical, or a repeating process. The cosmos is not permanent or created: It comes into existence and evolves for millions of years, after which time it decays and is destroyed. Another world system evolves, and the whole process begins again.

THREE POISONS
In the center of the wheel are the three Cardinal Faults, or poisons, of humanity: desire (represented by a cock), hatred (a snake), and ignorance (a pig).

WHEEL OF LIFE
The traditional way of illustrating the Buddhist cosmos is as the Wheel of Life. This shows the Six Realms of Existence into which a soul may be reborn. In fact, this is a simplification, since Buddhist writings describe heaven as being made up of many levels, of which five are called the Pure Abodes and contain beings that cannot be reborn on lower levels of the wheel.

Yama, the Tibetan lord of the dead, shows that everything inside the wheel is subject to decay and death.

Realm of the gods

Realm of asuras

Realm of humans

The Three Poisons

A TIBETAN REPRESENTATION OF THE WHEEL OF LIFE

Realm of animals

Realm of hungry ghosts

Realm of hell

EIGHTFOLD PATH
Buddhists follow the Eightfold Path in order to overcome suffering. The eight parts of the path are right understanding, right thought, right speech, right behavior, right occupation, right effort, right contemplation, and right concentration. Each part is represented by a spoke on the Wheel of Dharma (Law).

SILA
Morality, or sila, embraces the parts of the **Eightfold Path** that deal with everyday actions: proper speech, action, and livelihood. Sila also includes obeying the **Five Precepts**.

A THAI MONK PRACTICES SILA.

SIX REALMS OF EXISTENCE
At the bottom of the wheel is hell, a realm of torment from which the soul will eventually be released by rebirth. Above hell are the realms of animals and ghosts. In the next levels live the *asuras* – a race of mighty beings forever at war – and humans. At the top is the realm of the gods, a divine place of happiness that souls inhabit until their good **karma** runs out.

TWELVE STAGES OF LIFE
Around the rim of the wheel are the 12 conditions of existence, from ignorance to consciousness, which determine the human life cycle.

PRAJNA
Wisdom, or prajna, encompasses the first two parts of the **Eightfold Path**, right understanding and right thought. Prajna indicates a direct and intuitive understanding of the truth, as outlined in the **Three Marks of Existence**.

SAMADHI
Concentration, or samadhi, forms the key element in those parts of the **Eightfold Path** that deal with **meditation**: correct effort, contemplation, and concentration. Intense concentration is essential in order to achieve **enlightenment**.

FIVE PRECEPTS
The *Panca Sila*, or Five Precepts, are a series of moral rules by which Buddhists live. The first precept is not to harm living things, which has led many Buddhists to become vegetarians and pacifists. The other precepts are not to take what has not been given, to avoid sexual misconduct, to avoid unworthy speech (such as lying and speaking harmfully of others), and to avoid drugs and alcohol (which cloud the mind).

A TIBETAN MONK PRACTICES THE FIVE PRECEPTS.

SEE ALSO

WORSHIP AND FESTIVALS

THE BUDDHA WAS A TEACHER RATHER THAN A GOD. Consequently, Buddhist worship follows a pattern different from that of other faiths. Worship – whether at home, in a temple, or in a monastery – includes paying homage to the Buddha and reciting sacred prayers such as the Three Jewels. Festivals provide further opportunities for worship. Monasteries are very important in Buddhism, and the Sangha, or monastic community, plays a major part in the spiritual life of Buddhists. In countries such as Thailand, young men may become monks for a few years, as part of their spiritual education; in other places, monastic vows are more permanent.

THERAVADAN MONKS

MONKS AND NUNS
Buddhist monks and nuns live according to the Monastic Rule outlined in the Pali Canon. They observe the **Five Precepts**, plus additional rules that prescribe eating times, ban them from taking part in entertainments such as dancing and singing, and forbid them to lie on a luxurious bed. The Rule also instructs on other aspects of monastic life, such as the kind of robes that should be worn.

MERIT
Buddhists believe that when people perform good deeds they acquire good **karma**. For lay Buddhists, meritorious actions include helping others – especially the poor and members of the **Sangha**, attending religious services and festivals, and practicing the **Five Precepts**.

THREE JEWELS
Ceremonies often begin with worshipers reciting the Three Jewels, in which they are said to "take refuge." The Three Jewels are the Buddha himself, the **dharma**, and the **Sangha**.

INITIATION
To be accepted into the **Sangha**, monks undergo a series of initiation rituals, including having their heads shaved, and casting off any fine clothes so that they may enter the monastery in poverty. They are also tested on their suitability by older monks.

DHARMA
For Buddhists, dharma is the true reality. It symbolizes both the law of the universe and the teachings of the Buddha. In accepting the dharma, Buddhists acknowledge the **Four Noble Truths** and the **Eightfold Path**.

RITUALS

Buddhist rituals vary from one school to another. Traditionally, they include honoring the Buddha and reciting the Three Jewels and Five Precepts. Worship may occur in a shrine at home, or in a temple.

PRAYERS
In **Mahayana Buddhism**, prayers may be offered to the **bodhisattvas**. Saying such prayers, or turning a prayer wheel to symbolize a repeated **mantra**, is another way of gaining merit. Praying, rather than being a way of asking for something as in many other religions, is instead an attempt to combine one's inner thoughts with good forces.

ALMS
Monks and nuns live a life of poverty. They rely for their survival on alms given by laypeople. Each day, monks collect alms from their local community. Donating food or clothing is a popular way for lay Buddhists to acquire **merit**.

A BURMESE NOVICE MONK RECEIVES ALMS.

OFFERINGS
Buddhists make symbolic offerings – such as flowers, candles, and incense – at temples and shrines. Flowers symbolize the fleeting nature of earthly life; the flame of a candle indicates the light of **enlightenment**; the smell of incense reflects the spread of the **dharma**.

Saffron robes represent wisdom, concentration, knowledge, and morality.

MEDITATION

The bell symbolizes wisdom, and is rung during certain ceremonies

TIBETAN PRAYER BELL

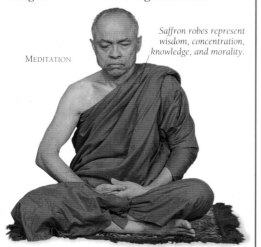

MEDITATION
The Buddha attained **enlightenment** while meditating, and Buddhists regard meditation as the main way of achieving **nirvana**. Meditation usually includes two stages: *samatha*, which develops concentration, and *vipassana*, which leads to insight.

A JAPANESE WORSHIPER PROSTRATES HERSELF BEFORE THE BUDDHA.

PROSTRATION
Although the Buddha is not worshiped as a god, Buddhists pay homage to offer thanks for his teachings by bowing, kneeling, and prostrating themselves before his image.

CIRCUMAMBULATION
Walking around a sacred site is a common ritual in Tibetan Buddhism. Pilgrims might walk three times around a monastery or shrine to symbolize the **Three Jewels**.

VIHARA

The monastery, or vihara, is the most important center for Buddhist worshipers. Viharas offer the opportunity for spiritual growth, and are also centers of learning and study. In the vihara, **monks** follow a life of devotion and **meditation**. They teach the **dharma** and provide for the spiritual needs of the lay population. Monks also take part in ceremonies at key stages in life, especially birth and death.

WAT PHRA KEOW, A VIHARA ATTACHED TO THE ROYAL PALACE IN BANGKOK

THAT LUANG FESTIVAL, VIENTIANE, LAOS

STUPAS AND PAGODAS

After the death of the Buddha, his relics were divided up. The early Buddhists created burial mounds, or stupas, in which they interred these relics. Other stupas were built to house remains of later Buddhist teachers and **bodhisattvas**. These mounds, encased in stone and adorned with statues of the Buddha, were treated with great reverence, and became places of worship and pilgrimage. In Southeast Asia, Japan, and China, stupas evolved into pagodas – great constructions the parts of which symbolize different aspects of the Buddhist universe. The great eighth-century Buddhist shrine of Borobudur is shaped like a great stupa, and has a pinnacle consisting of many smaller stupas.

STUPA ADORNING THE BUDDHIST MONUMENT OF BOROBUDUR, JAVA

Inside each stupa is a Buddha statue, representing the quest for enlightenment.

FESTIVALS

Buddhists celebrate numerous festivals, the most important of which are linked to the life of the Buddha. Celebrations vary in different parts of the Buddhist world, with festivals based on the agricultural year more popular in southern countries, and the festival of the rainy season, or **Asalha**, widely observed throughout Southeast Asia. Buddhist festivals are usually restrained and quiet events.

WESAK DAY

The birth, **enlightenment**, and death of the Buddha are said to have occurred on the same day in the month of Wesak (May–June). Buddhists celebrate these events on Wesak day. People decorate their houses and make offerings. An important part of the festival is the use of candles and other lights, which symbolize the enlightenment of the Buddha.

UPOSATHA DAYS

Days related to the phases of the moon, plus other special days in the lunar calendar, are called Uposatha days. Uposatha means "entering to stay": On such days laypeople may wear special clothes (most often white robes) and enter their local monastery. Here, they join the monks in chanting and meditating, and may also practice extra moral precepts, thereby gaining additional **merit**.

ASALHA

During the rainy season, or Asalha, Buddha is said to have ascended to heaven and taught the **dharma** to the gods. Travel is difficult, so the **monks** remain in their monasteries studying and meditating. At the end of Asalha, the monks perform a special ceremony where they ask forgiveness of their fellows if they have offended them.

PILGRIMS AT BODHGAYA

Shoes are always removed when entering a temple or sacred site.

PILGRIMAGES

Buddhists go on pilgrimages to places linked with the life of the Buddha. The most important are the Buddha's birthplace at Lumbini in Nepal; Bodhgaya, the place of his **enlightenment**; **Varanasi** (Benares), where the Buddha preached the **first sermon**; and Kusinara, the place of his death. There are also many local pilgrimage sites throughout the Buddhist world.

FUNERAL RITES

Buddhists are either cremated or buried. A variety of customs and rites prevail in different parts of the Buddhist world. Those close to a dying person usually try to help them prepare for death, which is thought to be a state of blissful rest. Monks are often employed by the family to pray for the deceased and perform funeral rites.

Coffin is carried under a red tent.

FUNERAL PROCESSION NEAR HANOI, VIETNAM

CHINA, JAPAN, AND TIBET

MAHAYANA BUDDHISM IS PREDOMINANT IN CHINA, JAPAN, AND TIBET. This form of Buddhism places more emphasis on compassion than the Theravada school. Mahayana Buddhists believe that when people achieve enlightenment, they remain in the world as bodhisattvas to help others toward the same goal. They do this because of their great compassion and wisdom, which are the qualities of those who have attained enlightenment. Countless different bodhisattvas are revered in the Mahayana Buddhist countries. They are seen as a force for good in the world and provide Buddhist worshipers with an ideal to emulate. Bodhisattvas are also a source of everyday help – people may pray to a bodhisattva when they have a particular problem in their lives.

LOHAN, OR "WORTHY ONE"

Elongated earlobes indicate enlightened status.

Cross-legged in lotus posture

CHEN YEN AND SHINGON

In China, Chen Yen – a school of **Tantric Buddhism** – was founded in CE 716 but never became deeply established. However, during the ninth century, the Japanese Buddhist leader Kukai visited China and returned with some of the teachings of Chen Yen. These ideas grew into the influential Shingon school of Japanese Buddhism. Shingon Buddhists believe that the Vairocana Buddha (the Buddha of infinite light) is the source of all existence.

CH'AN

This school of Chinese Buddhism has its origins in the sixth century CE, when an Indian prince called Bodhidharma became a Buddhist monk and traveled to China. Bodhidharma's teachings combined ideas from Mahayana Buddhism with those of Taoism. He discouraged the idea of merit-making, and concentrated on the process of **meditation** (Ch'an in Chinese). This form of Buddhism provided the foundation of the Japanese **Zen** school.

BODHIDHARMA, FIRST PATRIARCH OF CH'AN

LOHAN

In China, a person who has become enlightened is called a Lohan, or "worthy one." The Chinese Buddhist texts tell of 18 disciples of the Buddha who became Lohan. They are widely portrayed in Chinese Buddhist art.

ZEN

Introduced to Japan by monks returning from China during the 12th century, Zen emphasizes a simple lifestyle, **meditation**, and the avoidance of complex teachings. There are two main Zen groups: Rinzai, which is known for its use of koans, or riddles; and Soto, which emphasizes pure meditation as a route to **enlightenment**.

TENDAI

This school of Japanese Buddhism was brought from China in the ninth century. Its founder, Saicho, based his teaching on the *Lotus Sutra*, holding that it is possible to achieve Buddhahood by many different methods. Tendai contributed to the development of three important schools: **Nichiren**, **Zen**, and **Pure Land**.

PURE LAND SCHOOL

The Chinese monk Hui Yuan (CE 334–417) founded the Pure Land school of Buddhism. Pure Land Buddhists revere the bodhisattva Amitabha, ruler of a "pure land" where his devotees hope to be reborn. During the ninth century, Pure Land Buddhism came to Japan, where Amitabha is known as Amida. His devotees repeat the phrase, "I put my faith in Amida Buddha."

THIRTEENTH-CENTURY AMIDA BUDDHA AT KAMAKURA

NICHIREN

This Japanese Buddhist school is named after its founder, Nichiren, who lived during the 13th century. It is also known as the "Lotus sect," because of the importance placed on the *Lotus Sutra*. There are many sub-sects in Japan today, the largest of which is Nicheren Shoshu. Nicheren Buddhism has often been controversial, claiming to be superior to other religions. **Soka Gakkai** is a new international religion based on Nichiren's teachings.

AVALOKITESHVARA

The **bodhisattva** of compassion, Avalokiteshvara, is the most popular of all the bodhisattvas in the Mahayana tradition. Having attained **enlightenment**, he vowed to help others reach the same state. However, the task was so great that Avalokiteshvara's head was said to have split into a thousand pieces, which had to be reassembled to make his eleven heads. He is also said to assist others in their daily lives.

AVALOKITESHVARA, BODHISATTVA OF COMPASSION

TIBETAN BUDDHISM

Buddhism in Tibet is Mahayana Buddhism combined with a greater emphasis on texts called tantras. The tantras place a special stress on sacred sounds called mantras, mystical diagrams known as mandalas, and ritualistic gestures, or mudras, reflecting the three aspects of a person – speech, mind, and body.

TANTRIC MANDALA

PADMASAMBHAVA

Vase containing the elixir of immortality

The prayer wheel contains hundreds of rolled-up mantras.

A PRAYER WHEEL IS SPUN WHEN RECITING MANTRAS.

A LAMA'S HEADDRESS DEPICTING FIVE BUDDHAS

PADMASAMBHAVA
Known as "the second Buddha," the sage Padmasambhava, who lived during the eighth century, was one of the founders of Tibetan Buddhism. He was said to have been born from a lotus flower in the Indus River, and was invited to Tibet to exorcise demons who were preventing the spread of Buddhist teachings.

TANTRIC BUDDHISM
This form of Buddhism is based on the tantras, or ritual texts. These were said to be the words of the Buddha himself. The tantras cover a range of religious practices, from ritual magic to **meditation**, that aim to bring direct experience of **enlightenment** in this world.

LAMAS
Tibetan Buddhist teachers are called lamas. To reach **enlightenment**, a person must be initiated by a lama and follow his teachings. According to Tantric Buddhism, there are many Buddhas. These include the five Buddhas of Meditation, each of whom stands for an aspect of divine being. These are often featured on lamas' headdresses.

DALAI LAMA
The leader of the Gelugpa, or Yellow Hat, order of lamas is known as the Dalai Lama. Each Dalai Lama is thought to be a **reincarnation** of the first Dalai Lama and an incarnation of the **bodhisattva Avalokiteshvara**. The Dalai Lamas have been the spiritual leaders and political rulers of Tibet since the 17th century.

TIBETAN BOOK OF THE DEAD
This text is a manual used by **lamas** when carrying out funeral rites. The dying are taught to prepare themselves for death. Traditionally, the body is exposed to the elements.

RELICS
The physical remains of the **bodhisattvas** and lamas are important to Tibetan Buddhists. After a lama dies, his ashes are mixed with clay and made into a tablet that is preserved and revered.

MANTRAS
Mantras are sacred phrases used in **meditation** and devotion that have a special effect. One famous mantra, *Om mani padme hum* ("Hail to the jewel in the lotus"), is associated with **Avalokiteshvara**.

MANJUSRI

KUAN YIN
In China, the male **bodhisattva** Avalokiteshvara became known as the female Kuan Yin, meaning, "Hearer of the prayers of the world." As the protector of women and children, she retains her male ancestor's compassion. In Japan she is known as Kannon.

MANJUSRI
The **bodhisattva** Manjusri is a bringer of wisdom. He is usually shown carrying a sword of wisdom in one hand and a book in the other. He is widely revered in China, where the wisest rulers have sometimes claimed to be **reincarnations** of him.

TARA
Popular in Nepal and Tibet, the female **bodhisattva** Tara is a figure of compassion and bestower of long life. She was said to have been born from tears shed by **Avalokiteshvara**. At least 21 different Taras exist. Tara is regarded both as a bodhisattva and as a spiritual essence present within the mind, which a believer can develop by means of **meditation**.

TARA

Three eyes – in the forehead and the palms of the hands – indicate her all-seeing nature.

SEE ALSO

BODHISATTVA 59
ENLIGHTENMENT 56
MAHAYANA BUDDHISM 59
MAHAYANA SUTRAS 59
MEDITATION 62
MANTRAS 42
REINCARNATION 60
SOKA GAKKAI 119
TANTRIC HINDUISM 41

CHINESE AND JAPANESE RELIGIONS

China and Japan are geographically close, and have been in contact with each other for thousands of years. China, the larger of the two countries, has had a long-standing influence on Japan, in areas including agriculture, language, and, especially, religion. Of China's three great religions, or "ways" – Confucianism, Buddhism, and Taoism – the first two were taken to Japan by traders and missionaries.

CHINESE RELIGIONS

CHINESE TAOIST

China is a vast country with several different religious traditions. The two best known native Chinese religions are Confucianism, named after its founder Confucius (551–479 BCE), and Taoism. Buddhism also has a long history in China. These faiths combine together in Chinese popular religion, in which hundreds of different immortals – including Confucius and the Buddha – receive the prayers of their devotees.

RELIGIONS OF JAPAN

Japan has its own native religion, Shinto, which has just over 2.5 million followers. Shintoists believe in a host of spirits, many of whom represent forces of nature. Many Japanese people, however, follow faiths that have come into Japan from overseas. Buddhism – in the form of Zen Buddhism – is still popular and influential in Japan. Confucianism also arrived in Japan from China.

CONFUCIANISM

THE IDEAS OF THE SAGE K'ung Fu-tzu (551–479 BCE), known in the West as Confucius, are, together with Taoism and Buddhism, the most important in Chinese thought. However, Confucius did not originally intend to found a religion. His aim was to provide moral instruction, and to teach people to live well according to the values of duty, courtesy, wisdom, and generosity. One of the most important ideas for Confucius was that children should honor and respect their parents, both when they are alive and after they have died. For this reason, Confucius encouraged the practice of ancestor worship, which already formed part of Chinese religion. Later sages, such as Mencius (c.372–289 BCE) and Zhu Xi (1130–1200 CE) developed the ideas of Confucius into a religious system.

Yang

YIN AND YANG SYMBOL

YIN AND YANG
In Chinese thought, everything in the universe is made up of two opposite qualities, called yin and yang. Yin represents qualities that are feminine, receptive, and yielding. Yang is masculine, active, and unbending. Both need to be kept in balance.

Yin

CONFUCIUS HOLDING THE FIVE CLASSICS

Confucius

CONFUCIUS CONSULTS THE I CHING.

TEACHINGS OF CONFUCIUS
Confucius taught the importance of the **family** and respect for one's elders. He valued learning and insisted that his followers use the correct **rituals** during religious and other ceremonies. He looked to heaven and the deified ancestors as the source of goodness in the world, and, like other religious leaders, told people to treat others in the way that they wanted to be treated themselves.

FIVE CLASSICS
The five books known as the *Five Classics*, sometimes also called the Confucian canon, make up China's oldest body of literature. The individual books are *History*, *Poetry*, *Rites*, *Changes* (*I Ching*), and the *Annals of Spring and Autumn*. Said to have been edited by **Confucius**, they were probably composed long before his lifetime. Confucius encouraged his followers to read the Five Classics, and for thousands of years they were the basic texts used for training Chinese civil servants. Their use in education was only abandoned when imperial rule ended in China in 1911.

I CHING
The *I Ching*, or *Book of Changes*, is one of the *Five Classics*. It includes 64 diagrams called hexagrams, each consisting of six divided or undivided lines, which are used for divination. This was both a way of predicting problems in the world and of ensuring that the gods approved of human actions.

FIVE RELATIONSHIPS
Confucius identified five relationships that were of vital importance in Chinese society. These were between father and son, husband and wife, elder brother and younger brother, emperor and minister, and friend and friend. Of these relationships, only that between friend and friend was equal. In all other cases, there was seen to be a "senior partner." All these relationships were considered by Confucius to be fundamental to a stable, happy society, and they are still the most valued in China and Japan today.

A son serving his parents

FAMILY
For **Confucius**, happy families made for a harmonious world. The whole family should work together to help and support each other. Parents should teach virtue, so that their children grow up to be good citizens, while children should honor their parents and help them whenever they can. According to Confucian thought, this mutual support and respect leads to balanced, contented households, which in turn make possible a society that is properly ordered and well governed.

CHILDREN
Chinese society attaches special importance to children and their position in the **family**. Married couples usually wish for children so that they can create a full and secure family unit, which is the Confucian ideal. In ancient times, children were expected to obey and respect their parents' authority without question.

ANCESTOR WORSHIP
A form of filial piety, ancestor worship was seen as vital to a harmonious society. The honor given to parents when they are alive should therefore continue when they die. Funerals and offerings to the ancestors are still among the most important Chinese **rituals**.

Children represent harmony and fertility.

CHINESE FAMILY COMPOUND

HEAVENLY MANDATE

A ruler who worshiped his royal ancestors in heaven and gained their goodwill received a seal of approval known as the Heavenly Mandate. This meant that the natural order on earth, and the proper balance of **yin and yang**, would be maintained. This resulted in rich harvests, a good food supply, and **prosperity** and successful rule for the emperor and his civil servants.

CHINESE PAINTING SHOWING SOCIAL ORDER

According to Confucian ideals, a subject must respect his ruler.

SOCIAL ORDER

For thousands of years, China was an ordered society, with a hierarchy of social levels from peasant farmers to the emperor. All were expected to work hard to support their families and to serve the state. Although no single class was more important than another, Confucian thought placed special emphasis on two key classes: farmers, who provided food, and scholar-officials, who kept the state running efficiently.

PROSPERITY

Traditional Chinese families always aspired to being prosperous. To a Confucian, prosperity and plentiful harvests mean that the cosmos is in harmony, that evil forces are under control, and that life is following a steady, ordered course. For most of its history, the people of China have relied on rice for their staple food. The usual Confucian symbol of prosperity is therefore a full rice bin.

Red is a traditional Chinese bridal color.

MARRIAGE PROCESSION

FENG SHUI

The ancient Chinese art of feng shui, meaning "wind and water," is used to select sites for buildings, and to arrange their contents, in a way which allows Earth's vital energy, or ch'i, to flow smoothly. Good feng shui will foster health and harmony in a building, whereas bad placement may lead to bad luck or ill health.

Feng shui determines whether this is a good site for a building.

FENG SHUI

RITUALS

Confucianists celebrate many life cycle rituals. Marriage is especially significant, since it is seen as the relocation of the bride to a new family, her husband's. To symbolize this, the bride enters a special carriage and is led by the groom to his house in an elaborate wedding ritual procession. There are also calendar festivals in the odd-numbered, yang months, making up the Chinese ritual year.

WORSHIP

Confucius encouraged veneration of the ancestors, and the practice continues in modern Communist China. The ancestors may be worshiped at shrines in the home or at special altars in temples. The most important form of worship is by making offerings.

THE TEMPLE OF HEAVEN AT BEIJING

FOUR BOOKS

The four texts at the heart of Confucian thought, called the *Four Books*, are the *Analects, Mencius, The Great Learning,* and *The Doctrine of the Mean.* The books became the basis of Chinese education – students had to memorize them before studying the **Five Classics**.

ZHU XI

The 12th-century philosopher Zhu Xi wrote a series of commentaries on the **Four Books**. These works inspired neo-Confucianism, which encouraged both learning and morality.

LI

The term li has two meanings. According to **Confucius**, it represented correct personal behavior, or the proper ritual. **Zhu Xi** saw li as having a much deeper meaning – he said that it represented the supreme force or essence underlying all existence.

SEE ALSO

CHINA, JAPAN, AND TIBET 64–65
SHINTO 72–73
TAOISM 70–71
THE SPIRIT WORLD 28–29

TAOISM

THE FOLLOWERS OF TAOISM AIM TO PURSUE A SPIRITUAL PATH, or Tao, laid down by ancient Chinese thinkers. However, the Tao is more than a path – it is also defined as the source of everything in the world. By following the path, the Taoist aims to achieve unity with the Tao, and therefore with the forces of the natural world. This involves leaving behind the cares and concerns of the material world to concentrate fully on the path, thus reaching a balance and harmony in one's own life, and attaining the peace that comes through understanding. People who achieve these goals are said to become immortal after physical death. Modern Taoist thinkers distinguish two closely related forms of Taoism. These are religious Taoism, which involves the pursuit of Tao and worship of the Taoist deities, and Taoism as a complete lifestyle, embracing traditional ideas on health, meditation, and exercise.

LAO-TZU MOUNTED ON A BUFFALO

TAO
"The Way" or "Tao" represents the path every individual should try to follow. Following the Tao is said to enable a person to live in harmony with others, and a ruler who follows the Tao will rule wisely.

TEXTS
The two most important Taoist texts are the *Tao Te Ching*, said to have been written by **Lao-tzu**, and the *Chuang Tzu*, named after its author. The *Tao Te Ching* is a political text, using the **Tao** to help rulers rule wisely. The *Chuang Tzu* presents a philosophy of life that ordinary people could understand and follow.

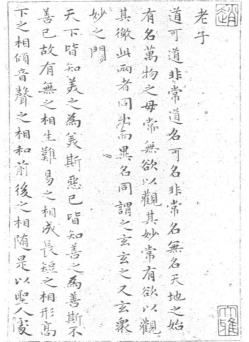

TEXT FROM THE TAO TE CHING

PERSONAL GODS
The personal gods of Taoism are people who have achieved **immortality** and godly status because of their great deeds during their lifetimes on earth. They include people who were ascetics, scholars, and warriors. Taoists pray to the personal gods to request help, and try to follow the examples the gods set while living.

LAO-TZU
The sage Lao-tzu ("The Old One") is said to be the founder of Taoism, and is looked upon as a god by religious Taoists. According to tradition, Lao-tzu grew in wisdom throughout his life, and was consulted by many about religion and politics. It is traditionally believed that the *Tao Te Ching* was written by Lao-tzu.

The peach of immortality

HSI WANG MU, THE HEAVENLY EMPRESS

SHOU HSING, GOD OF LONG LIFE

THREE STAR GODS
Among the most popular of Chinese deities are the Three Star Gods, and their statues are often seen in homes as well as temples. The trio – Shou Hsing, god of long life, Lu Hsing, god of wealth and official rank, and Fu Hsing, god of happiness – symbolize qualities that most people strive for. Lu Hsing is also revered as a bringer of male children, and is often portrayed carrying a young boy.

PA HSIEN
The Pa Hsien, or Eight Immortals, are spiritual role models who achieved **immortality** as a result of success in a variety of fields. Chung-li Ch'uan was a general, Chang Kuo-lao a scholar and advisor to emperors, Han Hsiang-tzu a musician, and Li T'ieh-kuai a healer and apothecary.

TAOIST DEMON

KUEI
Taoist demons, called Kuei, may be the spirits of people who died violent deaths, or those who were buried without proper ceremonies. Kuei must be placated with elaborate rituals, or they may harm the natural world by causing sickness and unhappiness.

HSI WANG MU
Hsi Wang Mu, the Heavenly Empress, is said to hold in her hands a peach of **immortality** that ripens only once every 3,000 years. Her cult has a long history, and she was once worshiped as a mother goddess and as ruler of the immortals.

WU-WEI
"Not-doing," or wu-wei, involves letting go of everyday thoughts and actions so that one may find the **Tao**. Emptying the mind leads to a higher state of consciousness and harmony with **nature**.

THREE TREASURES
The three treasures of Taoism are the qualities of vitality, energy, and spirit. None of these can exist without the other two. Taoists aim to keep all three in equal balance.

HARMONY AND BALANCE
Chinese thought sees everything in the world as made up of two opposite forces, **yin** (feminine, yielding, receptive) and **yang** (masculine, hard, active). The aim is to keep the two in harmony and balance.

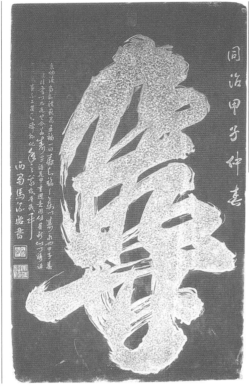

IMMORTALITY
The ideal Taoist life – following the **Tao**, letting go of material things, and living in harmony with **nature** and one's body – is said to lead to immortality, or infinite life. A person who achieves this goal is known as a chen jen, or perfected person. Immortality leads to spiritual liberation.

LONGEVITY
Taoists believe that living a long life by following the **Tao** will help them achieve **immortality** in the present life. Spiritual activities such as **yoga** and **meditation** provide the means to prolong life. The Chinese traditionally look up to old people, prizing their wisdom.

CHINESE CHARACTER FOR LONGEVITY

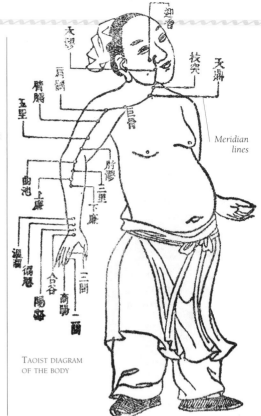

Meridian lines

TAOIST DIAGRAM OF THE BODY

HUMAN BODY
Chinese thought sees the body as an energy system; it is crossed by invisible channels called meridians, along which flows vital energy, or ch'i. By following a life in which everything is balanced and harmonious, Taoists aim to maintain a constant flow of ch'i through their bodies.

CHINESE LANDSCAPE

NATURE
Taoists have always appreciated the beauty of nature as something of greater worth than the material world, seeing mountains and pine trees as symbols of **immortality** and **longevity**. Landscapes are seen as symbolizing the constant change and motion of life.

RITUALS
Taoist rituals are intended to remind participants of the harmony of **Tao** and the balance between heaven and earth, and to promote health and **prosperity** in the community. They are often colorful, lively events. The most basic Taoist ritual is Chiao, or "offering." This can consist of a simple offering at a family altar, or a much more elaborate ritual to celebrate a special occasion.

TAOIST TEMPLE RITUAL

MEDITATION
One important way in which Taoists can let go of the material world is meditation. By emptying the mind of all everyday thoughts, a person may achieve harmony with the universe. Some forms enable the meditator to achieve unity with the **Tao**.

FESTIVALS
Annual festivals are important to Taoists because they reflect the constant renewal of the cosmos. This renewal is celebrated at various times of the year, particularly during the winter months. Most Taoist festivals also mark the birthday of a god or heavenly being.

EXERCISE
In Chinese thought, exercise is a vital way of keeping a healthy body, mind, and spirit. At the center of a person's health is his or her breathing, and systems such as Tai chi ch'uan provide gentle, graceful exercise to control a person's breath.

T'AI CHI CH'UAN IN CHINA

HUNGRY GHOST FESTIVAL

Ornate joss sticks outside a Taoist temple

SHINTO

THE NATIVE RELIGION OF JAPAN IS CALLED SHINTO, which means "the way of the gods." It was given this name in the sixth century, to distinguish it from Buddhism. At the center of Shinto are divine beings or forces of nature called kami, which are worshiped both in the home and at public shrines. There are thousands of shrines, from the large, nationally important ones at Ise and Izumo to small local shrines all over Japan. People may visit Shinto shrines for regular worship, at festivals, or if they have some special favor to ask of the kami. In each case, the correct ritual is important for communication with the kami to be successful.

The sanctity of this stone is denoted by the straw rope tied around it

SACRED STONE, SEEN AS A KAMI, AT A SHINTO SHRINE

KAMI
According to Shinto, the universe is full of sacred spirits or powers called kami. Some of the most important are the deities of Shinto mythology. Any especially powerful or impressive natural object or being, from mountains and rivers to birds and animals, can be seen as kami, as can a person or ancestor.

HACHIMAN
The deity Hachiman began as a god of farmers and fishermen. By the 12th century, he had become a god of war and warriors, and patron deity of the Minamoto, the family who ruled Japan during the late 12th and 13th centuries. Hachiman has three major shrines dedicated to him – at Usa, Kyoto, and Kamakura.

TORII
Shinto shrines have one or more gateways, called torii. These symbolize a separation between the sanctity of the shrine and the outside world. People entering the shrine bow as they pass through the torii.

TORII SYMBOL

STONE FOX STATUE, AT A SHINTO SHRINE TO INARI

INARI
The rice god, Inari, is associated with fertility and agricultural **prosperity**. His shrines usually have stone statues of foxes, thought to be his messengers, at their entrances. Inari's main shrine is the Fushimi Inari at Kyoto.

Amaterasu holding a moon that contains a hare

AMATERASU, THE SUN GODDESS

AMATERASU
The sun goddess, Amaterasu, is the principal Shinto **kami**, and is said to be ruler of heaven. She was said to have shown the people of Japan how to cultivate rice, and to have invented the craft of weaving with the loom. Amaterasu sent her grandson, Ninigi, to rule Japan, establishing the country's imperial line. Japanese emperors therefore worshiped her as an ancestor, especially at her shrine at Ise.

SHICHI FUKUJIN
The Seven Gods of Good Fortune, or Shichi Fukujin, are popular deities said to bring good luck. Each one is linked with a particular area of life that may bring happiness or **prosperity**. They are Benten, the love goddess, Bishamonten, a war god, Hotei-Oshu, god of generosity, Jurojin and Fukurokuju, gods of long life, Daikoku, god of wealth, and Ebisu, god of work.

SHIP WITH THE SEVEN GODS OF GOOD FORTUNE ABOARD

TENJIN
The ninth-century scholar and poet Sugawara no Michizane became the **kami** Tenjin or Tenman, and is worshiped as the god of learning. He has many shrines, known as Tenmangu, which are especially popular with students who go there to pray for success in exams.

YASUKUNI SHRINE
Situated in central Tokyo, the Yasukuni shrine is dedicated to the people of Japan who have died in war. Some 2.5 million people, who were killed in conflicts between 1869 and 1945, are enshrined as **kami** at Yasukuni. There is great controversy over the shrine in Japan, because some of those enshrined there were war criminals. The shrine does not receive public funding.

YASUKUNI SHRINE TO THE WAR DEAD

SHINTO FESTIVAL COSTUMES

MATSURI

Festivals, or matsuri, are held to honor and give thanks to the **kami**. Each shrine may have several festivals a year, with one or two major ones, often in the spring at rice-planting time, and to mark the autumn harvest. Matsuri provide the opportunity for the community to come together and for major shrines to attract tourists.

OFFERINGS

An important part of Shinto worship is the act of offering. A worshiper may offer money or objects to the **kami** in the hope that a request may be granted. Another form of offering is to perform a ceremonial dance called a kagura, to entertain the kami.

CHILDREN AT THE SHICHI-GO-SAN FESTIVAL

LIFE CYCLE RITES

Shinto has many life cycle rites, including two unique rites for young people. Hatsumiyamairi marks the new baby's first visit to a shrine, when the child becomes a member of the community. Shichi-go-san, or 7-5-3, is a festival for boys aged five, and girls aged seven and three.

GION FESTIVAL

In July at Kyoto, the Gion festival, which began during the ninth century, is held. Its original aim was to enlist the help of the **kami** in keeping away diseases. At the end of the festival, many beautifully decorated floats are washed to symbolize the purification of disease and are pulled by hand through the streets of the city.

BOY DRESSED AS SAMURAI WARRIOR AT GION FESTIVAL

PROCESSIONS

Shinto festivals often involve a whole community in worship and celebration. Processions and parades form an integral part of the proceedings and feature colorful floats and **mikoshi** as part of the festival entertainment. Processions provide people with the opportunity to take part in a communal religious experience.

FLOAT FOR A SHINTO FESTIVAL

MIKOSHI

At many festivals, the **kami** of a shrine is carried through the

REBUILDING OF ISE SHRINE

The two main shrines at Ise are greatly revered, and all Japanese people hope to visit them once in their lifetime. Every 21 years, the shrines are dismantled and rebuilt with much ceremony and at great expense. These regular rebuildings have taken place since the seventh century.

RITUALS

Shinto rituals are designed to praise and honor the kami, and to enlist the help and support of the deity. At the shrine, a priest presides. There are usually four stages to temple worship – purification, offerings and worship, prayer, and a sacred feast.

HARAE

Rituals called harae are purification ceremonies, most commonly used on entering a shrine, to prepare for worship. Harae usually involve the use of water for washing the hands and mouth.

O-MIKUJI

Small divination slips, called o-mikuji, are often left at shrines. They bear predictions of the future or requests, which are addressed to the gods.

EMA AND FUDA

An offering in the form of a picture is called an ema, which means "horse picture," and comes from the belief that horses were the gods' messengers. Amulets called fuda, bearing the name of the deity or shrine, are often left as offerings.

FUDA

豊川閣霊験順守

EMA

Tenjin, god of learning

加賀之國兼六園

MODERN SHINTO ROADSIDE SHRINE

SHINTO TODAY

Although a fall in rural population has meant that many smaller local shrines are unable to support their own priests, Shinto remains popular in Japan. Many people still attend the major shrines, and roadside shrines are also common.

SEE ALSO
CHINA, JAPAN, AND TIBET 64–65
CONFUCIANISM 68–69
RITUALS AND PRACTICE 30–31
SACRED PLACES AND RITUAL 12–13
TAOISM 70–71
THE SPIRIT WORLD 28–29

JUDAISM

The Jewish people trace their ancestry, and their faith, back to the early leaders of their people, such as Abraham. They believe that God made a covenant, or agreement, with their ancestors, and that it is their duty to live faithfully under God. Jews believe in one God, as indicated in the opening words of the declaration called the Shema, which is recited daily: "Hear O Israel, the Lord our God, the Lord is One."

PEOPLE OF THE BOOK

THE MENORAH –
A JEWISH SYMBOL

Judaism is based on the words of the Hebrew Bible, especially the Torah, which is the name given to its first five books. Over thousands of years, prophets, rabbis, and other spiritual leaders have added a huge body of commentary to the Torah, together with writings that discuss the commentaries. These collections of texts provide advice and moral leadership on a vast variety of situations, and their complexity can seem daunting to outsiders. The whole essence of the Torah, however, has been summed up in one sentence: "That which is hateful to you, do not do unto your neighbor."

JEWISH DIASPORA

The Jewish faith has never laid particular emphasis on the recruitment of new converts. However, because the Jews have often been exiled from their homeland in Israel, they have spread all over the world in the Diaspora, or dispersion. Although they have faced persecution throughout history, Jewish people have made a positive contribution to the societies in which they have lived. Today, around one-third of all Jews live in Israel.

THE HEBREW BIBLE

JUDAISM IS THE OLDEST RELIGION to teach a belief in one single, all-powerful, all-knowing God. Jews believe that God selected them as his Chosen People, and that he revealed his words to them in the Torah – the first five and most important books in the Hebrew Bible. The Bible contains most of the surviving Hebrew texts written down before *c*.150 BCE. It provides Jews with numerous instructions on how to behave and also describes the early history of the Jewish people – from the creation of humankind to the establishment of Jerusalem as a religious center with the first Temple of Solomon. The Jews are historically called Israelites after the Patriarch Jacob, who after a mysterious struggle with God, was renamed "Israel," or "he who strives with God." He gave this name to his descendants.

HASHEM
Jews refer to God as HaShem, "the Name." The Hebrew equivalents of the four letters YHWH represent the name under which God made himself known to the **prophets**. Jews think this name too holy to use, and say HaShem instead.

TANAKH
The Hebrew name for the Bible is the Tanakh. It is made up of three groups of books – the **Torah**, **Nevi'im**, and **Ketuvim**. The name Tanakh derives from the initial letters of these three parts. The Tanakh tells the story of God's covenant with his people.

TORAH
The first five books of the Bible are known as the Torah, which Jews believe God first revealed to **Moses**. Torah means "guidance" and "teaching," but it also translates as "law." As well as history, the Torah contains 613 commandments on which Jewish life is based.

Torah scrolls covered by an embroidered mantle

Hebrew text reads "Crown of the Torah."

Crown symbolizes the Torah as the crowning glory of Jewish life.

Lion is a symbol for the tribe of Judah.

Handle for raising the scroll

PATRIARCHS

ABRAHAM DEPICTED IN STAINED GLASS

The forefathers of the Jews are known as the Patriarchs. The first was Abraham, followed by his son Isaac, his grandson Jacob, and Jacob's 12 sons from whom the 12 tribes of Israel originate. Their lives are described in the Book of Genesis.

ABRAHAM
Genesis tells how God made a covenant, or agreement, with Abraham. God promised Abraham that He would be faithful to the people of Israel, who must serve Him and obey His laws. In turn, Abraham would become the father of a great nation, and God promised Abraham a land "flowing with milk and honey." Abraham left his homeland in Mesopotamia (now modern Iraq) and traveled to the "Promised Land" of Canaan. For many years, Abraham had no children, and wondered how God's promise could be fulfilled. But when Abraham was 100 years old, his wife Sarah gave birth to their son **Isaac**.

ISAAC
To test his obedience, God asked Abraham to sacrifice his only son, **Isaac**. Abraham obeyed, but at the moment when he was about to kill Isaac, God intervened and told him to sacrifice a ram instead.

JACOB DREAMS OF GOD AND A LADDER OF ANGELS.

JACOB
In a dream, God told **Isaac**'s son Jacob that the land he lay on would always belong to him and his descendants. Later, God renamed Jacob "Israel."

NEVI'IM
This section of the Bible is known as the Prophets. The first part, the Former Prophets, draws moral and spiritual lessons from its historical narratives. The second, the Latter Prophets, contains mainly prophetic speeches, covering many themes – from God's moral demands to a prediction of the time when he will rule with peace on earth.

KETUVIM
The third part of the Bible, known as the Ketuvim, or Writings, contains a wide range of different types of text – from historical narratives to the poetry of the psalms and the wisdom of the proverbs. The psalms are used regularly in **synagogue** worship, and other books of the Ketuvim are read on festival days.

NOAH
Disappointed with mankind's evil ways, God sent a great flood to destroy humanity. Only the virtuous Noah, his family, and a selection of animals were saved, by building an ark. A similar flood story was told of a Babylonian character in the epic of **Gilgamesh**.

EZRA
The religious leader Ezra led Jews home from exile in Persia. A religious reformer, he encouraged people to obey the Jewish Law.

MOSES

The Book of Exodus describes how the Jews spent years in exile as slaves in Egypt. Moses their prophet led them out of Egypt to the Promised Land. On the journey, God gave Moses the tablets containing the Torah and the Ten Commandments – the laws by which all Jews must live.

EXODUS
When **Moses** led the Israelites out of Egypt, they began a long period of wandering. They were pursued by Egyptian soldiers, but God sent a wind to help them cross the Sea of Reeds, or the Red Sea, before the waters flowed back to drown Egypt's army.

MOSES AND THE JEWS

TEN COMMANDMENTS
When the Israelites camped in Sinai, God gave **Moses** the Commandments by which Jews must live, and all the **Torah**. To keep safe the tablets on which the Ten Commandments were written, the Israelites made a wooden chest, called the **Ark** of the Covenant.

Moses receives God's word.

GOLDEN CALF
When **Moses** came down from Mount Sinai, the Israelites had made an idol of a golden calf, and were worshiping it. Angered by these actions, Moses broke the **Ten Commandment** tablets. The words had to be written again on new tablets.

BOOKS OF THE BIBLE

The Hebrew Bible is divided into three parts: the Torah, the Prophets, and the Writings. The five books that make up the Torah were thought to have been divinely inspired, written after God revealed them to Moses.

BOOK OF GENESIS
The first book of the Bible, Genesis, deals with the creation story, in which God created the world in six days and rested on the seventh day. Genesis tells of the origins of the human race from Adam and Eve, the first man and woman, to the wanderings of the **Patriarchs** and the slavery of the Jews, who were led by **Jacob**, in Egypt.

ADAM AND EVE IN THE GARDEN OF EDEN

BOOK OF PSALMS
The Book of Psalms, now used regularly in **synagogue** worship, is a collection of 150 poems on different themes – praise of God, lamentation, and kingship. Originally, it was thought King **David** had written the psalms, but we now know they had several authors.

BOOK OF ISAIAH
It was the prophet Isaiah who predicted the period of **Exile** that resulted after the Babylonian conquest of **Jerusalem**.

RUTH
Ruth was a Moabite woman who, when her Israelite husband died, moved to Judah with her mother-in-law Naomi. To support Naomi, Ruth gleaned leftover corn in the fields of Boaz, who showed Ruth great kindness and married her. In this important story, Ruth's selfless love for Naomi and righteousness are rewarded by God, even though she is a non-Jew. Traditionally, the Book of Ruth is read at **Shavuot**.

WHEATSHEAF AND SICKLE, SYMBOLS OF RUTH'S MEETING WITH BOAZ

SLING AND STONES

DAVID
A military leader who won fame by killing Goliath, the gigantic champion of the Philistines, David was the first ruler of Judah. Later, he was chosen as the king of all Israel. David conquered **Jerusalem** and made it his seat of government and religious center. He brought the **Ark** of the Covenant there and set it beneath a tent.

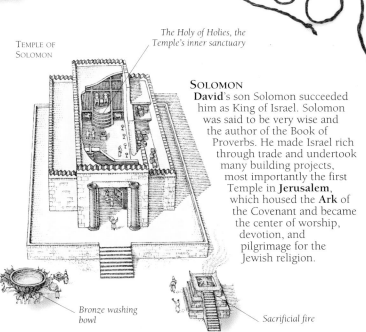

TEMPLE OF SOLOMON

The Holy of Holies, the Temple's inner sanctuary

Bronze washing bowl

Sacrificial fire

SOLOMON
David's son Solomon succeeded him as King of Israel. Solomon was said to be very wise and the author of the Book of Proverbs. He made Israel rich through trade and undertook many building projects, most importantly the first Temple in **Jerusalem**, which housed the **Ark** of the Covenant and became the center of worship, devotion, and pilgrimage for the Jewish religion.

EXILE
During the seventh century BCE, the Babylonians conquered much of the Middle East. The Jewish state was destroyed and its leaders lived in exile in Babylon. But the Jews clung to their faith and, eventually, when the Persians defeated Babylonia, they were allowed to return to their homeland and rebuild their temple in **Jerusalem**.

MESSIAH
Since the time of the prophets, Jews have looked forward to the coming of the Messiah, or Anointed One. The Messiah will establish God's kingdom on Earth, scatter Israel's enemies, and rule with justice for all time. **Orthodox** Jews await this coming of the Messiah.

Reform Jews hope for a time of righteousness and peace for all people.

WRITINGS AND HISTORY

THE WORDS OF GOD form the basis of the Jewish religion. Jews believed that the Torah was the word of God, whereas the other books of the Bible were written by people who were inspired by God. Jews therefore believe that the Bible deserves the most careful study. As time went on, Jewish scholars and rabbis wrote commentaries to explain the results of their Bible studies. After the Bible, these commentaries are Judaism's most important books, and their importance explains why Jews have always set a very high value on learning.

TALLIT, OR
PRAYER SHAWL

Tefillin (leather boxes)

BOOKS

Judaism has always valued learning. For thousands of years, rabbis have studied the Torah and set down the results of their work in commentaries that have provoked further scholarly writings. The most important of all these works is the Talmud, which contains guidance on Jewish Law and Biblical narrative.

TORAH
SCROLL

MIDRASH
The term Midrash means "to search out or expound." It is used to describe the process of explaining the Hebrew Bible, and the large body of explanatory texts that have been written about it. The Midrash uses a wide range of stories, parables, legends, and puns to explain the scriptures.

MISHNAH
A collection of writings about Jewish Law, the Mishnah has six sections – Seeds (agriculture), Women (marriage law), Damages (civil and criminal law), Holiness (offerings and sacrifices), Purities (ritual purity and impurity), and Seasons (set feasts).

TALMUD
When the **Mishnah** was completed, **rabbis** added their comments. Their studies, or the Gemara, alongside the Mishnah, became the Talmud, the most important Jewish text after the **Bible**. There are two versions – Palestinian and Babylonian.

HALAKAH
Meaning "that by which one walks," Halakah is the name for all the laws in the **Talmud** that govern civil or religious practices in the Jewish community. It is thought these rules may go back to **Moses** at Sinai.

HAGGADAH
Haggadah, meaning "storytelling," examines the stories of the Bible, explaining their apparent contradictions, suggesting different interpretations of biblical passages, and throwing light on subjects such as the nature of God and the **Messiah**. A special Haggadah, the Passover Haggadah, is read at the **Pesach** meal.

ILLUSTRATED HAGGADAH

PHARISEES
During the Roman period, the Pharisees were among the most important Jewish minorities in Palestine. They were well known for their scholarship and skill in interpreting the Bible. Many historians believe that the Pharisees had an important influence on later **rabbis**, whose teaching led to an increase in scholarship.

HILLEL
A great teacher, Hillel lived in **Jerusalem** in the first century BCE. This prominent **Pharisee** passed on his wisdom by word of mouth rather than by writings. Hillel helped the poor and stressed the importance of being kind to others.

SHAMMAI
The leading **Pharisee**, Shammai lived in the first century BCE. He founded a school that fostered a literal interpretation of the Jewish Law. Known for his strict moral views, Shammai's influence encouraged the Jews of Palestine to oppose Roman rule. In later centuries, the more moderate **Hillel** was more influential.

JUDAH THE PRINCE
The patriarch or leader of the Jews of Palestine at the beginning of the second century CE, Judah ha-Nasi was known as a cultivated and holy man and a great scholar. Judah had good relations with the Roman rulers of Palestine. Because of his qualities, he was known as ha-Nasi – "The Prince." His most notable achievement was collecting all the oral laws that the scribes, scholars, and **Pharisees** had created over the centuries, and editing them to produce the **Mishnah**.

RASHI
Rabbi Shlomo Yitzhaqi (Rashi) was born in France in CE 1040. He taught in Troyes for many years and wrote detailed commentaries on the Bible and the **Talmud**. These became standard textbooks and are still read today.

MAIMONIDES
The philosopher Moses ben Maimon, known as Maimonides, lived in the 12th century CE. He settled in Cairo, where he was physician to the Egyptian Sultan. He wrote the famous *Guide to the Perplexed*, which tried to reconcile Judaism with the thinking of the Greek philosopher Aristotle.

KABBALAH

The term Kabbalah is the name given to a collection of Jewish mystical ideas, passed on by word of mouth and kept secret. The two branches are practical (prayer) and speculative (mystery).

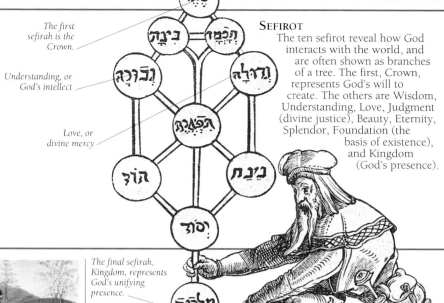

The first sefirah is the Crown.

Understanding, or God's intellect

Love, or divine mercy

ZOHAR

The Book of Splendor, or Zohar, is the main text of the Kabbalah. While it was reputed to be the teachings of a second-century sage, scholars have since argued that Moses de Leon, a 13th-century Kabbalist in Spain, wrote the texts. The Zohar introduced new rituals and describes the **sefirot**, attributes of God from which he created the cosmos.

SEFIROT

The ten sefirot reveal how God interacts with the world, and are often shown as branches of a tree. The first, Crown, represents God's will to create. The others are Wisdom, Understanding, Love, Judgment (divine justice), Beauty, Eternity, Splendor, Foundation (the basis of existence), and Kingdom (God's presence).

The final sefirah, Kingdom, represents God's unifying presence.

SEFIROT AS THE BRANCHES OF A TREE

HISTORICAL VIEW OF JERUSALEM

GOLDEN AGE

In many parts of Europe where Jews settled, they were highly successful, as in medieval Spain, where Jewish art, culture, commerce, and scholarship flourished for centuries. Gifted with languages, Jews became authorities on law and were valued diplomats. Anti-Jewish violence erupted in the 14th century, with Jews later expelled from Spain in 1492.

EXPULSIONS

Conquests of Palestine, emigration, and the attractions of foreign trade have scattered Jews all over the world, especially in Europe and North Africa. They have often been persecuted and sometimes expelled from their homes, both in Palestine and elsewhere. During Roman times, a group of Jewish Zealots held out in the fortress of Masada, by the Dead Sea. They committed mass suicide rather than surrender to the Roman army.

HASKALAH

An enlightenment, or haskalah, of Jewish scholarship and culture took place during the 18th century, inspired by the great philosopher Moses Mendelssohn. The Jews of the haskalah wanted to be better educated and to play a more positive role in society than before.

Black hat is a sign of respect for God.

HASIDIC JEW

JERUSALEM

Jerusalem has always been the most important city for the Jews. It has been a city of the Canaanites, the capital of King **David**, the site of **Solomon**'s Temple, and of a later temple after the Babylonians destroyed the first. As capital of modern Israel, it is a place of pilgrimage and a devotional center for the Jewish faith. However, Jerusalem is also sacred to the Christian and Islamic faiths, causing religious disputes in the city for hundreds of years.

HASIDISM

During the 18th century, Hasidism, a popular mystical movement, emerged. Hasidic Jews value religious devotion. They worship separately, wear distinctive, dark clothes, and grow a long earlock of hair. The Hasidic movement is still strong in Israel and the US.

HOLY DAYS

THROUGHOUT THE YEAR there are many important religious festivals commemorating key events in the history of Judaism. By bringing people together to celebrate Jewish beliefs, festivals strengthen the synagogue, family ties, and the wider community of Jews around the world. They give a regular pattern to the year, as does the cycle of readings from the Torah, whose ending and new beginning are commemorated in a festival. Similarly, the day of rest on Shabbat gives a pattern to the week.

SHABBAT CANDLES AND KIDDUSH (WINE GOBLET)

SHABBAT
The Jewish day of rest, or Shabbat, begins at sunset on Friday. A time of joy, Shabbat marks God's creation and his rest afterward. The celebration begins with the lighting of the Shabbat candles. Jews should not work on this day or go on long journeys. Fires should not be lit, although one started the previous day may be left burning. Jewish people go to **synagogue** on Shabbat, then share a special meal. The end of Shabbat is signaled with a ceremony called **havdalah**.

SHABBAT TABLE

SHABBAT MEAL
Prepared in advance, a family Shabbat meal begins with a blessing over a braided loaf, or challah. The family sings special songs and ends the meal with a Shabbat grace.

Scent of burning spices lifts the soul as Shabbat departs.

Spices reflect sweet feeling of Shabbat.

SPICEBOX

HAVDALAH
The ritual marking the end of **Shabbat** involves a blessing, dousing a candle with wine, and burning sweet-smelling spices. As the smoke of the spices rises, it feels as if the Shabbat' spirit is ascending with it.

PESACH

The spring feast of Pesach, or Passover, celebrates the exodus of the Israelites from Egypt. The name Passover derives from the tenth plague of Egypt, when the first-born sons of Egypt died, but the angel of death "passed over" the homes of the Israelites. There are special songs and prayers, and the story of the Exodus, as set out in a special service book called a Haggadah, is recounted.

SEDER
Originally, the special **Pesach** meal, or Seder, consisted of Passover lamb, eaten with unleavened bread (matzah) and bitter herbs (maror). All Seder foods are symbols of the **Exodus** story. Unleavened bread is the "bread of affliction" eaten by Israelites in Egypt. Traditionally, a place is laid at the table for the prophet Elijah, who will usher in the **Messiah**.

Matzah shows haste when Israelites fled Egypt.

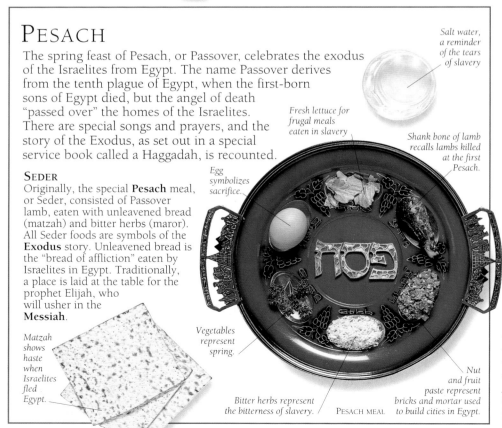

Salt water, a reminder of the tears of slavery

Fresh lettuce for frugal meals eaten in slavery

Egg symbolizes sacrifice.

Shank bone of lamb recalls lambs killed at the first Pesach.

Vegetables represent spring.

Bitter herbs represent the bitterness of slavery.

Nut and fruit paste represent bricks and mortar used to build cities in Egypt.

PESACH MEAL

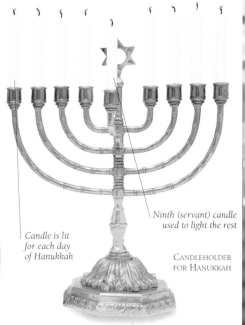

Candle is lit for each day of Hanukkah

Ninth (servant) candle used to light the rest

CANDLEHOLDER FOR HANUKKAH

HANUKKAH
Taking place in December, Hanukkah, meaning "the festival of lights," celebrates the rededication of the Temple in **Jerusalem** in 164 BCE, after Judas Maccabeus defeated the Syrians. Because a single cruse (earthenware container) of oil lasted for eight days in the Temple after the victory, Hanukkah is celebrated for eight days.

ROSH HASHANAH

New Year's Day, or Rosh Hashanah, occurs in the autumn to celebrate both the world's creation and the Day of Judgment, when God will judge people on their past lives. At this festival, people rededicate themselves to God's service, and a shofar, or ram's horn, is blown to call people to appear before God. It begins ten days of repentance that end with **Yom Kippur**.

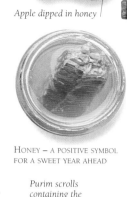

Apple dipped in honey

HONEY – A POSITIVE SYMBOL FOR A SWEET YEAR AHEAD

Purim scrolls containing the Book of Esther

Hebrew script

SILVER FISH HOLDS THE BOOK OF ESTHER.

PURIM

In February or March, the joyful feast of Purim commemorates the story of Esther, when the Jews in Persia were saved from death. The Book of Esther, which is read in the **synagogue** at Purim, tells how Haman, an official, plotted to kill the Jews and drew lots, or purim, to decide when to do so. Esther helped to bring about Haman's downfall, and he was eventually hanged on the gallows meant for Esther's cousin Mordecai. During the reading of the Book, people in the synagogue stamp their feet or make a noise with rattles whenever Haman's name is mentioned.

YOM KIPPUR

The Day of Atonement, or Yom Kippur, is a day of fasting when people pray and confess their sins. In ancient times, the high priest made a sacrifice on behalf of the people. Today, people repent their sins, often spending all day in the **synagogue**. The shofar (ram's horn) is blown at the end of the fast.

RAM'S HORN, OR SHOFAR

Hebrew script

YOM HA-SHO'AH

After **Pesach** is a period of seven weeks' austerity and mourning, when Jews remember the tragedies in their history, such as their failed revolt against Rome in the second century, the killings during the **Crusades** in the Middle Ages, and Sho'ah (the **Holocaust**), when millions of Jews were tortured and massacred by the Nazis during World War II. The government of Israel has set aside one particular day – Yom ha-Sho'ah (the Day of the Holocaust) – so Jews can remember the Holocaust's victims.

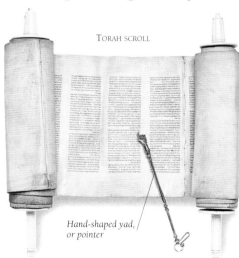

HOLOCAUST SCULPTURE FROM YAD VASHEM, ISRAEL

TISHAH BE'AV'

Another day of mourning is Tishah be'Av', the ninth day of the Jewish month of Av. On this day, Jews remember the destruction of the first Temple by **Nebuchadnezzar** in 586 BCE and that of the second Temple by the Romans in 70 CE. Decorations are removed from the **synagogue**, and there is general fasting to show repentance.

TORAH SCROLL

Hand-shaped yad, or pointer

SIMCHAT TORAH

The name Simchat Torah means "rejoicing in the law." This celebration in the **synagogue** marks the end of the yearly cycle of readings from the **Torah**. The last verses of the Book of Deuteronomy are read, followed once more with the opening of the Book of **Genesis**. Both Books are blessed. The Torah scrolls are paraded around the synagogue seven times amid much singing and dancing.

SHAVUOT

Fifty days after the second day of **Pesach** comes Shavuot, the Festival of Weeks (or the Fifty-Day Festival). It celebrates the giving of the **Torah** and the **Ten Commandments** to **Moses** and is also a harvest festival, when the **synagogue** is decorated with shrubs and flowers.

Citrus fruit, a symbol of the heart

ETROG, A CITRUS FRUIT

SUKKOT

The autumn festival of Sukkot (Tabernacles) commemorates the way in which God cared for the Jews on their way to the Promised Land. People eat their meals and sometimes sleep in temporary tabernacles that are roofed with branches and leaves. Palm, myrtle, willow, and etrog mark the end of the agricultural year.

FLAG OF ISRAEL

YOM HA-ATZMA'UT

The modern state of Israel was founded in 1948 on the fifth of Iyyar, second month in the Jewish calendar. Jews now celebrate this day as Yom ha-Atzma'ut (the Day of Independence). The flag of Israel bears the Star of **David**, known in Hebrew as Magen David (David's Shield), a symbol of God protecting his people.

Lulav, or palm frond

Myrtle

Leaves (of palm, myrtle, and willow) symbolize the shelter that God gave the Jews.

LULAV, CARRIED IN PROCESSION AT SUKKOT

LIFE AND WORSHIP

RELIGION AFFECTS EVERY ASPECT of Jewish life, from eating specially prepared food to the rituals surrounding the main events in life from birth to death. Prayer is seen as a way of serving God and attaching oneself to him. Religious Jews pray three times a day – at morning, noon, and night. Ideally, a group of at least ten people (a minyan) is required before prayers can take place, usually in the synagogue, where prayer services include the Shema (the assertion of faith) and a series of blessings called the Amidah, meaning "standing prayer."

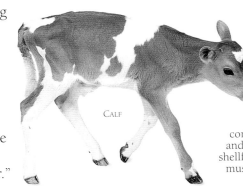

CALF

KOSHER FOOD
Traditionally, Jews eat food that is chosen and prepared according to strict dietary laws – such food is said to be kosher, or fit to eat. For example, only animals that chew the cud and have a cloven hoof are kosher, and these must be slaughtered in the correct way. Fish with both fins and scales may be eaten, but not shellfish. Meat and dairy products must be prepared separately and must not be eaten together.

STAGES OF LIFE

Judaism marks the key events of life with special ceremonies. Some of the most important stages are circumcision (for eight-day-old boys), Bar Mitzvah (for 13-year-old boys, and Bat Mitzvah (for 12-year-old girls), and marriage.

CIRCUMCISION
The practice of circumcision (removal of the foreskin) is carried out on Jewish baby boys by a mohel, or a trained circumciser. Also present are the boy's father and godfather. Circumcision is a sign that the child is Jewish and a reminder of God's covenant with his Chosen People.

Jewish boy reading the Torah

BAR MITZVAH CEREMONY

Jewish marriage contracts are often highly decorated.

MARRIAGE CONTRACT

BAR MITZVAH
The traditional Jewish coming-of-age ceremony is the Bar Mitzvah. A Jewish boy is said to reach adulthood at age 13. On the first **Shabbat** after his 13th birthday, he is called to read from the **Torah** in Hebrew, and receives his father's blessing. There is a celebratory meal, then the boy makes a speech. A similar ceremony for 12-year-old girls, called the Bat Mitzvah, has also developed.

MARRIAGE
A marriage ceremony has two parts: the first (erusin, or betrothal) was originally a pre-wedding ritual. The bride accepts a ring from the groom, the couple is blessed, and the **rabbi** reads the marriage contract aloud. The second part, under a chuppah, or canopy, symbolizes the new home the couple will make together. The seven blessings of marriage are recited. Then the groom breaks a wine glass beneath his feet, in remembrance of the destruction of the Temple in **Jerusalem**.

DEATH
The dead are buried in plain coffins. Jews observe a period of seven days of intense mourning, when a prayer (the Kaddish) is recited. Over the next 23 days, the mourners gradually return to normal life.

MEZUZAH
A mezuzah is a small container fixed at a slanting angle to the doorpost of a Jewish home. It contains a paper or parchment printed with verses from the **Bible**. The texts include the **Commandment** to serve God faithfully, to teach one's children God's laws, and to observe these laws both at home and away. It is traditional to touch the fingers to the lips and then to the mezuzah when entering or leaving the house.

Tiny parchment scroll

Star of David, Israel's greatest king

MEZUZAH CASE

PRAYERS
Jews believe that humankind was made in God's image, so it is possible by means of prayer for people to communicate with God. Prayers from the **prayer book** may be used, or the person praying may use his or her own words. People may pray to praise God or to give him thanks, to confess their sins, or to ask for his help.

The first part of the Biblical text of the Shema

שְׁמַע יִשְׂרָאֵל יְהֹוָה אֱלֹהֵינוּ יְהֹוָה אֶחָ֑ד וְאָהַבְתָּ אֵת יְהֹוָה אֱלֹהֶיךָ בְּכָל לְבָבְךָ וּבְכָל נַפְשְׁךָ וּבְכָל מְאֹדֶ֑ךָ וְהָיוּ הַדְּבָרִים הָאֵלֶּה אֲשֶׁר אָנֹכִי מְצַוְּךָ הַיּוֹם עַל לְבָבֶךָ וְשִׁנַּנְתָּם לְבָנֶיךָ וְדִבַּרְתָּ בָּם בְּשִׁבְתְּךָ בְּבֵיתֶךָ וּבְלֶכְתְּךָ בַדֶּרֶךְ וּבְשָׁכְבְּךָ וּבְקוּמֶ֑ךָ וּקְשַׁרְתָּם לְאוֹת עַל יָדֶ֑ךָ וְהָיוּ לְטֹטָפֹת בֵּין עֵינֶ֑יךָ וּכְתַבְתָּם עַל מְזוּזֹת בֵּיתֶךָ וּבִשְׁעָרֶיךָ

The Shema is the Jewish declaration of faith.

SHEMA

SHEMA
Affirming that there is only one God, the Shema is the most important of all **prayers** and is recited twice a day. It is named after the first word, and begins, "Hear, O Israel, the Lord is our God, the Lord is One." Traditionally, this is the first phrase taught to a Jewish child, the last prayer a person says before **death**, and by all believers before going to sleep at night.

SILVER PRAYER BOOK

A Jewish prayer book can be used at home or in the synagogue.

SYNAGOGUE

The synagogue, a center for worship and study, is the main meeting place in any Jewish community. It is usually rectangular, with seats on three sides; the fourth side faces toward Jerusalem. The building contains the Ark (cupboard for the Torah scrolls) and also has rooms for meetings, study, and offices. Orthodox synagogues contain a separate women's gallery.

CROSS-SECTION OF A SYNAGOGUE

Ark

RABBI

Bimah, from which a service is conducted

Yad, or pointer

PRAYER BOOKS
The first Jewish prayer books were probably written during the ninth century, but before this, **prayers** were passed on by word of mouth. Since printing was invented in the 15th century, many different prayer books have been produced, serving the needs of the different strands of Judaism. Prayer books are often given as presents when a person comes of age.

TEFILLIN
During **prayers** Jewish men may wear two small leather boxes strapped to their upper left arms and foreheads. These boxes – called tefillin – contain pieces of parchment on which are written words from the **Shema** and three other passages from the **Bible**. Attaching these to the forehead is said to make the wearer think of his faith; attaching them to his arm makes him act on his beliefs.

PRAYER SHAWL
Jewish men wear the prayer shawl, or tallit, during **prayers**. The shawl is white with blue stripes and has a tassel at each corner. The tassels recall the instruction in the scriptures that the Israelites should attach tassels to their clothing, to remind them of the **Ten Commandments** of the Lord. The stripes represent the 12 tribes of Israel.

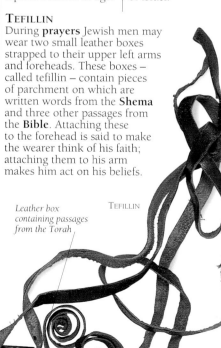

Leather box containing passages from the Torah

TEFILLIN

RABBI
The rabbi is first and foremost a teacher, one who studies the **Torah** and applies it to daily life. Although a rabbi is not a priest, he fulfills many of the roles taken by priests in other faiths – he may preach, visit the sick, console the bereaved, and advise members of his congregation on spiritual matters.

CANTOR
Any congregational member may lead the **prayers**, but in larger **synagogues** a paid official, or cantor, does this. It is traditional for prayers and scriptures to be chanted, without any musical accompaniment.

ETERNAL LIGHT
A light always burns in every **synagogue**, to remind a congregation of God's eternal light. It cannot be held, but illuminates the world.

When the Ark's doors are open, people stand as a mark of respect.

ARK
The scrolls of the **Torah** are kept in a cupboard (the ark), positioned behind a curtain on the **synagogue's** wall facing toward **Jerusalem**. The curtain, solemnly opened before removing the scrolls, recalls the veil that concealed the Holy of Holies in the Temple in Jerusalem.

ARK

SKULL CAP
When a Jewish man prays at home or in the **synagogue**, he normally covers his head with a hat or a skull cap, called a yarmulkah or kippah, as a mark of respect for God. Men also cover their heads when studying the sacred texts and when eating, and **Orthodox** Jewish men may cover their heads at all times when outside. It is also traditional for women to cover their hair in the synagogue and in other public places.

SKULL CAP

MODERN JUDAISM

THEODORE HERZL

DEPRIVED OF THEIR OWN HOMELAND for hundreds of years, Jews spread all over the world in the movement known as the Diaspora. In the 20th century this spread continued, so that there are now Jews in every part of the world, living and working beside non-Jews, while preserving their own faith and way of life. During the last 100 years, two of the most momentous events in Jewish history occurred. The Holocaust, when millions of Jews were murdered by Germany's Nazi regime during World War II, was followed by the establishment of the modern state of Israel, providing the Jews with a national homeland for the first time since the Roman period.

Black grapes

CROPS GROWN ON A KIBBUTZ

Figs

Pomegranates

DIASPORA
For many centuries, but especially since the destruction of the Second Temple in CE 70, Jews have been dispersed around the world. This Diaspora has occurred as a result of war and **exile**, but also through travel and commerce.

ZIONIST MOVEMENT
Writer Theodor Herzl (1860–1904) saw the damage done by anti-Semitism when he was working as a journalist in Paris and Vienna. At the first **Zionist Congress** in 1897, Herzl founded the Zionist Movement with the purpose of creating a Jewish national state as the homeland of Judaism in Palestine.

ALIYAH
The Hebrew word aliyah (going up) describes immigration to the land of Israel. The first modern settlers arrived between 1880 and 1914 and set up the first kibbutzim. A kibbutz is a collective farm where everyone lives as equals, according to socialist values. When the state of Israel was founded, many Jews formed kibbutzim.

Soldier's arm is bound by tefillin.

SOLDIER IN ISRAEL

BALFOUR DECLARATION
The British foreign secretary Arthur Balfour (1848–1930), wrote a letter in 1917 declaring that his government supported the formation of a "national home for the Jewish people" in Palestine. This declaration was an important step in the creation of the independent state of Israel.

WESTERN WALL, JERUSALEM

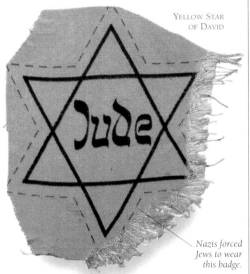

YELLOW STAR OF DAVID

Nazis forced Jews to wear this badge.

WAR OF INDEPENDENCE
After World War I, Palestine was governed by the British, and the **Balfour Declaration** was included in the terms of British rule. Violence broke out between Arab Palestinians and the Jews. The United Nations voted to create separate Arab and Jewish states in the area. The British withdrew, and an independent Israel was proclaimed in 1948.

HOLOCAUST
The term Holocaust (Sho'ah) is used to describe the mass murder of European Jews by the Nazis during World War II – Hitler's so-called "final solution" to the Jewish question. Persecution of the Jews began in the early 1930s, when the first concentration camps were set up. During the War, the Nazis massacred some six million Jews, remembered each year by **Yom ha-Sho'ah**.

SABRA, OR PRICKLY PEAR

SABRA
The fruit known as the sabra is a kind of prickly pear that grows in Israel's coastal regions. It has spines on the outside and soft flesh inside. Israeli men often use it to describe their own character – a hard outer surface, but soft within.

WESTERN WALL
For Jews today, **Jerusalem**'s most sacred place is the Western (Wailing) Wall, which contains stones from the retaining wall of the Second Temple. People come to pray at the wall, and leave **prayers** written on pieces of paper pushed into gaps between the stones. Israel upholds religious freedom in the city.

SEPHARDIM

The Jews of the Mediterranean region are known as Sephardim (from the Hebrew word for Spain), because many Jews moved to Spain during the Middle Ages. Here, they lived side by side with Muslims. They developed their own strong intellectual culture, and a language called Ladino, a mixture of Spanish and Hebrew.

SEPHARDIC SYNAGOGUE

ASHKENAZIM

The Jews of northern and eastern Europe are known as Ashkenazim (from the Hebrew word for northern France and Germany). From these areas they moved eastward to Poland and Russia, where they developed a rich culture based around their language of **Yiddish**.

FALASHAS

The Jewish people of Ethiopia are called Falashas, from an Ethiopian word meaning "stranger." They follow the traditions of Judaism, but read the Bible in an Ethiopian dialect known as Geez.

YIDDISH

The language of the **Ashkenazim** is a mixture of German, Hebrew, and some Slavic expressions, but is written using the Hebrew script. Up to World War II, Jews in central and eastern Europe spoke Yiddish; Jews today are more likely to speak the language of the country in which they live.

MODERN HEBREW

As Jews spread around the world, the ancient Hebrew tongue declined as a spoken language, but lived on in the **Torah** and **Talmud** texts and as a literary language. In the late 19th century, there was a revival of spoken Hebrew, and the tongue became the official language of the modern state of Israel. It is still written in the ancient Hebrew alphabet, which reached its current form during the sixth century BCE. The modern language includes many words from ancient and medieval Hebrew.

THE FIRST TEN LETTERS OF THE HEBREW ALPHABET

CONSERVATIVE

Some Jews felt that **Reform** Judaism had gone too far, so the Conservative movement began as a way of returning to traditional values – but without retreating completely from the ways of modern life. Conservative Judaism began in the US, where it is still particularly strong.

ORTHODOX

Orthodox Jews refer to themselves as observant Jews and believe that because the **Torah** consists of God's own words, they should obey it exactly. For Orthodox Jews, the Torah affects every aspect of life – food, dress, work, and family life. Orthodox Jews often live apart from the rest of the community and wear dark clothes.

ORTHODOX JEWS

JEWISH CULTURE

The Jews have developed a rich culture, a result of living in exile. They speak different languages from those around them, and value scholarship, stressed by their faith.

EUROPE

The Jews have enriched the cultural heritage of Europe by producing many noted writers, artists, and musicians.

UNITED STATES

The US has seen the largest flowering of Jewish culture since World War II – in the arts, academia, law, politics, business, and entertainment. Jews are part of the wider community, **synagogues** flourish, and there is widespread support for Israel.

BAGELS, TRADITIONAL JEWISH-AMERICAN BREAD

FEMALE RABBI, REFORM JUDAISM

REFORM JUDAISM

Reform Judaism, a radical movement begun in the late 18th century, holds that the **Torah** was written by a number of human authors. Although they still consider it a supremely important text, Reform Jews do not obey the Torah to the letter. This has enabled them to adapt to modern life – for example, by dropping some religious practices, accepting modern science, and becoming more integrated into modern society.

LIBERAL

The most recent Jewish movement, known as Reconstructionism, was founded by Mordecai Kaplan (1881–1983) and is especially strong in North America. This branch of Judaism places great stress on the Jews as a people, reinterpreting the laws in terms of the experience of Jews everywhere.

B'NAI B'RITH

Founded in New York in 1843, B'nai B'rith, meaning "sons of the covenant," is a Jewish organization that promotes humanitarian work all over the world. From its many lodges, or branches, it has organized and funded projects such as hospitals, orphanages, and college departments of religion, as well as helped with Israel's agricultural development, and provided worldwide aid and disaster relief.

WORLD ZIONIST CONGRESS

In 1897, the first World Zionist Congress met at Basel, Switzerland, where it was convened by Theodor Herzl. Subsequently, conferences met regularly – at first, every year, later every two years – to publicize the need for a Jewish state in Israel. By making speeches, publishing pamphlets, and creating newspapers, the members of the Congress raised support for the cause of Zionism.

ANTI-DEFAMATION LEAGUE

In 1913, **B'nai B'rith** created the Anti-Defamation League to act as a watchdog against the anti-Semitism that Jews encountered all over the world.

CHRISTIANITY

Christianity is the religion of the followers of Jesus Christ. Christians believe Jesus to be the Son of God and the Messiah, whose coming was promised in the Old Testament of the Bible. Christians believe that humankind has been in a state of sin ever since Adam and Eve disobeyed God. They believe that through his life, death, and resurrection, Jesus brought his followers salvation from this sinful state.

CHRISTIAN MESSAGE

Christians believe in one God, who exists in three forms – Father, Son, and Holy Spirit – making up the Holy Trinity. They follow the teachings of Jesus, which place a high value on love and forgiveness. Jesus' life and teachings, together with the story of his death and resurrection, are described in the opening books of the Bible's New Testament.

THE CROSS – SYMBOL OF CHRISTIANITY

A WORLD RELIGION

Some 300 years after the death of Jesus, Christianity became the official religion of the Roman empire. The faith spread from Palestine to Europe, Western Asia, and northern Africa, and through constant preaching and teaching, it has continued to spread worldwide ever since. During the 17th century, the early European settlers in America took their Christian faith with them, and in the 19th century, the religion saw a large expansion when missionaries followed European colonists into many parts of Africa and Asia. Now there are almost 2 billion Christians in all parts of the world. They belong mainly to three broad groupings – Catholic, Orthodox, and Protestant – which differ on points of doctrine and ritual, but share basic Christian beliefs.

JESUS CHRIST

TWO THOUSAND YEARS AGO, Jesus lived in Judaea, which was a province of the Roman empire in the area now covered by Syria and Israel. Christians believe that Jesus is the Son of God, and the Christian religion is based on his life and teachings. Nearly all that we know about Jesus comes from the first four books of the Bible's New Testament, the Gospels of Matthew, Mark, Luke, and John. These concentrate on the story of Jesus' years of preaching and teaching in Galilee. They also tell the story of his death and resurrection. This is the most important of all the stories about Jesus, since Christians believe that by sacrificing his son, God gave them salvation and the chance of everlasting life.

JESUS OF NAZARETH
Known as Jesus of Nazareth after the town in **Galilee** where he grew up, Jesus is also called the Son of God, and the Son of Man. The name Christ is the Greek translation of the Hebrew word **"Messiah,"** which means "the anointed one," who would help to free Israel from its enemies.

JESUS CHRIST

BIRTH OF JESUS

Jesus was born in Bethlehem to Mary and Joseph, in around 4 BCE, during the reign of Herod the Great.

ANGEL GABRIEL
Luke's Gospel tells how the angel Gabriel was sent to visit Mary. Gabriel told Mary that she had found favor with God, and that she would give birth to a child, the Son of God, whom she should call Jesus. This visit is known as the Annunciation.

MARY AND BABY JESUS

MARY
Born in **Jerusalem** or Sepphoris, Mary was brought up in Nazareth. At the time of Jesus' birth she was betrothed to the carpenter Joseph, who was descended from King **David**, and the **Gospels** say that she was a virgin. As the mother of **Jesus**, she is the most revered of all the Christian **saints**.

BETHLEHEM
The **Gospels** of Matthew and Luke describe how the Roman Emperor called a census to register people and their property for taxation purposes. As a result, Joseph and **Mary** had to go to Joseph's home city of Bethlehem, where **Jesus** was born. In the busy city, there was no room at any inn, so Jesus was born in a stable.

SHEPHERDS PRESENT AT THE BIRTH OF JESUS

WISE MEN
Matthew's Gospel tells that a group of Wise Men, or Magi, from the east followed a star until they found **Jesus**. They worshiped the baby, and gave him precious gifts of gold, frankincense, and myrrh.

SHEPHERDS
Soon after the birth of **Jesus**, an angel visited a group of shepherds in the fields near **Bethlehem**. The angel told them of the Savior's birth, and the shepherds were the first to go to the stable to see the child.

INCARNATION
Christians believe that God came to Earth in the form of **Jesus** Christ. This is known as the Doctrine of the Incarnation. On Earth, Jesus lived as a human being, and had to cope with many human problems, such as suffering and doubt. However, as God in human form, Jesus also had special powers, which he used to help others. For example, he could heal the sick, and raise the dead.

SEA OF GALILEE

GALILEE
Jesus grew up in the area called Galilee, in northern Palestine. He was probably educated in the **synagogue** school and learned Joseph's trade of carpentry. When he was around 30, he began to preach and teach in the Galilee area.

JOHN THE BAPTIST

JOHN THE BAPTIST
John was a popular preacher who believed that people should repent for their sins and return to God. He baptized his followers in the Jordan River. When **Jesus** visited John, he too asked to be baptized, and this marked the beginning of Jesus' ministry.

SERMON ON THE MOUNT
Jesus explained most of his central teachings in one sermon, which, in Matthew's description, he preached on a mountain. The sermon begins with a series of blessings on groups of people such as the poor in spirit, the meek, and the merciful. It then teaches about obeying God's law, about loving one's enemies, and about setting aside concern for material things. The sermon also includes the words of the Lord's Prayer.

MIRACLES
Jesus used miracles to help the unfortunate. He healed the sick, exorcised devils, and raised people from the dead. Other miracles were intended to demonstrate the power of faith in God, such as the occasion when he walked on water at the Sea of **Galilee**. The miracles also have another meaning. They are fulfillments of **Old Testament** prophecies, confirming Jesus was God working on Earth.

THE DEVIL
TEMPTS JESUS.

TEMPTATIONS

At the start of his ministry, **Jesus** spent a period of 40 days fasting in the wilderness. During this time, the devil tried to tempt Jesus by offering him power over the world, and taunted him, saying that God would protect him from danger. Jesus refused the devil's offers of power and glory, but the temptations are a reminder to Christians that believers may still be tempted.

DISCIPLES

Jesus' 12 closest followers were his disciples. Jesus chose these men to help with his ministry, and to continue it after his death. The disciples had ordinary backgrounds – several were fishermen and one was a tax collector.

JESUS AND THE
TWELVE DISCIPLES

JERUSALEM

At the time of **Passover**, **Jesus** rode into the city of Jerusalem on a donkey. He was welcomed by the people, many of whom apparently hoped that he would become a national leader against the rule of Rome. Instead, Jesus carried on his life of preaching and teaching.

JUDAS ISCARIOT

It was the disciple Judas who betrayed **Jesus** to the Romans, for an unknown reason. In return for 30 pieces of silver, Judas led the Roman soldiers to the garden of Gethsemene, where Jesus was praying. Judas told the soldiers that they would know whom to arrest when he kissed Jesus.

PASSION

Each of the four Gospels tells the story of the last days of **Jesus** in **Jerusalem**. This narrative describes Jesus' last meal with his **disciples**, his betrayal by **Judas**, his trial by **Pontius Pilate**, his **crucifixion**, and his burial. This sequence of events is known as the Passion (from a word meaning "suffering"). Christians commemorate the Passion every year during **Holy Week**.

LAST SUPPER

Jesus and his **disciples** gathered together for a final **Pesach** meal. During the meal, Jesus warned the disciples that the time of his death was drawing near. He took bread, broke it, blessed it, and asked the disciples to eat it, saying, "This is my body." Jesus then told the disciples to drink wine, saying, "This is my blood." This was the beginning of the Christian ritual of the **Eucharist**, or Holy Communion.

SIXTH-CENTURY BYZANTINE
MOSAIC DEPICTING THE
LAST SUPPER

PONTIUS PILATE

Governor of the Roman province of Judaea from CE 26 to 36, Pontius Pilate had control of the local Roman justice system, and of the occupying forces stationed in the region. When **Jesus** was taken for trial before Pilate, the governor ordered him to death at the request of the Jewish authorities.

HEROD

The Herodian dynasty was a royal family that ruled parts of ancient Palestine during the Roman period. Herod the Great ruled at the time of Jesus' birth. Herod Antipas reigned in **Galilee** at the time of the **Crucifixion**, and questioned Jesus at **Pilate's** request.

Jesus was nailed to the cross by his hands and feet.

JESUS ON
THE CROSS

CRUCIFIXION

Pontius Pilate ordered **Jesus** to be put to death by crucifixion, and the sentence was carried out on the day now known as **Good Friday**. Jesus was made to carry his cross to a hill called Golgotha, thought to be just outside **Jerusalem**. Here he was crucified, along with two thieves. This event plays a vital part in the Christian religion: Christians believe that Jesus died to cleanse them of their sins.

RESURRECTION

After his death, **Jesus** was buried in the tomb of Joseph of Arimathaea, one of his followers. The gospels tell that on the Sunday after the **Crucifixion**, a number of women went to the tomb, discovered that it was empty, and were told that Jesus had risen from the dead. The Resurrection is the greatest of all the Christian **miracles**, showing them that they can believe in a living Christ who will one day return to rule in peace.

THE RESURRECTION

ASCENSION

After the Resurrection, **Jesus** made several appearances to Mary Magdalene and his **disciples**. Mark and Luke describe how some time later he ascended into **heaven** to sit at God's right hand.

HISTORY AND SCRIPTURE

AFTER JESUS' CRUCIFIXION AND ASCENSION TO HEAVEN, his disciples preached to the Jewish people of the eastern Mediterranean, and wrote down their beliefs as scriptures, helping to spread Christianity. With the work of the missionary St. Paul (died 65 CE), the religion advanced, gaining a foothold in the Roman empire. Like the empire itself, Christianity developed two branches: western, based in Rome, and eastern, based in Constantinople (modern Istanbul). These two strands form the origins of the modern Roman Catholic and Orthodox Churches. Much later, with the movement of change known as the Reformation, a third branch of Christianity, Protestantism, evolved. The three branches have become the dominant strands of the Christian religion, giving a rich variety and wide distribution to the faith today.

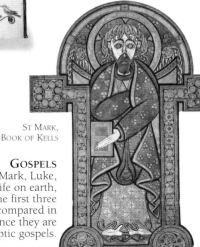

PETER

BODY OF CHRIST
The early Christian community was called the Body of Christ. The first Christians were persecuted for their beliefs and therefore usually worshiped in secret.

CATACOMBS
When the faith spread to Rome, Christians were persecuted even more, and many were put to death. Christians took to worshiping in the catacombs, a network of underground burial places. Later, the catacombs were used for memorial services for Christian **martyrs**.

St. Paul the missionary arrives by boat.

PAUL

PAUL
Originally a persecutor of Christians, Saul of Tarsus converted to Christianity after seeing a vision of **Jesus** on the road to Damascus. He changed his name to Paul, and went on a series of missionary journeys around the Mediterranean. Paul founded churches in Asia Minor, Syria, Cyprus, and Greece, which he returned to in order to help them in their work. He also wrote a famous series of letters that now form part of the **New Testament**.

PETER
Jesus called his **disciple** Simon by the name Peter, meaning "rock." This showed that Peter was to be the foundation of the early church. After Jesus' ascension, Peter became the leader of the Christians, preached widely, and, according to tradition, founded the Christian church in Rome.

SCRIPTURES

The Christians added the New Testament to the existing scriptures of the Hebrew Bible. This name indicates that these writings tell of a new covenant, or agreement, with God. The original New Testament books were written in Greek.

BIBLE
The Christian Bible is divided into two sections, or Testaments. The **Old Testament** consists mainly of the Hebrew writings that make up the body of Jewish sacred writings. The **New Testament** contains Greek writings, mainly about the life of **Jesus** and early Christianity, collected by the first Christians.

BIBLE

EPISTLES
Most of the epistles, or letters, were written by St Paul to the members of the various churches he founded around the Mediterranean.

APOCRYPHA
A number of **Old Testament** books, known as the Apocrypha, are not accepted by several branches of the Church as fully authoritative, and so are often printed as a separate section.

OLD TESTAMENT
The Old Testament tells the story of the Israelite people, from the creation of the universe up to the second century BCE. It also includes writings of the Jewish prophets, which early Christians interpreted as fore-telling Jesus' coming.

OLD TESTAMENT WRITINGS FROM THE DEAD SEA SCROLLS

NEW TESTAMENT
In the second century CE, early Christians gathered together many of the writings that make up the New Testament. These writings are the four **Gospels**, the Book of Acts, which describes the work of the apostles after Jesus' ascension, a series of letters, and the Book of Revelation.

PENTATEUCH
The first five books of the **Old Testament** are known to Christians as the Pentateuch. Many people think that these were written by **Moses**.

ST MARK, BOOK OF KELLS

GOSPELS
The Gospels of Matthew, Mark, Luke, and John describe **Jesus'** life on earth, but differ in many details. The first three are similar and can be compared in side-by-side "synopses"; hence they are called the synoptic gospels.

ROMAN EMPIRE

After years of persecution, the fortune of the Christians changed in Rome during the fourth century. The emperor Constantine I (c. CE 274–337) converted to Christianity, and in 313 he ordered that persecution should cease and that Christians throughout the empire should be granted their civil rights. In 324, Christianity became the official religion of the Roman empire.

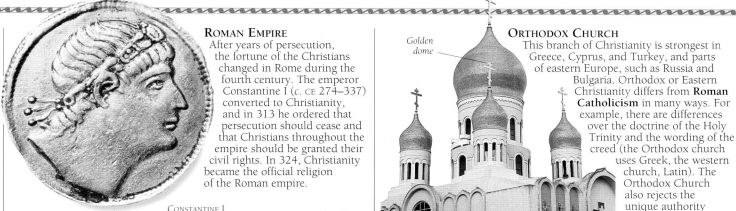

CONSTANTINE I
GOLD COIN

POPE JOHN-PAUL II

ROMAN CATHOLICISM

The Roman Catholic Church grew from the early Christian community in Rome, claiming **St Peter** as the city's first **bishop** and first **pope**. After the fall of Rome, the church survived in western Europe to become the dominant form of Christianity in this area. Today, Roman Catholicism is practiced all over the world.

SCHISM

The Western church, based in Rome, and the Eastern Church, based in Constantinople, disagreed over certain matters of belief, and they split in 1054. This split is known as the Great Schism, or separation.

POPE

The leader of the Roman Catholic Church is the pope. Roman Catholics believe that the pope is a direct successor of St Peter, and that he is therefore Christ's representative, or "vicar," on earth.

ORTHODOX CHURCH

This branch of Christianity is strongest in Greece, Cyprus, and Turkey, and parts of eastern Europe, such as Russia and Bulgaria. Orthodox or Eastern Christianity differs from **Roman Catholicism** in many ways. For example, there are differences over the doctrine of the Holy Trinity and the wording of the creed (the Orthodox church uses Greek, the western church, Latin). The Orthodox Church also rejects the unique authority of the **pope**, seeing all **bishops** as equal.

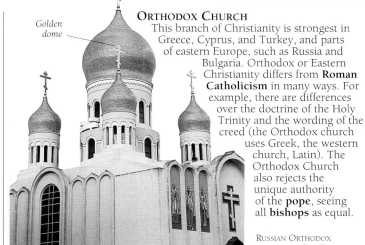

Golden dome

RUSSIAN ORTHODOX CATHEDRAL, SAN FRANCISCO

PATRIARCH

The leaders of the **Orthodox** Church are known as patriarchs. The original patriarchs were the leaders of Christian districts, or sees, based on the provinces of the Roman empire. With the setting up of the Orthodox Church, the patriarch of Constantinople became the senior leader, although all patriarchs are said to have equal status.

Armed knight

Monk

CRUSADES

REFORMATION

During the early 16th century, there was criticism of the corruption of the Roman Catholic Church, and some of its practices. Reformers such as the Frenchman John Calvin and the German Martin Luther urged Christians to go back to the teachings of the Bible, even if this meant ignoring church traditions.

MARTIN LUTHER

Perhaps the greatest of the reformers was Martin Luther. Luther disapproved of the church's practice of selling indulgences, which promised God's forgiveness of sins. He wrote out 95 theses, or arguments, protesting this practice, and nailed the document to a church door at Wittenberg. Luther translated the scriptures into German, so that ordinary people could understand them, and the reform movement he began spread across Europe.

MARTIN LUTHER PREACHING

MEETING OF THE PROTESTANT FATHERS

PROTESTANTISM

The Protestant churches that grew up as a result of the **Reformation** stressed that the words of the **Bible** had more authority than church traditions. Protestant churches came to dominate northern Europe, especially Britain, Germany, and Scandinavia.

CRUSADES

During the Middle Ages there were a number of military campaigns, called Crusades, on behalf of Christianity. These campaigns were an attempt by the Christians to take control of **Jerusalem**, and to ensure the safety of Christian pilgrims who wanted to visit the city. They degenerated into a series of wars between Christians and Muslims, bringing little benefit to either side.

HERESY

People who rejected some church doctrines while claiming to be Christians were known as heretics. In the Middle Ages, the **Roman Catholic** Church set up the Inquisition, a body whose job it was to investigate and root out heresy.

BELIEFS AND PRACTICES

CHRISTIANITY DEVELOPED AMONG THE ANCIENT JEWS and owes much to Jewish ideas, such as a belief in one God, a belief that humankind was made in God's image, and the idea that one day God will send a Messiah, his representative, to rule in righteousness on earth. However, the coming of Jesus as the Messiah marks a fundamental difference between Christian and Jewish belief. For Christians, the death and resurrection of Christ began a new covenant, or agreement, between God and humankind, where salvation was possible through Christian love. Christians believe salvation is possible for all who believe in Jesus as the Son of God and who live according to his teaching.

ADAM AND EVE IN THE GARDEN OF EDEN

CREATION
The creation story in the Book of **Genesis** tells how God made the world in six days and created the first humans, **Adam and Eve**. However, modern science has demonstrated that the universe evolved over millions of years. Today, many Christians do not accept the Biblical account of creation, although they still believe that God is the creator of the universe.

SIN
An offense against God and his laws is known as sin. Christian teaching holds that humanity has been permanently flawed, or in a state of "original sin," ever since **Adam and Eve** were expelled from the Garden of Eden for disobeying God. Christians repent for their own sins and pray to God for forgiveness. They believe that the death of **Jesus** makes this forgiveness possible.

EVIL
Christians believe that evil in the world is the result of the intervention of Satan, or attribute it to the ignorant and sinful actions of people.

SALVATION
According to Christian thought, humankind moved away from God and became **sinful**; however, Christ's death offered people the chance to return to God and "save" themselves. As a result, there will be salvation – or eternal life with God – for those who believe in Jesus, repent for their **sins**, and live correctly.

St. John the Baptist

DAY OF JUDGMENT
Many Christians believe that **Jesus** will return to earth to judge humanity. On this day, the dead will rise up and be sent to either **heaven** or **hell**. The church also developed the belief that a judgment will take place at the end of each person's life. The good would be sent to heaven and the sinful to hell.

A SECTION OF MICHELANGELO'S VISION OF THE LAST JUDGMENT

Jesus, with the Virgin Mary to his right

The 12 Disciples, at Christ's left hand

HOLY TRINITY
Christians believe in one God who exists in three persons – Father, Son, and Holy Spirit. The Holy Spirit is often invoked as an inspirational presence for prophets.

MEDIEVAL CRUCIFIX

Christ

CRUCIFIX
The cross recalls **Jesus'** death by **crucifixion**, and is the universal symbol of Christianity. It usually takes the form of a crucifix, with Jesus on the cross. An alternative symbol is an empty cross, reminding believers of the **Resurrection** and **Ascension** of Jesus.

HEAVEN
The Christian heaven is both a state of being – in which the bond between God and humankind is realized through the fulfillment of Christian life – and a place, inhabited by God, where those who have reached **salvation** go after death.

HELL
Traditionally, hell was seen as a place of punishment and torment, where those who were not saved dwelled after death. Modern Christian thought more commonly looks on hell as a state in which God is absent.

CREEDS
Christian belief is summed up in texts called creeds. Since 325 CE, The **Orthodox** and **Roman Catholic** Churches have recited the Nicene Creed. Most **Protestant** churches use the earlier Apostles' Creed, based on their teachings.

SAINT

People who suffered or died for their faith, or whose lives were particularly religious in some other way, are called saints. Some Christians believe that saints in **heaven** have the power to intercede on behalf of people on earth. This belief is strong in the **Roman Catholic** and **Orthodox** Churches, where there is a tradition of venerating saints.

ST. MENAS, AN EGYPTIAN SAINT, DEPICTED ON A 17TH-CENTURY PALESTINIAN ICON

MARTYR

People who die for their religious beliefs are known as martyrs. During the early years of Christianity, when believers were persecuted, there were many martyrs who were given the status of **saints**. There were also many martyrs in later periods of persecution. The term "martyr" comes from a Greek word meaning "witness." Jesus' 12 **disciples**, who were literally witnesses to his life and ministry, were also originally known as martyrs.

ECSTASY

Certain **saints**, and some **prophets**, are said to have experienced ecstasy. This religiously inspired feeling can include states of frenzy, inspiration, and a state of bliss where a person feels he or she is transcending the body. In such mystical states, prophets claim to receive messages from God or the saints, and temporarily achieve union with the divine.

STIGMATA

Miraculous marks on the body, like the wounds of **Jesus** when he was crucified, are called stigmata. They may appear on a person who has experienced ecstasy, and may be permanent. They are said to indicate an especially close relationship with God.

CHRISTIAN VOCATION

Some Christians have a strong conviction that they must dedicate their lives to serving God. Such a conviction, or vocation, leads men and women to become **priests**, pastors, or **missionaries**, or join one of the **monastic orders**.

ST. JOAN OF ARC, RELIGIOUS MARTYR

MONASTICISM

People who want to pursue a Christian vocation may leave the everyday world behind them and join a monastic order. Monks and nuns dedicate their lives to God through prayer, and through charitable work such as nursing or teaching.

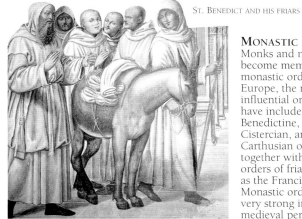

ST. BENEDICT AND HIS FRIARS

MONASTIC ORDERS

Monks and nuns become members of monastic orders. In Europe, the most influential orders have included the Benedictine, Cistercian, and Carthusian orders, together with the orders of friars, such as the Franciscans. Monastic orders were very strong in the medieval period.

MONKS AND NUNS

Monks and nuns live in single-sex **monasteries**. They obey their order's rules, which cover every aspect of their lives from the clothes they wear to when and how often they worship.

VOWS

When **monks** or **nuns** join an order, they make several promises, or vows. The most important of these are poverty (a monk should have no personal possessions), chastity, and obedience to the abbott or abbess.

OFFICES

Prayer and worship dominate the monastic life. Monks and nuns take part in different services, or offices, at set times of the day from dawn to midnight.

MONASTERIES

Most Christian monasteries consist of a series of rooms arranged around a courtyard, or cloister, next to a church. Many of these rooms are for communal activity – for example, a frater where the monks eat together, a chapter house where they discuss business, and a dormitory in which they all sleep.

ROMANIAN MONASTERY

MOUNT ATHOS

In a remote part of Greece, this mountain has some 20 **monasteries**. They form the most important religious community in the **Orthodox Church**.

MISSIONARIES

Christianity has always been spread by **missionaries**, or preachers and teachers, who have tried to convert unbelievers to the faith. This tradition goes back to the time of **St Paul**, with his journeys around the Mediterranean. Traveling missionaries flourished when European countries gained colonies in Africa and Asia during the 19th century.

MISSIONARY DEPICTED ON A NIGERIAN CARVING.

FESTIVALS AND HOLY DAYS

THE CHRISTIAN YEAR IS ORGANIZED around a series of festivals that celebrate the life of Jesus Christ. The best known of these, Christmas and Easter, provide the main focus of the year, with special services in church and celebrations at home. Different branches of the church give different emphasis to the celebration of festivals. Some Protestant churches concentrate on the major holy days, while in Catholic countries, the church also stresses saints' days. In Christian countries as a whole, however, the importance of these festivals extends well beyond the church itself. Almost everyone celebrates Christmas, children still receive eggs at Easter, and many adults receive time off from work at major religious festivals.

SUNDAY
Christians keep Sunday as the Sabbath, the day on which God rested after creating the world. In Christian countries Sunday is kept special. Some people go to **church**, many have the day off work, schools and stores close, and families eat special meals.

Slits in bell tower allow the sound of ringing bells to escape.

FRENCH TIMBER-FRAMED CHURCH

CHRISTMAS

Christmas marks the birth of Jesus Christ and is a time of peace, joy, and goodwill. It is important to Christians because it is a celebration of God sending his only Son to earth in order to bring everlasting life to humanity. Christmas is the most widely celebrated of all Christian festivals.

ADVENT
The four weeks before Christmas are known as Advent, the festival of the coming of Jesus. In many churches, a special candle is lit on each **Sunday** until the four form a circle. Children have Advent calendars, which mark the days from the first day of December until **Christmas Day**.

ADVENT CALENDAR

NATIVITY SCENE

CHRISTMAS DAY
The birth of Jesus is celebrated on December 25 by most Christians, but the **Orthodox Church** celebrates it on **Epiphany**. **Churches** are decorated with a model of the stable where **Jesus** was born, with figures of Jesus, **Mary**, Joseph, and the shepherds and **wise men**. Special services are held in church, homes are decorated, people eat celebratory meals, and presents are exchanged.

EPIPHANY
Christmas ends with Epiphany, usually celebrated on January 6. It marks the visit of the magi (**wise men**), or three kings, who brought gifts of gold, frankincense, and myrrh to baby **Jesus**. The visit of the magi is important because it signals Jesus' importance to non-Jews, showing that he is Savior of the whole world.

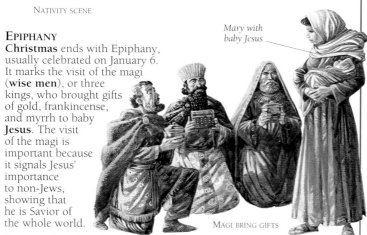

Mary with baby Jesus

MAGI BRING GIFTS

MARDI GRAS CARNIVAL IN RIO DE JANEIRO, BRAZIL

SHROVE TUESDAY
The day before the beginning of **Lent** is known as Shrove Tuesday or Mardi Gras. It was traditionally a day on which Christians went to **church** to confess their sins and receive absolution, or forgiveness. A person was said to be "shriven" after confession. Also on Shrove Tuesday, rich foods not needed over Lent were used up in a spree of pancake making – a tradition that has continued in some countries. In some parts of the world, people celebrate Mardi Gras with lavish carnivals before the solemn period of Lent. Today, the liveliest carnivals are held in New Orleans, Rio de Janeiro in Brazil, and Nice in France.

Palm leaves are used to make the Palm Sunday crosses that are burned on Ash Wednesday.

PALM BRANCH

ASH WEDNESDAY
The first day of **Lent** is called Ash Wednesday. It gets its name from a ritual in which the **priest** uses ashes to make the sign of the cross on worshipers' foreheads as an indication that they have repented for their sins. The use of ash is a reminder that people are no more than ash compared with God, and that Christians depend on God's grace for their salvation. The ash used in this ritual traditionally came from burning the previous year's palm crosses.

LENT
The 40-day period before **Easter**, Lent, is a time of fasting or giving up luxuries to remember the 40 days Jesus spent in the wilderness, when he was tempted by the devil and ate only simple foods.

MOTHERING SUNDAY
In the United Kingdom, the fourth **Sunday** of Lent is a celebration of the role of women, especially the Virgin **Mary** and Mary Magdalene, in Jesus' life. People honor their own mothers on this day by giving them presents.

EASTER

Easter, the festival of Christ's arrest, trial, crucifixion, and resurrection, takes place in the spring. Since Christians believe that Jesus' death will bring eternal life to all believers, Easter is the most important of all Christian festivals.

CHRIST ENTERS JERUSALEM.

PALM SUNDAY

Signifying the start of **Holy Week**, Palm Sunday, also called Passion Sunday, commemorates Jesus' ride into **Jerusalem** on a donkey. People lining the street strewed cloaks and palm leaves on the road to make a path for their **Messiah**. Today, in special **church** services, palm crosses are given out as a reminder of this.

HOLY WEEK

During the last week of **Lent**, Christians remember the story of Jesus' life, from his entry into **Jerusalem** to his burial. Each day, part of the story is read in **church**.

MAUNDY THURSDAY

On this day, Christians celebrate Jesus' **Last Supper** with his **disciples**. The **Eucharist** (also called holy communion) is performed according to Jesus' wishes to remember him.

HOT CROSS BUNS

GOOD FRIDAY

The most solemn day of the Christian year, Good Friday, commemorates Jesus' **crucifixion**. Christians perform rituals, such as processions, **pilgrimages**, and bowing to the cross. The fast of **Lent** may be broken with special foods; in the United Kingdom, hot cross buns are popular.

EASTER SUNDAY

Jesus' **resurrection** is celebrated on Easter Sunday. In the Eastern Church, the celebration begins at midnight on Saturday, when lighted candles are passed around the **church**, and people look for Jesus' body in an empty tomb. In many countries, joyful **Easter** parades are held and people decorate eggs, or eat chocolate ones, as a symbol of new life.

EASTER PARADE IN GUATEMALA

ASCENSION DAY

According to the **Bible**, Jesus spent 40 days on earth with his **disciples** after his **resurrection** from the dead. He then ascended to heaven from the Mount of Olives to join God the Father and sit at his right hand. Ascension Day commemorates this event, and asserts the belief that Jesus' spirit exists outside space and time. Ascension Day is celebrated on a Thursday, the 40th day after **Easter**.

HARVEST FESTIVALS

In many countries, Christians give thanks to God for a successful harvest in a special **church** service of thanksgiving. Farmers, fishermen, and growers bring a selection of their produce to the church to be blessed. The food is then distributed to the poor and needy in the community.

God the Father and creator

The Holy Spirit, represented by a dove

The Son, Jesus Christ

THE HOLY TRINITY

PENTECOST

Held on the seventh **Sunday** after **Easter**, the feast of Pentecost, or Whitsunday, celebrates the point at which Jesus' disciples were given the Holy Spirit. This marked the start of the holy church. Traditionally, Pentecost was a time for **baptism** and, since people wore white, it became known as White Sunday, or Whitsunday.

St. Francis is remembered for his love of animals.

St. Francis was simply dressed, like Jesus.

ST. FRANCIS OF ASSISI

SAINTS' DAYS

Special days in the **church** calendar mark the lives of the saints. These days began as commemorations of those who died for their faith, such as martyrs. Today, each saint has his or her own day when church services are held and colorful processions take place. In some countries, saints' days are national holidays – for example, St. Patrick's Day in Ireland. Some of the most popular saints' days are those of St. **John the Baptist** (June 24), St. **Peter** and St. **Paul** (June 29), and St. Francis (October 4).

ALL SOULS' DAY

This day, falling on November 2, is when Christians remember the dead. In **Roman Catholic** churches, masses and **prayers** are offered for souls in purgatory. In some countries, people place flowers on the graves of the dead or put up decorations such as colored streamers. These are symbols of life, reminding people of Jesus' promise of eternal life to his followers.

WORSHIP AND RITUALS

THE COMMUNITY OF CHRISTIAN BELIEVERS is called the "church," which is also the name of the building in which Christians worship. People join the Christian community in the ceremonies of baptism and confirmation. Christians gather together for regular services, most commonly on Sundays. These services include several elements – for example, prayers to God, the singing of hymns in his praise, readings from the scriptures, and sermons. The central Christian ritual is the Eucharist or Mass, which was initiated by Jesus himself.

Red is worn for services that commemorate martyrs.

A PRIEST'S CEREMONIAL VESTMENTS

PRIEST
The **Roman Catholic**, **Orthodox**, and **Anglican** Churches have officials called priests. Priests officiate at religious ceremonies, particularly the **sacraments**, and administer to a parish. The word vicar, meaning "substitute," is also used in the Anglican church. **Protestant** churches do not have priests, insisting that there is a "priesthood of all believers."

BISHOP
Ministers who rank above priests in the church hierarchy are called bishops. A bishop normally has responsibility for a large area called a diocese, centered on a cathedral. He supervises the clergy in the diocese, and has the authority to ordain priests and to confirm members of the church. The **Roman Catholic**, **Orthodox**, and many **Protestant** churches have bishops.

CHURCHES AND CATHEDRALS
Western churches and cathedrals contain a nave for the **congregation**, and a **choir**, from which the services are led by a **priest**. For most rituals, the focal point is the **altar**. Additional areas, such as aisles, provide extra seating. Other features include the **pulpit**, the lectern (for reading the scriptures), and the font (for **baptism**). A cathedral also contains a bishop's throne.

Spire

Nave

CONGREGATION
People who come to church to worship together are called the congregation. They sit in the nave to listen to the **sermon** and readings, stand to sing hymns, and kneel to pray.

ALTAR
In **Roman Catholic** and Orthodox Churches, the bread and wine used for the **Eucharist** are prepared and set down on a structure known as an altar. In **Protestant** churches it is called the "table." It has been customary to celebrate private masses: As a consequence, some churches have several altars, the main one being called the high altar.

PULPIT
Sermons are read from a raised platform called a pulpit. Traditionally, it is placed at the eastern end of the nave, to one side of the center. In **Protestant** churches, the pulpit may have a more central position.

HYMNS
The singing of sacred songs, or hymns, by the **congregation** forms an important part of Christian worship. Hymns were originally sung in Greek or Latin: However, since the **Reformation**, they have mostly been sung in the mother tongue of the congregation.

NOTRE DAME CATHEDRAL, PARIS

Choir

CHOIR
Many churches have a choir of trained singers who both lead the **congregational** singing and sing parts of the service, such as the anthem, independently.

When reciting Hail Mary, the beads are counted as part of the prayer sequence.

ROSARY BEADS

PRAYER
Christians pray in order to praise God and to ask for divine help and favors. Prayer therefore forms a central element of all Christian worship. When praying, Christians often adopt a special posture: It is common to kneel, with eyes closed and hands held together in supplication.

SERMON
A sermon is an address on a religious topic, by a priest or a lay preacher. It is often based on an extract from the **Bible**, which may be read before the sermon from the lectern. When a person preaches a sermon, they are said to be preaching "the Word of God." For this reason, sermons are especially important in **Protestantism**.

MEDIEVAL LECTERN

LORD'S PRAYER
When Jesus instructed his followers how to pray, he gave them this prayer, also called the "Pater Noster," or "Our Father," after its opening words. It is the most popular of all prayers used in Christian worship. In combining praising God, seeking his kingdom, and asking for God's help with human needs, whether spiritual and physical, the Lord's Prayer sets a pattern for other Christian prayers.

HAIL MARY
This prayer to the Virgin **Mary** is popular in the **Roman Catholic** church. It has been used in worship since the 11th century. Part of the prayer is a quotation from the **Bible**, based on the words of the angel **Gabriel** to Mary. It is often sung in Latin in Roman Catholic ceremonies.

SACRAMENTS

The most solemn Christian ceremonies are called sacraments. The sacraments are rituals which, if performed by the faithful in the correct way, channel the grace of God toward a specific person or group. The Roman Catholic Church recognizes seven sacraments, covering major points in a person's spiritual life. The Protestant churches recognize only two: Baptism and the Eucharist.

BAPTISM

People are formally admitted into the church through the rite of baptism. The ceremony usually involves water, recalling the ancient practice of baptizing in rivers. In most churches, infants are baptized at the font, where the priest pours holy water over the child's head. In some **Protestant** churches, adults are baptized by immersion.

BAPTISMAL FONT

CONFESSION AND PENANCE

Roman Catholics are required to confess their **sins** to a priest at least once a year, and show remorse for their bad actions. The **priest** may tell the person that they should perform a penance, or punishment, for their sins, and that God will forgive them only after this.

EUCHARIST

The consecration of bread and wine by the **priest** and its consumption by the **congregation** is at the heart of Christian worship. The ceremony is known by several names, including the Eucharist, Mass (Roman Catholic), Holy Communion, and Lord's Supper (Protestant), and is understood in different ways by the Catholic and Protestant Churches. The bread and wine symbolize **Jesus'** body and blood, and recall the **Last Supper** with his **disciples**.

MARRIAGE

Christian marriage takes place when a couple exchange vows in a **church**, in the presence of a **priest**, and symbolically, in the presence of God.

BREAD AND WINE

CONFIRMATION

Initiation into the church begins with confirmation. In the **Orthodox** Church, this happens immediately after baptism. **Roman Catholics** are normally confirmed at around age seven, while the early **Protestant** rite takes place during adolescence. In Western churches, the ceremony is carried out by a **bishop**, who anoints the child, or performs the laying-on of hands.

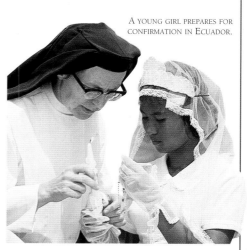

A YOUNG GIRL PREPARES FOR CONFIRMATION IN ECUADOR.

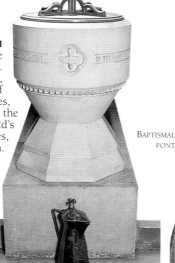

FIFTEENTH-CENTURY PAINTING OF A PRIEST ADMINISTERING EXTREME UNCTION

EXTREME UNCTION

The practice of anointing the sick is known as unction. The ritual was traditionally carried out when a person was dying, when it was known widely as extreme unction. Today, in the **Roman Catholic** Church, the rite of anointing the sick is linked more closely with healing. **Priests** also administer the last rites to the dying, offering them the opportunity for a final **confession** before death.

ORDINATION

A new **priest** is confirmed in office in an ordination ceremony. This is usually carried out by a **bishop**, who may lay his hands on the candidate and present him with symbols of his new office, such as a **Bible**.

ORTHODOX ICONOGRAPHY

In **Orthodox** churches, there is a nave where the congregation stands and a sanctuary that contains the **altar**. A screen, or iconostasis, separates these two areas and is opened during services. Images of Christ and the saints are displayed on the screen. The screen is intended as an aid to devotion by invoking the presence of God and the mysteries of the faith.

A 14TH-CENTURY GREEK ICON OF MARY AND CHILD

MYSTERIES

The **sacraments** are called the Mysteries in the **Orthodox Church**. The Mysteries include rites that correspond to the seven Western **sacraments**, as well as blessing, funeral and memorial ceremonies, and admission to one of the **monastic orders**.

LITURGY

Any formal religious service is called a liturgy. It can include words (**prayers**), music (**hymns**), actions, and symbolic visual aids (icons). Liturgies take a wide variety of forms, depending on the needs of different religious communities.

CHRISTIANITY TODAY

INTERNATIONAL MONUMENT TO THE REFORMATION, GENEVA

TODAY THERE ARE CHRISTIANS IN ALL PARTS OF THE WORLD. Christianity accompanied the early European settlers to South and North America in the 16th and 17th centuries. Missionaries followed European colonizers to Asia and Africa in the 18th and 19th centuries. Many local Christian churches developed in these new countries, and some have become very important in the everyday lives of their communities. In the developing world, the church has been at the forefront of education and poverty relief. Spread worldwide and engaged in so many activities, today's churches have great variety.

ROMAN CATHOLIC CHURCH TODAY
The oldest Christian church is still the largest, with more than one billion believers worldwide. The church is strongest in South and Central America, where festivals can still draw hundreds of thousands of worshipers.

ECUMENISM
Founded in 1910 following the Edinburgh Missionary Conference, the ecumenical movement seeks cooperation between the various Christian churches in the hope that they will eventually be united. The Ecumenical Council meets regularly and claims to have the authority of the whole Christian church. Discussions of doctrinal and social issues has led to some cooperation and the reduction of tension between the **Roman Catholic** and **Orthodox** Churches.

ORTHODOX CHURCH TODAY
With 250 million adherents, the Orthodox Church remains the chief religion in Russia, Eastern, and Southeastern Europe, despite persecution by various communist regimes over the last 70 years.

A LUTHERAN MINISTER CHRISTENS A BABY.

WORLD COUNCIL OF CHURCHES
Established in 1948 as part of the ecumenical movement, the World Council of Churches also works for church unity. Most Christian churches, except for the **Roman Catholic** Church, are members. The Council's headquarters is in Geneva, Switzerland.

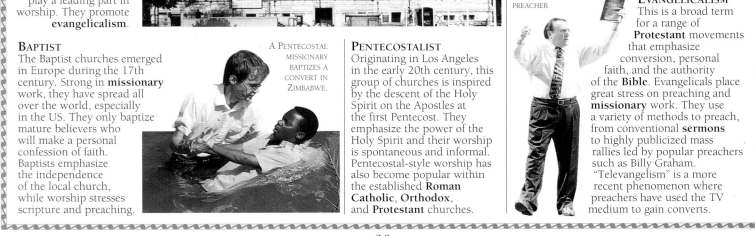

THE METHODIST CENTRAL HALL, LONDON

METHODIST
Founded in Britain by John Wesley, Methodism was a part of the **Anglican Church**, but separated in 1795. Wesley stressed living "according to the method laid down in the **Bible**." Methodists seek a close, personal relationship with God. Lay preachers often play a leading part in worship. They promote **evangelicalism**.

BAPTIST
The Baptist churches emerged in Europe during the 17th century. Strong in **missionary** work, they have spread all over the world, especially in the US. They only baptize mature believers who will make a personal confession of faith. Baptists emphasize the independence of the local church, while worship stresses scripture and preaching.

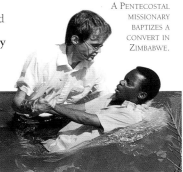

A PENTECOSTAL MISSIONARY BAPTIZES A CONVERT IN ZIMBABWE.

PENTECOSTALIST
Originating in Los Angeles in the early 20th century, this group of churches is inspired by the descent of the Holy Spirit on the Apostles at the first Pentecost. They emphasize the power of the Holy Spirit and their worship is spontaneous and informal. Pentecostal-style worship has also become popular within the established **Roman Catholic**, **Orthodox**, and **Protestant** churches.

LUTHERAN
The Lutheran churches were inspired by the teachings of the 16th-century German theologian, **Martin Luther**. These Protestant churches stress the importance of scripture, personal faith, and the "priesthood of all believers." Lutheranism began in Germany and northern Europe, but has spread throughout the world, especially in North America.

PRESBYTERIAN
This church originated as a result of the **Reformation** in Scotland. It is distinguished by its government, which is by councils containing both ordained ministers and lay people, or "Elders." There are numerous Presbyterian churches around the world, many of which belong to a unifying body, the World Alliance of Reformed Churches.

MAORI ANGLICAN MINISTER, NEW ZEALAND

ANGLICAN CHURCH
The Anglican Church, or Church of England (the Episcopal Church in the US), was formed during the 16th century, when King Henry VIII split from **Roman Catholicism**. Worship and practice now contain both Catholic and **Protestant** elements. As a result of colonization and **missionary** activity, this church has spread throughout the world.

EVANGELICAL PREACHER

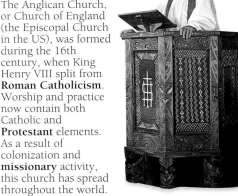

EVANGELICALISM
This is a broad term for a range of **Protestant** movements that emphasize conversion, personal faith, and the authority of the **Bible**. Evangelicals place great stress on preaching and **missionary** work. They use a variety of methods to preach, from conventional **sermons** to highly publicized mass rallies led by popular preachers such as Billy Graham. "Televangelism" is a more recent phenomenon where preachers have used the TV medium to gain converts.

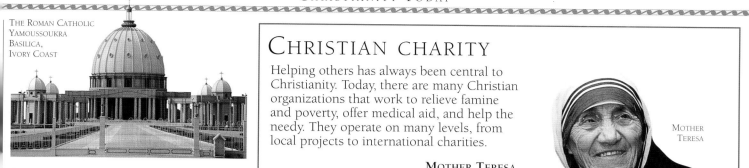

THE ROMAN CATHOLIC
YAMOUSSOUKRA
BASILICA,
IVORY COAST

AFRICAN CHURCHES

European **missionaries** brought many Christian churches to Africa during the 19th century, and many **Protestant** and **Roman Catholic** communities became established in every part of the continent. However, these churches have since developed in a variety of ways. Some mix traditional African beliefs with Christianity, while others reject this approach, returning to a closer study of the **Bible**.

COPTIC WALL HANGING

COPTIC CHURCH

The Christian church of Egypt, the Coptic Church, has a long history, dating back to when it broke away from the **Orthodox Church** in 451. Although Egypt is now a Muslim country, there are still several million Coptic Christians living there. The Coptic Church maintains its ancient **liturgy** in the Coptic Egyptian language, and has developed impressive religious art.

ETHIOPIAN ORTHODOX CHURCH

Christianity came to Ethiopia in the fourth century. Since then, the spread of **Islam** isolated Ethiopia from the Christian world, causing the church to develop separately. Consequently, it includes some unusual features, such as the keeping of the Sabbath and circumcision – both Jewish customs.

ETHIOPIAN
ORTHODOX PRIEST

CHRISTIAN CHARITY

Helping others has always been central to Christianity. Today, there are many Christian organizations that work to relieve famine and poverty, offer medical aid, and help the needy. They operate on many levels, from local projects to international charities.

MOTHER TERESA

The Albanian nun Mother Teresa set up a **Roman Catholic** religious order, the Missionaries of Charity, to help the poor, homeless, and dying. Her work began among the poor of Calcutta, but today the Missionaries of Charity work all over the world. Mother Teresa was awarded the Nobel Peace Prize for her work.

MOTHER
TERESA

AID WORKERS
BUILD A WELL
IN AFRICA.

RED CROSS

This organization was found in 1863 by the Swiss humanitarian Jean Henri Dunant. Its original aim was to give medical aid to war victims. Today, it also helps victims of disasters, aids refugees, and provides services such as first-aid training. Since 1986, it has been united with its equivalent Muslim organization, the Red Crescent.

CHRISTIAN AID

Formed in response to the hardships of World War II, this charity group works for development and poverty relief in more than 70 countries.

OXFAM

Founded in Oxford in 1942, Oxfam worked to reduce famine during World War II. It now works to end poverty all over the world.

SOCIAL RESPONSIBILITY

Being a responsible member of society is a key Christian belief. In the 20th century, this has often led to radical action: for example, Martin Luther King, Jr., campaigned for black people's rights in the US, and Bishop Tutu's struggle against apartheid in South Africa.

PACIFISM

Jesus taught that Christians should reject violence in order to live a Christian life. In response to Christ's teachings about loving one's neighbors, treating others as you wish to be treated, and nonviolence, many Christians are pacifists.

PILGRIMAGES

For centuries, Christians have gone on pilgrimages, making journeys to sacred places. The sites of the birth of **Jesus**, his ministry, and his **crucifixion** – Bethlehem, **Galilee**, and **Jerusalem** – have always been important places of pilgrimage. Other popular routes include the sites of miraculous healings – such as Lourdes in France – and shrines where the relics of saints are preserved, such as Santiago de Compostela in Spain, and the Virgin of Guadaloupe in Mexico.

PILGRIMS PAY HOMAGE TO THE
VIRGIN MARY IN EL ROCEO, SPAIN.

CHURCH OF SOUTH INDIA

Formed in the 1940s when the **Anglican**, **Methodist**, and Reformed churches combined, this church emphasizes **missionary** activity and social work.

ISLAM

The followers of Islam are called Muslims. The word Islam means "submission," and the faith involves unconditional submission to the will of God, who is known to Muslims as Allah, an Arabic word meaning "the God." Muslims believe that their faith was revealed to the prophet Muhammad by God, whose words were later collected into the Islamic holy book, the Qur'an.

THE HILAL, OR CRESCENT
MOON, THE SYMBOL OF ISLAM

ISLAMIC BELIEFS

Muslim belief is expressed in a formula called the shahada, or Profession of Faith: "There is no god but God, and Muhammad is the Prophet of God." Muslims believe in a final judgment followed by an afterlife in heaven or hell. They take their spiritual guidance from the words of the Qur'an and from the Hadith, the words and deeds of Muhammad and his companions.

THE ISLAMIC WORLD

Soon after the faith was revealed to Muhammad, Islam spread rapidly through the Middle East and to northern Africa. The Middle East is still at the heart of the Islamic world, and in this region, Islam is the dominant religion in every country except Israel. All Muslims face toward Mecca whenever they pray, and hope to make the pilgrimage to the city at least once in their lives. There are also many Muslims in northern Africa and parts of eastern Asia, such as Indonesia. Islam is the fastest-growing of all the world religions, because of both missionary activity and population growth in Muslim countries. Today, there are more than 1 billion Muslims in the world.

HISTORY OF ISLAM

MUSLIMS BELIEVE THAT ISLAM HAS ALWAYS EXISTED as a way of life that God intended for humankind. He sent a series of prophets, such as Musa (Moses), to call the people to the true faith, culminating with Muhammad as the messenger of God. The Islamic faith was revealed to Muhammad during the seventh century CE. In the time of Muhammad and his immediate followers, Islam spread rapidly through western Asia and northern Africa. Later, the travels of Arab merchants, the learning of Muslim scientists, and the conquests of Muslim soldiers carried the faith all over the world.

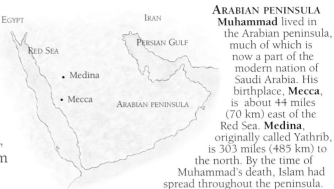

ARABIAN PENINSULA
Muhammad lived in the Arabian peninsula, much of which is now a part of the modern nation of Saudi Arabia. His birthplace, **Mecca**, is about 44 miles (70 km) east of the Red Sea. **Medina**, originally called Yathrib, is 303 miles (485 km) to the north. By the time of Muhammad's death, Islam had spread throughout the peninsula.

MUHAMMAD
The prophet Muhammad (570–632) was born in the city of **Mecca**, in modern Saudi Arabia. He was born an orphan and brought up by his grandfather and uncle. Later, he worked as a trader and was employed by a widow named Khadija to lead caravans throughout the **Arabian peninsula**. On his travels, Muhammad met many people who believed in one God, in contrast to the people of Arabia, who were polytheistic. When he was 25 years old, Muhammad married Khadija, and they had four children.

MECCA
When **Muhammad** was born, **Mecca** was a thriving trading city and an important religious center. The **Ka'ba**, a sanctuary in the city, contained statues of tribal gods and goddesses, which were worshipped by the Arabs.

NIGHT JOURNEY
Muhammad was instructed by the angel Jibril (**Gabriel**) that he was to be the messenger of God. According to tradition, Jibril took him from **Mecca** to **Jerusalem**, where he made his ascent to heaven, or Mi'raj, from a rock on a temple, later the site of the Dome of the Rock. God gave Muhammad instructions about daily prayer and practice.

REVELATION ON MOUNT HIRA

MUHAMMAD'S ASCENSION TO HEAVEN

REVELATION
By the time he was 40 years old, **Muhammad** was troubled by the variety of gods worshiped in Arabia. He often went to Mount Hira, outside **Mecca**, to meditate on the nature of God. Here, he received a revelation from God brought by the angel Jibril, or **Gabriel**. Muhammad's revelations were later collected in the **Qur'an**.

HIJRA
In **Mecca**, **Muhammad** preached a belief in one god – **Allah** – which brought him into conflict with local religious leaders. In 622, Muhammad left Mecca. His migration to **Medina** is known as the Hijra, and marks the beginning of the Islamic calendar.

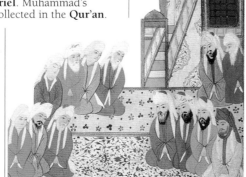

FAREWELL PILGRIMAGE

MEDINA
In **Medina**, **Muhammad** converted most of the population to Islam and became the leader of an organized Muslim community. There was still opposition from **Mecca**, which led to bloody battles between the two cities. Muhammad captured Mecca in 630, seized the **Ka'ba**, and removed the statues of the old gods.

FAREWELL PILGRIMAGE
By 632, **Muhammad's** influence had spread all over the **Arabian peninsula**. He made the annual pilgrimage to the **Ka'ba** at **Mecca**, which was restricted to Muslims only. On the tenth day of the pilgrimage he preached his last sermon, in which he urged Muslims to treat each other as brothers and sisters and maintain the unity of Islam. Muhammad died in the arms of his favorite wife, A'isha. A mosque in **Medina** was rebuilt to incorporate his tomb.

UMMA
The community of Islam is called the "umma." Originally, Arabs had priority within the umma, because **Muhammad** was seen as a prophet to the Arab nation. However, with the spread of Islam, umma has come to refer to all Muslims, regardless of ethnicity, nationality, and ideology. The umma provides religious solidarity in the face of challenges to traditional Islam from secularism.

AFTER MUHAMMAD

After the death of Muhammad, Islam spread rapidly throughout northern Africa and into Spain, especially under the Umayyad dynasty of caliphs. However, under the Abbasids, areas such as Spain were partially lost as the empire shrank.

CALIPHATE
Caliphs led the Islamic world after the death of **Muhammad**. The first was Abu Bakr, the father of the Prophet's wife, A'isha. Abu Bakr was called Al Sadiq, "the truthful." He was followed by 'Umar, 'Uthman, and 'Ali, who was the Prophet's cousin and son-in-law.

UMAYYADS
The first dynasty of hereditary caliphs was the Umayyads (661–750), who ruled from Damascus. Kinsmen of 'Uthman, they were opponents of 'Ali. Their conquests established Islam in much of Central Asia, northern Africa, and Spain. Incursions into France were halted at the battle of Tours in 732.

ABBASIDS
Based in Baghdad, the Abbasid dynasty (750–1258) ruled a huge Muslim empire in a period of brilliant cultural development.

MONGOL WARRIOR

MONGOLS
Formed from a group of tribes in Mongolia, the powerful Mongol army swept through much of Asia to form a vast empire by 1211. The Mongols destroyed the Abbasid dynasty by sacking Baghdad in 1258.

MUGHALS
The Mughal dynasty ruled India from 1526 to 1857. At their height, during the reign of Akbar the Great in the 16th century, the Mughal emperors presided over a period of great learning and artistic creation.

SAFAVIDS
Ruling Persia from 1501 to 1732, the Safavids were descended from a leader of a **Sufi** order called the Safavi. They established a powerful **Shi'a** dynasty that rivalled the vibrancy of the **Mughal** and **Ottoman** empires.

OTTOMANS
The Ottoman empire (1342–1924) became established on the Anatolian peninsula (modern-day Turkey). At the height of their power, the Ottoman sultans controlled an area that included most of southeastern Europe, North Africa, and the Middle East.

SULEIMAN THE MAGNIFICENT, OTTOMAN RULER (1520–1566)

SUNNIS
Approximately 90 percent of all Muslims are Sunnis. Their name comes from the word "sunna," or "path," meaning the way of **Muhammad**, as demonstrated by his sayings and deeds. Unlike some **Shi'is**, Sunnis recognize the early caliphs as the rightful successors of Muhammad. Sunni orthodoxy emphasises the views and customs of the majority of the **umma**, as distinguished from the views of minority groups.

SUNNI TRADITIONS
Many groups have broken away from the Sunni mainstream. As far back as the seventh century, the Kharijis differed over theological issues and definitions of faith. Some small groups survive today, such as the Ibadi people of Oman and East Africa. The Yezidis venerate Melek Taus, the fallen angel who they believe was pardoned by God.

SHI'I
Shi'ism is one of the major branches of Islam. The name derives from the Arabic words, "Shi'at Ali" ("party of Ali") – Shi'as believe that Ali and his descendants are the true leaders of the Islamic community. They place more emphasis on suffering, and Ali's son, Husayn, is revered for his martyrdom at **Kerbela** (680 CE). Shi'ism has developed its own system of law. A more radical Shi'i consciousness was awakened by the **Iranian Revolution**.

SHI'I TRADITIONS
Shi'as are the majority in Iran and southern Iraq. There are several groups within Shi'i Islam, some of which developed from a group called the Isma'ilis. The latter include the Druzes in Lebanon, and the Nizaris, a widespread group led by the Aga Khan.

SUFISM
The mystical branch of Islam is called Sufism. Sufis emphasize a personal relationship with God as a complement to following God's law. They try to become closer to God by using rituals involving music, chanting, dancing, and breathing exercises to reach a mystical state. Sufism emphasizes the virtues of humility and caring for others.

SUFI ORDERS
Sufism is organized into many separate orders, each under a spiritual leader, or shaykh. The orders have both lay followers and full members, who may be known as faqirs or dervishes. A brotherhood of Turkish Sufis became known as "whirling dervishes" because of their energetic dancing style.

WHIRLING DERVISH, PERFORMING FOR THE BENEFIT OF VISITORS AT THE MEVLEVI MONASTERY, ISTANBUL

SHI'I STANDARD, BEARING THE NAMES OF GOD, MUHAMMAD, AND ALI

TEACHINGS AND SCRIPTURE

THE BASIS OF THE ISLAMIC FAITH is the Qur'an, the holy scripture that for Muslims represents the words of God. The Qur'an tells of God and his greatness, the need to obey God and his wrath toward those who do not obey him, and the role of Muhammad as God's messenger. The Qur'an also contains a wealth of teaching about the family and community. This material is complemented by the sunna, or "custom," which is the sum of Muhammad's deeds and sayings, contained in the Hadith. Together, the Qur'an and sunna constitute the main sources of Islamic law.

ALLAH'S NAMES
The Muslim name for God is Allah ("the God"). Allah is the one, unique God. Allah's oneness is his most important quality – he was not created, nor is there any other being like him. The creator of the cosmos, he is all-powerful, but he is also merciful and compassionate. Muslims believe Allah will reward those who believe in him with a place in paradise, but will punish those who do not. He has 99 names, known as the Most Beautiful Names, which are recited during worship.

Each bead represents one of the 99 names of Allah.

JINNS
Taking a variety of forms, jinns (genies) are fire spirits who inhabit desert regions. According to official doctrine, jinns are a distinct creation from men and angels. Jinns that are unbelievers are demons and are therefore harmful.

PRAYER BEADS (MISBAH)

MALAK (ANGEL)

MALA'IKA
Known in Arabic as mala'ika, angels are the winged messengers of **Allah**, who created angels before creating human beings. The angels are God's servants and always obey him. Only one angel, Iblis (Satan), refused to obey Allah; Allah told him to bow down before the newly created **Adam**, but Iblis refused.

PROPHETS
Muslims recognize two types of prophets. The *nabi* is a prophet, while a *rasul* brings a new religious message. Muslims consider Ibrahim (Abraham), Musa (Moses), 'Isa (Jesus), and Muhammad to be *rasul* prophets. They believe that Ibrahim, Musa, and 'Isa were misinterpreted by their followers, but the final prophet, Muhammad, was the seal of the prophets.

SACRED TILE DEPICTING THE PLACE OF IBRAHIM, FROM THE SACRED MOSQUE IN MECCA

IBRAHIM
Muslims believe Ibrahim (**Abraham**) to be the first Muslim. Allah instructed him to go to the valley of **Mecca**, where he rebuilt the **Ka'ba** after its destruction in the flood. The black stone at the eastern corner of the Ka'ba became a symbol of the divine covenant. Ibrahim also began the practice of the pilgrimage to Mecca, although this tradition was abandoned until revived by **Muhammad**.

The black stone of the Ka'ba

The pavement of the Ka'ba, where pilgrims perform the tawaf, *or circuits*

'ISA
Known as 'Isa ibn Maryam ("**Jesus**, son of Mary"), 'Isa was conceived by the power of **Allah**. 'Isa was one of a number of prophets who brought the message of God's uniqueness and foretold the arrival of another messenger, **Muhammad**. Unlike Christians, Muslims do not believe 'Isa was the son of God. The **Qur'an** states that Allah "raised him to himself," as one of his prophets.

THE PROPHET ISA IS CARRIED TO HEAVEN.

ARCHANGEL JIBRIL

ARCHANGELS
Angels of special importance are called archangels. Four archangels have special significance. Jibril, who is known as **Gabriel** to Christians, helped to bring the **Qur'an** to the world. Mika'il, with Jibril, was the first archangel to bow down before Adam; he was also said to have helped the Muslims achieve their first military victory. Israfil will blow the trumpet at the end of time, to announce the **Day of Judgement**, while Israil is the angel of death.

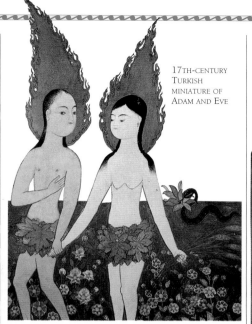

17TH-CENTURY TURKISH MINIATURE OF ADAM AND EVE

QUR'AN

Muslims believe that the Qur'an is the word of God. Sent directly from heaven, this holy scripture was revealed to **Muhammad** by the angel Jibril over a period of 20 years. Muslims recite the Qur'an in Arabic, the language in which it was revealed. Qur'an means "recitation" and Muslims often learn its Arabic text by heart.

SURAS AND AYAS

The **Qur'an** contains 114 chapters, or suras, each divided into smaller sections called ayas. The book begins with a short sura, al Fatiha, or The Opener, after which the suras are arranged in order of length, the longest first. The Qur'an covers many topics, first focusing on the oneness of God; later suras deal with social issues such as family, marriage, and law.

QUR'AN

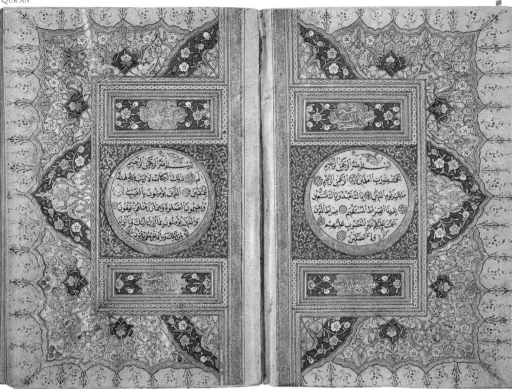

ADAM AND EVE

The first humans, created by **Allah**, were Adam and Eve. Like the biblical Adam and Eve, they were tempted by Iblis and disobeyed Allah. Later, Adam traveled the world, making the pilgrimage to Mecca, where he is said to have built the first **Ka'ba**.

RESURRECTION

As proof of the creative and sustaining power of **Allah**, the **Qur'an** teaches that at some point in the future al-Dajjal, the Antichrist, will appear, only to be destroyed by the returning **'Isa**. The bodies and souls of the dead will be reunited and two angels will call humans and jinns to a final **Judgment** before Allah.

DAY OF JUDGMENT

According to the **Qur'an**, immediately after the **resurrection**, there will be a Day of Judgment. On that day, the dead will rise and the world will cease to be. The book that records each person's life will be opened, and their deeds will be judged by God according to their conduct and belief.

AFTERLIFE

Souls that receive a favorable final judgment go to al-jannah, or paradise. This is described as a beautiful garden, where the blessed exist close to **Allah**. Those who are condemned go to hell, which is believed to be a place of torment.

TAFSIR AND TAWIL

Commentary that provides background information and explanations of the **Qur'an** is known as *tafsir*. Another kind of commentary – *tawil* – provides esoteric analysis of the essence of the Qur'an.

SHARI'A

THE SULTAN HASSAN MOSQUE IN CAIRO HOUSES THE FOUR SUNNI SCHOOLS.

Muslim law is the shari'a, the path that a Muslim must follow in life. The Qur'an and the Hadith provide the basis of the shari'a. If a particular issue is not covered here, the principle of analogy may be used, or guidance may be taken from the Muslim community.

HALAL FOOD

SUNNI SCHOOLS OF LAW

Four schools of law were founded to interpret and apply the shari'a. These are the Shafti, Hanbali, Hanafi, and Maliki. **Shi'i** Muslims have a separate legal school.

DIETARY RULES

Shari'a provides instructions about food and prescribes the kinds of animals that can be eaten. Animals must be ritually slaughtered for the meat to be considered halal, or permitted.

HADITH

The Hadiths, or "sayings," are a traditional collection of teachings thought to derive from **Muhammad** or from one of his companions. They are second in authority to the **Qur'an**, and provide guidance on many aspects of life.

RITUALS AND FESTIVALS

RITUALS FORM THE BACKBONE OF ISLAMIC PRACTICE. The most important are the Five Pillars of Islam – actions that all Muslims should perform. They range from daily prayers and observing the annual fast to making a once-in-a-lifetime pilgrimage to the holy city of Mecca. Rites of passage, rituals that mark the different stages in the life of the individual and family, are also important. The family is the core of the Islamic community, and religious ceremonies often include the whole extended family. Rituals include birth ceremonies, naming ceremonies, and rituals to mark the beginning of the child's religious education. In addition to these ceremonies, there are many Islamic festivals that are observed annually throughout the Muslim world. Festivals are often sober affairs and a time for people to strengthen community ties and reassert their faith.

JIHAD
This means "striving for God's cause." In one sense, jihad is a striving against temptation and wrong-doing within oneself. Jihad may also involve defending the community of Islam against attack. A Muslim may do this with words or with arms, but should only fight defensively.

FIVE PILLARS OF ISLAM

All Muslims are required to perform prescribed actions known as the Five Pillars of Islam as part of their obligation to God. Each Pillar is considered a part of the supporting structure of Islam, which provides a firm foundation for the religion. The most important is the first Pillar, the profession of faith.

ZAKAT – MONEY FOR THE POOR

PULPIT TILE WITH TEXT INCLUDING THE SHAHADA

SHAHADA
The first Pillar of Islam is the shahada, the profession of faith. Its words proclaim the uniqueness of God and the importance of the Prophet: "There is no god but God (Allah) and Muhammad is the messenger of God." Shahada is the testimony of the faith of Islam and provides the basis of conversion – by sincerely reciting these words, a person proves his or her acceptance of the faith.

SALAT
Salat (ritual prayer) is the second Pillar of Islam. A Muslim should pray five times every day, facing toward **Mecca**. A congregational prayer, Jum'a, takes place in the mosque every Friday at noon. The times for salat are called by the muezzin from the **mosque**.

ZAKAT
Muslims are obliged to help the needy by giving alms. This is known as zakat, or purification, and is the third Pillar of Islam. Zakat embodies the notion that God can be worshiped indirectly, by showing gratitude for God's favor.

SAWM
Fasting, or sawm, is the fourth Pillar of Islam. Sawm is performed during Ramadan, the ninth month of the lunar year. Muslims will not eat or drink from dawn until dusk, first breaking the fast at sunset, often with dates and water before eating an evening meal at home.

HAJJ
Muslims who are able enough must make the hajj, or pilgrimage, to **Mecca** at least once in their lifetime. This is the fifth Pillar of Islam. It is performed in the 12th month of the year, known as **Dhu al-Hijja**. Pilgrims wear white unsewn clothes (ihrams), which they later use as a burial shroud.

PILGRIMS WEARING IHRAMS

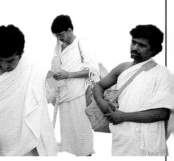

FESTIVALS

Muslim festivals are held in response to commands in the Qur'an or to celebrate events in the life of the Prophet. Two major festivals stand out – 'Id al-Adha, at the end of the pilgrimage to Mecca, and 'Id al-Fitr, at the end of the fasting month of Ramadan. Both of these are celebrated with large gatherings at the mosque or out of doors.

A Jordanian card celebrating the end of Ramadan

CARD AND SWEETS CELEBRATING 'ID AL-FITR

DAY OF HIJRA
The Islamic year begins on the Day of Hijra, the day on which **Muhammad** started his journey from **Mecca** to **Medina** in 622. On this day, **Shi'a** Muslims also remember the martyrdom of Husayn, the Prophet's grandson.

DHU AL-HIJJA
The last month of the Islamic calendar is Dhu al-Hijja, during which people go on **Hajj**, or pilgrimage, to **Mecca**. Pilgrims prepare themselves by cutting their hair and wearing ihrams. On arrival, they walk seven times around the **Ka'ba**, starting in the southeast corner.

'ID AL-FITR
This festival of 'Id al-Fitr marks the breaking of the fast at the end of Ramadan. At this joyful time, people give thanks for being strong enough to complete the fast. Streets and buildings are illuminated, sweet foods are sold in markets and bazaars, cards are exchanged, and people give gifts and money to children and the poor.

'ID MAWLID
The birthday of the Prophet, on the 12th day of the third month, is celebrated with feasting and the distribution of food to the poor. In cities there may be processions, and homes are decorated.

LAYLAT AL-BAR'H
The 15th day of the eighth month is Laylat al-Bar'h, or the Night of Forgiveness. God determines each person's fate for the coming year. People forgive each others' sins and spend the night in prayer.

MUHARRAM
In the first month of the Islamic calendar, **Shi'i** Muslims celebrate the 10-day festival of Muharram. Often, a religious play is performed and processions commemorate the death of Muhammad's grandson, Husayn, at the battle of **Kerbela** in 680. Some Shi'a parade through the streets, smearing themselves in animal blood to symbolize their sadness and grief at Husayn's suffering.

'ID AL-ADHA
The four-day Festival of Sacrifice, 'Id al-Adha, forms the climax of the pilgrimage to **Mecca**. Pilgrims make an animal sacrifice at a village called Mina, between Arafat and Mecca, remembering that Ibrahim was willing to sacrifice his son to God. After a sermon and prayers, an animal – such as a sheep or goat – is sacrificed. Some of the meat is given to the poor. The festival is also celebrated by those not on pilgrimage.

ANIMALS ARE SACRIFICED ON 'ID AL-ADHA.

LAYLAT AL-QADR
The Night of Power, toward the end of the month of Ramadan, celebrates the night when the **Qur'an** was first revealed to **Muhammad**. In imitation of Muhammad, many Muslims spend the night in prayer at the **mosque**.

YOUNG SHI'I MUSLIM SMEARED IN ANIMAL BLOOD

FATHER SHAVES A BABY'S HEAD.

BIRTH
Newborn children are welcomed into the community as a gift from **Allah**. Shortly after the birth, the baby's father whispers into its right ear the words of the adhan, or call to prayer, then places a little honey on the child's tongue. The head is often shaved as a symbol of purity.

MALAYSIAN WEDDING

MUSLIM BURIAL IN PAKISTAN

CIRCUMCISION
Muslim boys are circumcised. Although not mentioned in the **Qur'an**, this rite is said to have been carried from biblical times, to mark the covenant between God and humans. Circumcision can be performed on a child of any age between eight days and ten years.

MARRIAGE
According to local custom, Muslim marriages are often arranged, with parents finding suitable partners for their children. The **Qur'an** permits a man to have up to four wives, but in practice most Muslim marriages are monogamous. The wedding ceremony may take place at the house of either bride or groom, or at a **mosque**. An **imam** usually presides, and the ceremony includes readings from the Qur'an. There is a written contract, and the groom is expected to pay a dowry for his bride.

DEATH
When a Muslim dies, the corpse is wrapped in the ihram and carried to the **mosque** for funeral prayers. The body – which should be buried quickly out of respect for the deceased – is placed in a simple grave marked by a mound of earth.

WORSHIP

PRAYER IS THE MAIN FORM OF WORSHIP IN ISLAM. Muslims pray five times each day, at set times, which are called muezzin. At noon on Fridays, Muslims go to the mosque for a communal service that includes a sermon and special prayers led by a leader called an imam. The Qur'an instructs Muslims to "perform" their prayers, so physical posture is as important as the words. Ritual prayers involve a series of postures, from standing through bowing to prostration, in which the toes, knees, hands, and forehead must all touch the ground.

MOSQUE

The most important buildings in Islam are mosques. They are centers for the community and for education, as well as places of worship. Although designs vary throughout the world, most mosques have two main parts – an interior for prayer, and an outside space, usually a courtyard. The interiors of many mosques are plain and unadorned, since decorations are thought to distract the worshipers from prayers. However, some mosques are decorated with tiles and beautifully written quotations from the **Qur'an**.

PRAYER HALL

The prayer hall is the main area inside a mosque. This provides a clear space for the congregation and must face toward **Mecca**. There are no seats, because worship involves standing, kneeling, and prostrating. In larger mosques, there may be a balcony for the women; otherwise, women pray separately behind the men.

16TH-CENTURY SELIMIYE MOSQUE, ISTANBUL

Minaret

Prayer hall

Minbar

Mihrab

MINARET

Muhammad had a dream in which he heard a call to prayer. He therefore commanded one of his followers to call the faithful to prayer at set times every day. The caller became known as a muezzin. **Mosques** were built with special towers, called minarets, where the muezzin could stand and call the faithful. The opening words of the call to prayer – *Allahu akbar* ("God is great") – are called the adhan.

PERFORMING ABLUTIONS

ABLUTION AREA

Before praying, Muslims ritually clean themselves by washing their face, mouth, nostrils, hands, lower arms, and feet. A special washing area is provided at every **mosque** for Muslims to perform ablutions.

IMAM

The leaders of the religious community are called imams. Although not officially appointed, they are venerated for their knowledge of the **Qur'an** and usually lead prayers and officiate at weddings.

MIHRAB IN THE GREAT MOSQUE AT CÓRDOBA, SPAIN

MIHRAB

Inside the **prayer hall**, a niche called a mihrab indicates the direction of **Mecca**. This acts as a focal point during prayers, showing the faithful which way to face. While he is leading prayers, the **imam** stands to one side of the mihrab. A mihrab may be a simple, plain alcove, but in some mosques, the niche is beautifully decorated with intricate tiles. The prayer hall is designed so that as many people as possible can see the mihrab.

QIBLA

The direction that Muslims face when they pray is called the qibla. During the first two years of the Muslim community's existence, **Jerusalem** was the qibla. However, since 624, it has been **Mecca**.

ABU ZAID PREACHING FROM A MINBAR

MINBAR

The **imam** gives his Friday sermon from a stepped platform called a minbar. In a large mosque, the minbar may have many steps, but the imam never preaches from the top step – this is symbolically reserved for the Prophet.

PRAYER MAT
It is prescribed that Muslims should pray in a clean place, so worshipers are required to remove their shoes before entering a **mosque**. For reasons of hygiene, Muslims use prayer mats both in the mosque and when praying at home. A prayer mat may be decorated with abstract designs or with a picture of a mosque. Some mats even have a compass attached, so that the user can easily find the right direction to face during prayer.

Compass for indicating the direction of Mecca

PRAYER MAT

JERUSALEM
Muslims visit Jerusalem because of its associations with **Muhammad**. Jerusalem is the place where the Prophet arrived at the end of his **Night Journey**, and from which he ascended to heaven. The Dome of the Rock was built on the site of his departure. It was completed in 691 and is considered the third most sacred site in Islam, after **Mecca** and **Medina**.

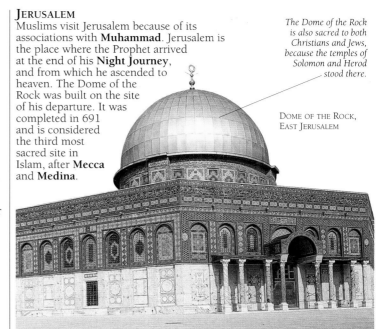

The Dome of the Rock is also sacred to both Christians and Jews, because the temples of Solomon and Herod stood there.

DOME OF THE ROCK, EAST JERUSALEM

PILGRIMAGE TO MECCA

When Muslims make the pilgrimage to the holy city of Mecca in fulfillment of the fifth Pillar of Islam, they leave luxury and worldly status behind. This means that they feel a sense of spiritual togetherness, strengthened faith, and equality before God.

KA'BA
Before entering the sacred area surrounding **Mecca**, pilgrims put on white robes called ihrams. As they enter this area, they cry "Labbayka," which means, "I am at your service." They then go directly to the Sacred Mosque and walk seven times around the Ka'ba. For many, this is the most moving part of the pilgrimage.

THE KA'BA AT MECCA

The gray stone rock of the Ka'ba is covered with a curtain on which the words of the shahada are written.

MECCA
More than one million pilgrims visit Mecca every year. They may perform the pilgrimage in one of two ways – as the 'Umra ("visit") to the Sacred Mosque, or as the **Hajj**, beginning in Mecca, but continuing also to Arafat. The 'Umra may be done at any time of the year, but the Hajj must be performed during the month of **Dhu al-Hijja**.

PILGRIMS CAMP NEAR MINA.

ARAFAT
On the ninth day of **Dhu al-Hijja**, pilgrims go to Mount Arafat, near Mecca. They pray quietly together and ask for forgiveness for their sins.

MINA
On the tenth day of **Dhu al-Hijja**, pilgrims visit the village of Mina. Here, they throw stones at three pillars symbolizing evil, to commemorate the unsuccessful temptations of **Ibrahim** and Ismail by the devil.

KERBELA
Shi'a Muslims have special places of veneration. The most important is Kerbela, in Iraq, where Husayn was martyred. The tomb of the eighth imam, 'Ali al-Rida, at Mashad in Iran, and that of his sister, Hazrat-i-Fatima, at Qom, Iran, are also important Shi'a sites.

MEDINA
Medina is an important center for pilgrimage. Quba', an oasis just outside Medina, was the site of the first mosque, built by **Muhammad**. Pilgrims today also visit the Mosque of the Prophet in the city.

TOMB IN HAZB, ALGERIA

SHRINES AND TOMBS
Notable holy people are known to Muslims as "friends of God" or "blessed ones," and are revered by Muslims. Although some conservative groups do not approve of this practice, pilgrimages to their tombs and places associated with their lives are not uncommon.

RELICS OF THE PROPHET
Physical remains of **Muhammad**, such as fragments of his bones and beard, used to be revered. Pilgrimages to places where relics were housed were once popular. Some believe that the footprint of the Prophet is visible at the Dome of the Rock.

KNOWLEDGE AND ART

MUSLIMS BELIEVE THAT GOD CREATED ALL THINGS – therefore, discovering the world is seen as learning about God's creation. For this reason, Islam has always valued knowledge and scholarship. The Islamic world expanded steadily between 600 and 1200 as Muslim merchants traveled across North Africa, Asia, and southern Europe. Muslim Spain became a thriving center of scholarship and artistic creativity, leading to the spread of Eastern and Islamic scientific developments throughout medieval Europe.

13TH-CENTURY ISLAMIC LIBRARY

ASTRONOMERS OBSERVE THE SKY.

Scholars examine a globe in a 16th-century observatory in Istanbul.

SCHOOLS AND LIBRARIES
By the tenth century, madrasas – places of higher education often attached to mosques – were flourishing in the Islamic world. Some are still operating today. They teach Islamic theology, interpretation of the **Qur'an**, Islamic law, and many other subjects. One of the oldest and most famous is al-Azhar in Cairo, founded in 972. In the tenth and 11th centuries, Muslim Spain became a major center for scholarship. In the city of Córdoba, for example, there were 70 libraries and 700 mosques.

An astrolabe enables the user to establish his or her latitude – useful for finding the direction of Mecca

MOORISH ASTROLABE

MEDICINE
Muslim physicians developed the work of the doctors of ancient Persia. They discovered how blood circulates around the body, and devised treatments for diseases such as smallpox. The most famous early Muslim doctor was the Persian Ibn Sina (980–1037), whose work, *The Canon of Medicine*, was a popular textbook.

SCIENCE AND MATHEMATICS
Between the ninth and 14th centuries, Muslim scientists and mathematicians laid the foundation for modern science. They pioneered the complex subject of algebra, made important advances in geometry, and developed trigonometry. As Islam spread around the world, they learned from other cultures. They adopted the concept of zero from India, and translated many ancient Greek scientific books into Arabic.

ASTRONOMY
Continuing the work of ancient Mesopotamian scientists and the Alexandrian astronomer Ptolemy, Islamic astronomers invented navigational aids such as the astrolabe. They used these instruments to make accurate maps of the stars and astronomical tables that were used for centuries. They named stars, like Betelgeuse and Aldebaran; the names are still used today.

ISLAMIC ART

Muslims believe that Allah is the divine creator and that it is therefore inappropriate for human beings to imitate God's power. Consequently, Islam forbids the representation of living things. While not all Muslim artists have obeyed this rule, abstract representations of living forms, calligraphy, and pattern-making have become highly developed.

CARVED WOOD FROM MOROCCO

Arabic calligraphy decorates this 14th-century Mamluk mosque lamp.

MOSQUE LAMP

CERAMIC TILE WITH ABSTRACT MOTIFS AND CALLIGRAPHY

CALLIGRAPHY
Stylized Arabic writing is used in place of images to adorn pottery, textiles, and buildings. Scholars developed several scripts for writing the **Qur'an** from the angular Kufic, used until the 11th century, to the more flowing Naskhi in use today.

CERAMICS
Abstract patterns ranging from plant and flower forms to geometrical designs are often used to decorate ceramics. The term "arabesque" derives from the swirling, intricate style of art best exemplified by the blue and white pottery from Iznik in Turkey.

WOOD CARVING
Wood carving has been a popular form of decoration for Islamic buildings and mosques since the Middle Ages. Highly intricate wooden latticework screens, called mashrabiyyas, exist in many mosques.

CARPET DESIGN
Prayer mats are used for Muslim prayers. Such rugs may have elaborate patterned decoration centered on an image of a **mihrab**. Iran, Turkey, and India are renowned for their rug making.

ISLAMIC ARCHITECTURE
The Islamic world combined different architectural styles, as exemplified by many **mosques**. There are two main styles, in which the prayer hall is either roofed by a dome or supported by pillars. Other features of Muslim architecture include pointed arches, inlaid masonry, decorative tiling, and pierced window screens. All these features can be seen at the Taj Mahal (c.1640) in India, the tomb built by the **Moghul** emperor Shah Jahan.

DOMED MOSQUE
In this type of **mosque**, a central dome, sometimes surrounded by semidomes, creates a vast, unbroken central space for the **prayer hall**. Although domed mosques appear throughout the Islamic world, some of the finest were built during the **Ottoman** period in Turkey. The Blue Mosque in Istanbul – named because of the blue tiles that adorn its interior – was designed by the great Ottoman architect Sinan during the 16th century.

BLUE MOSQUE, ISTANBUL

Outer domes support the vast central dome.

CALLIGRAPHY ON TILES

The words of the Basmala, meaning, "In the name of God, the Merciful, the Compassionate."

INTERIOR DECORATION
While many **mosques** have plain interiors, they can be decorated with abstract patterns and quotations from the **Qur'an**. These may appear on carved reliefs as painted decoration, or, most commonly, on ceramic tiles. **Calligraphy** is considered to be one of the most important art forms in the Islamic world, because it can be used to remind believers of the word of God.

PILLARED MOSQUE
This design uses pillars and arches to support the roof. One of the best-known pillared mosques, the huge Great Mosque of Córdoba in Spain, was built in 785.

INTERIOR OF THE GREAT MOSQUE, CÓRDOBA

MODERN MOVEMENTS

TODAY, THERE ARE MUSLIMS LIVING in more than 120 of the world's nations. While many countries, such as Iran, Indonesia, and Pakistan, have majority Muslim populations, there are also substantial minorities in others, such as France, Britain, and Germany. With improvements in communications and the spread of Islam, many Muslims have been influenced by modern Western thought. This in turn has led to a reaction in which some religious leaders have returned to the basics of the faith and their interpretation of the Qur'an. Followers of these movements are often known as fundamentalists. Today, they are very influential in some countries – such as Iran and Afghanistan – although many other Muslims have a more liberal view.

WAHHABIS

The conservative Islamic Wahhabi movement was founded in the 18th century by Ibn 'Abd al-Wahhab. He believed that Muslim society had become corrupted by non-Islamic ideas, and that Muslims should find guidance only in the **Qur'an** and **Hadith**. Wahhabis reject the veneration of saints and decoration of **mosques**. The Wahhabis have become strong throughout Saudi Arabia since Saudi leader Muhammad Ibn Saud joined the movement.

MUHAMMAD
IBN SAUD
(1880–1953)

FUNDAMENTALISM

Islamic fundamentalists believe that Islam is a total system including both public and private matters, where the **Qur'an** and **shari'a** should be applied to every aspect of life from family to politics, economics, and law. Partly, it is as a response to Western and **Islamic Modernism**. Islamic fundamentalism – like all fundamentalism – emphasizes the importance of scripture.

JAMA'AT-I-ISLAMI

This Islamic political movement was founded in India by 'Abdul al-A'la Mawdudi in 1941. Its aim was to establish an Islamic state based on the **Qur'an** in the newly independent Pakistan. Jama'at-i-Islami has been active in attempting to increase the influence of Islam in Pakistan. While the movement has remained influential, they have never succeeded in elections.

NATION OF ISLAM

Established among African-Americans during the 1930s, the Nation of Islam movement has worked to improve the lot of Black Muslims living in a mainly white, Christian society. They promoted the educational, social, and economic rights of its members, as well as the status of the religion. The movement was developed by Elijah Muhammad, but became well known as a result of the work of another leader, Malcolm X. An effective speaker and campaigner for Black Power, Malcolm X drew many followers to the movement before he was killed in 1965. Nation of Islam is not considered mainstream by many Muslims because of its unorthodox beliefs.

MALCOLM X
(1925–1965)

ISLAMIC MODERNISM

During the 19th century, many Muslim thinkers in India and Egypt began to encourage their fellow Muslims to respond to the challenges posed by Western science, technology, and ideas. They sought to reinterpret Islam in the light of the modern world. This led to changes in the interpretation of Muslim law and the abandonment of customs such as slavery and polygamy.

KEMAL ATATÜRK
WITH HIS WIFE IN
WESTERN DRESS

KEMAL ATATÜRK

The nationalist leader Mustapha Kemal Atatürk became the President of Turkey in 1923. He transformed an old-fashioned state into a modern secular republic, and in doing so became the father of modern Turkey. Atatürk reduced the power of Islam, for example, by banning **Sufi orders**. Modern Turkey has remained a Muslim country, but one that is open to non-Islamic influences, from the drinking of alcohol to the use of the Roman alphabet.

MUSLIM BROTHERHOOD

Founded in Egypt in 1928 by a schoolteacher, Hasan al-Banna, the **Sunni** Muslim Brotherhood aimed to reform society and reestablish the basics of the Islamic faith. The Brotherhood preached against Western influence, built schools, and founded hospitals. In Egypt, the movement became a major threat to the military government and was banned in 1954. However, its influence has spread to areas such as Syria, Palestine, and the Sudan.

REZA SHAH

Shah Pahlavi, first ruler of modern Iran,(1925-1941) allowed the secularization of schools and the law – areas previously dominated by Islam. These changes were later overturned in the **Iranian Revolution**.

WOMEN IN ISLAM

In Islam, women are spiritually equal to men. The **Qur'an** accords women great respect, and Muslim women have usually had good educational opportunities. In marriage, women keep their own property and their own names. They also have the right to receive a dowry of money or property from the groom before marriage. However, men and women have different roles in daily life. Women are traditionally seen as homemakers, while men work and are the head of their household.

Chador

FAEZAH HASHEMI, IRANIAN FEMINIST

WOMEN'S DRESS

While Islam requires modest dress for men and women, it does not specifically ask women to cover their bodies. Traditionally, however, they have covered the head, legs, and arms, often with a chador – a garment that envelops the body.

EGYPTIAN GIRL IN HEAD SCARF

WESTERN SCARF

Many Muslim women – especially in liberal countries or urban areas – choose to dress in a Western style, covering their head discreetly with a head scarf.

HIJAB

The hijab, or veil, has traditionally been worn for many centuries by Muslim women. In some areas of the Middle East it will be worn with a yashmak, or face screen.

Yashmak

SAUDI WOMAN

WORLD ISLAM

Muslims inhabit every part of the world, with the greatest numbers living in Asia and Africa. All these countries variously interpret Islamic practice according to local traditions and customs. However, all Muslims are united in keeping the Five Pillars of Islam and in their reverence for the words of the Qur'an.

BENAZIR BHUTTO, FORMER PRIME MINISTER OF PAKISTAN

ISLAMIC NATIONS

Some modern nations owe their very existence to the Islamic faith. Pakistan, for example, grew out of the desire for a Muslim state among Indian Muslims in the early 20th century, and led to the partition of India and the creation of Pakistan in 1947. East Pakistan, formerly the Muslim-dominated state of East Bengal, broke away in 1971 to form the independent nation of Bangladesh.

THE GREAT MOSQUE AT DJENNE, MALI

NEAR AND MIDDLE EAST

The part of the world where Islam first originated is still predominantly Muslim and includes many Islamic states, from Saudi Arabia to Iran. However, tensions in this region remain – both between Muslims and Jews in Israel, and between **Shi'i** Iranians and **Sunni** Iraqis, which led to war between the Iran and Iraq from 1980 to 1988.

SOUTHEAST ASIA

Islam was first brought to Southeast Asia by Arab merchants during the 15th century. Indonesia has the world's largest Muslim population of 170 million. Muslims are also the majority in Brunei and Malaysia, and are minorities in Thailand, Burma, Singapore, and the Philippines. In this region, Islam flourishes in societies that retain strong, local secular traditions.

EUROPE

Many European cities have small Muslim populations, but many more Muslims are concentrated in a few states in south-eastern Europe. Albania, Kosovo, and Bosnia became Muslim regions as a part of the great **Ottoman** empire during the 15th century. They remain true to the faith despite political pressures.

AFRICA

There are more than 300 million Muslims in Africa, most of whom live in the northern part of the continent. The spread of Islam in Africa has been influenced by many different forces, from the **Sufi orders** to the austere Islam of leaders such as Al-Mahdi of Sudan.

CHANGING WOMEN'S ROLES

Many Muslim women are striving for greater gender equality. Islamic feminists argue that conservative male interpretations of Islamic scripture have discriminated against women and that Islam, with its concern for social justice, should offer women equality. They also argue that in the time of the Prophet, women were given greater freedom.

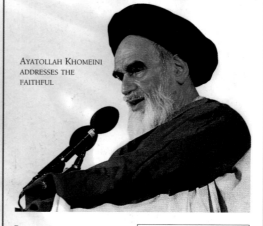

PALESTINIAN POLICEWOMAN

AYATOLLAH KHOMEINI ADDRESSES THE FAITHFUL

IRANIAN REVOLUTION

In the 1960s, Ayatollah Khomeini emerged as the leader of **Shi'i** Muslims who were opposed to the secular state in Iran. When the Shah's government collapsed in 1979, the Ayatollah returned from exile to establish an Islamic republic.

New Religions

Religion deals with the eternal and with everlasting truths, but no religion remains the same. Interpretations of sacred texts alter, and attitudes adapt as society changes. Sometimes there are divisions, and new groups or sects are formed within established faiths; occasionally a new, independent religion appears, with a fresh insight into life.

A religious revival

During the last two hundred years, new religious movements have flourished, and there may be a greater diversity of religious movements now than at any time before. Improved communications, from the railroads of the 19th century to today's mass media, have enabled new ideas to travel quickly across vast distances. As a result, new religions that began in eastern Asia have spread to the US, while new American Christian sects have had an influence in Europe.

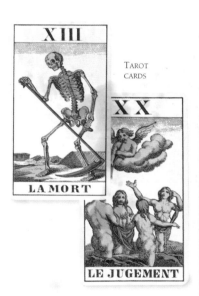

TAROT CARDS

Old beliefs, new interpretations

Few religions are totally new. Usually the prophet or founder of a "new" faith combines a personal vision with elements of a religion that already exists. In recent centuries, Christianity, Buddhism, Hinduism, and Islam, among others, have inspired new faiths and sects. Not all of these will last as long as the established religions that inspired them, but many will endure and grow, adding to the richness of beliefs around the world.

BAHA'ISM

THE BAHA'I FAITH WAS FOUNDED IN THE 1860s by Baha'u'llah, a self-declared prophet from Persia (modern Iran), who announced that he was an incarnation of God. Baha'u'llah brought a new message that was addressed to the whole world. His early followers, however, were mostly unorthodox Muslims or followers of another Persian spiritual leader known as the Bab. As a result, Baha'i doctrine and practice shares many common features with Shi'i Islam in particular. Today, it is a world religion with more than seven million followers, especially in southwestern Asia, Africa, and the American continent. Baha'is believe in one God. They avoid involvement in politics, but work for peace, encourage understanding between nations, and promote "green," or environmentally friendly, policies. Baha'is place a high value on education, family values, and personal conscience.

'ABDU'L-BAHA'

TOMB OF THE BAB, HAIFA, ISRAEL

THE BAB
Sayyid 'Ali Muhammad Shirazi (1819–1850), a merchant from Persia, was a spiritual leader who proclaimed himself to be the first of a new line of prophets, following from **Muhammad**. He called himself the Bab, or "gateway," to God. The Bab's teachings, especially regarding **shari'a** issues, were seen as a threat to the government. He was accused of plotting against the **Shah** of Persia and executed.

BAHA'U'LLAH
Baha'u'llah – meaning "the glory of God" – was born in 1817 in Persia. A leading Babi after the death of the **Bab**, he announced himself as a new messenger of God in the garden of **Ridvan** in 1863. Baha'u'llah was forced to live much of his life in exile, where he wrote many Baha'i texts. Under his leadership, Baha'ism broke from Islam to become a universal religion.

BABIS
The followers of the **Bab** – called Babis – were widespread in 19th-century Persia. They were originally seen as an unorthodox branch of **Shi'i** Islam. In 1848, however, they declared their separation from Islam and began to fight against the Persian authorities. After the death of the Bab, some of the Babis followed his successor, Subh-i Azal, while the rest became followers of **Baha'u'llah**.

'ABDU'L-BAHA'
Baha'u'llah's son, 'Abdu'l-Baha', led the Baha'is from 1892 to 1921. He played a crucial role in the expansion of Baha'ism beyond the Middle East, spreading the faith to North America and Europe. A noted teacher, speaker, and writer, 'Abdu'l-Baha' recorded his thoughts in thousands of letters to his worldwide following. He also campaigned for social reforms.

SHOGHI EFFENDI
'Abdu'l-Baha' chose his grandson, Shoghi Effendi (1897–1957), to lead the Baha'is after him. Shoghi Effendi built and extended shrines, translated many of **Baha'u'llah's** writings into English, improved the religion's organization, and helped Baha'ism grow.

SHOGHI EFFENDI

SCRIPTURE
The writings of **Baha'u'llah** are at the heart of the Baha'i faith. They are considered to be sacred texts inspired by God. Among the best known are ethical and doctrinal works such as *Hidden Words, Seven Valleys,* and *Book of Certitude.* The *Most Holy Book* deals with holy law. The interpretive works by **'Abdu'l-Baha'** are also considered sacred.

BAHA'I SCRIPTURES

PERSECUTION
As a new religion and alternative to Islam, the Baha'is have long suffered persecution in Iran (Persia). In the 1920s and 1940s, Baha'is were oppressed, culminating in the destruction of the Baha'i House in Shiraz in the 1950s. After the **Iranian Revolution** in 1979, the new Islamic government continued the trend, refusing to recognize Baha'ism as a religion. Persecution has led Baha'is to seek homes in many other parts of the world.

UNIVERSAL HOUSE OF JUSTICE

The governing body of the Baha'i faith is called the Universal House of Justice. It has nine members, who are elected every five years and meet at the Baha'i World Center in Israel. First formed in 1963 by the National Assemblies of the Baha'i community, the governing body is based on ideas from the writings of **Baha'u'llah**. Baha'u'llah said that when formed, this governing body would be guided by God, so its judgments are seen as having supreme and unifying authority.

BAHA'I WORLD CENTER

TEACHING BAHA'I BELIEFS IN INDIA

DOCTRINES AND TEACHINGS

The Baha'is believe in one God. God is in himself unknowable; however, God's purpose is revealed through various prophets, or "Manifestations of God," including **Abraham**, the **Buddha**, **Muhammad**, the **Bab**, and **Baha'u'llah**. Baha'is seek to understand the attributes of God seen in his manifestations. The Baha'i faith teaches that all humankind and all faiths are one. Cultural diversity is welcomed and gender equality promoted. Individuals are encouraged to seek religious truth for themselves. Marriages are monogamous and divorce is discouraged.

WORSHIP

Baha'i worship is similar to Islamic practice, the main rituals being prayer (**salat**), fasting (**sawm**), and pilgrimage (**hajj**). Worship is usually informal, and there are no officials (such as priests or imams) or initiation ceremonies. There is also no monastic tradition in Baha'ism. Local elected assemblies organize collective worship and other religious activities. Work, if performed in the right spirit, is also seen as a form of worship.

PRAYER

Prayer is performed daily, usually in the home. There are three different forms of prayer, which can be recited either once at noon, once a day, or three times a day. When Baha'is pray, they face in the direction of the tomb of **Baha'u'llah** in Acre, Israel.

BOY PRAYING

FESTIVALS

Feasts mark several important days in the Baha'i calendar. The calendar was devised by the **Bab**, and consists of 19 months each with 19 days. There is a feast – called a 19-day feast – on the first day of each month. This is the principal regular gathering for Baha'is. Feasts are usually held in three stages: Prayers and readings from the scripture are followed by discussions about community business and finally, a communal meal. There are nine other principal holy days in the year when adults must not work and children do not go to school.

PLACES OF WORSHIP

Baha'is usually worship together in simple halls or in the home of a community member. However, there are five grander custom-designed houses of worship, used mainly as regional centres. Each is round and roofed with a dome, with nine separate entrances.

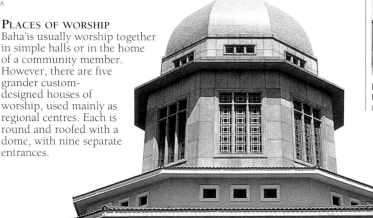

BAHA'I TEMPLE, UGANDA

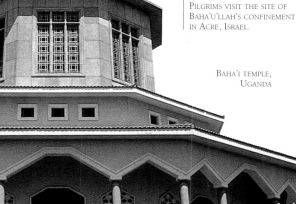

PILGRIMS VISIT THE SITE OF BAHA'U'LLAH'S CONFINEMENT IN ACRE, ISRAEL.

PILGRIMAGES

There are two main traditional pilgrimage sites, the house of the **Bab** in Iran and the house of **Baha'u'llah** in Iraq. In practice, it has not been possible for Baha'is to visit these places. Baha'is have therefore gone on pilgrimages to the tombs of the Bab and Baha'u'llah in Israel. In recent years, the grave of **Shoghi Effendi** in London has also become important.

DEATH

While cremation is accepted, Baha'is usually bury their dead. The grave should be within an hour's journey of the place of death. The body is placed so that the feet point toward the tomb of **Baha'u'llah**. Funeral ceremonies are the only times at which Baha'i prayers are recited in unison.

BAHA'I FAST

A consequence of its Islamic origins, Baha'ism prescribes an annual fast for the last month of the Baha'i year, which precedes the celebration of **Naw-Ruz**. The sick, and pregnant women, are not required to fast.

NAW-RUZ

The Baha'i new year, or Naw-Ruz, follows the annual fasting period. It is celebrated at the beginning of the month of Baha' (March 21 in the Western calendar), usually with prayers, dancing, and musical performances.

RIDVAN

The festival of Ridvan commemorates **Baha'u'llah's** announcement that he was the one whose coming had been prophesied by the **Bab**. This happened in the Garden of Ridvan ("paradise"), Baghdad.

MARTYRDOM OF BAB

The **Bab** was executed by the Persian authorities on July 9, 1850. This event marked the beginning of further persecution of Babis and Baha'is in Persia. Baha'is remember this time with special prayers.

BIRTH OF BAHA'U'LLAH

On November 12, 1817, **Baha'u'llah** was born. Baha'is celebrate his birthday on the same date every year. This is the most joyful of feasts – huge parties are held, and cards and gifts are exchanged.

OTHER RELIGIOUS MOVEMENTS

MANY NEW RELIGIOUS MOVEMENTS HAVE DEVELOPED over the last 300 years. Some have their origins in an existing faith but offer new interpretations of old beliefs. These movements – which include many Christian groups and faiths based on Eastern religions – vary greatly in size and distribution, from small groups like the Amish to worldwide organizations such as Krishna Consciousness. While some of these are controversial sects, other groups, like the Quakers, have won universal respect and recognition.

MILLENARIANISM

Some Christians believe that Jesus will return to earth to reign for 1,000 years. This belief, known as millenarianism, is founded on a prophecy in the *Book of Revelation*. Millenarian beliefs have a long history and are current among Christian groups such as the Plymouth Brethren, Anabaptists, and **Adventists**. Other groups, including some Buddhist sects in Thailand, hold similar beliefs about local holy men.

CHRISTIAN MOVEMENTS

Since the Reformation, and especially in the last 200 years, a number of new Christian groups have formed. Some of these are founded on literal or "fundamentalist" interpretations of the Bible, while others – such as the Mormons and Jehovah's Witnesses – were inspired by visions or revelations. They illustrate the great variety of Christian belief, especially in the United States.

QUAKERS

The Society of Friends, or Quakers, were founded in 17th-century England by George Fox. They do not have **priests** or **sacraments** – Christ is thought to be present when any group of Friends meets. The Quakers have a notable humanitarian record, campaigning for peace, women's suffrage, and prison reform.

A 17TH-CENTURY ENGRAVING OF A QUAKER MEETING

MENNONITES

Named after their first leader, the 16th-century Dutch reformer Menno Simons, most of today's one million Mennonites live in the US. Their faith is based closely on the **New Testament**. They are pacifists, and refuse to hold civil office. Communities of Amish people in the US come from the same tradition as the Mennonites.

AMISH WOMAN

JEHOVAH'S WITNESSES

Since the late 19th century, Jehovah's Witnesses have held the **millenarian** belief that Christ will return to earth and save the chosen few. Jehovah's Witnesses base their faith on a literal interpretation of the **Bible**. They refuse to do anything – such as take oaths or receive blood transfusions – that they believe to be against God's law.

SEVENTH DAY ADVENTISTS

This group began in the 19th century under the leadership of William Miller, who predicted that the world would end in 1843–1844. When this did not happen, members of the church concluded this was because too many people were not keeping the Sabbath.

MORMONS

The beliefs of the Church of Jesus Christ of Latter-day Saints, or Mormons, are base on the *Book of Mormon*, which its founder, Joseph Smith, claimed was inspired by God in 1822. Mormons assert that theirs is only true Christian church, and hold the **milllenarian** belief that Christ will establish a new Jerusalem in the US. Mormon doctrine differs from that of orthodox Christianity, and includes the belief that humans are literally God's children. The Mormon church has its center in Salt Lake City, Utah.

MORMON MONUMENT

WAY INTERNATIONAL

Developed in the 1950s and 1960s, Way International describes itself as a biblical research and teaching ministry. It rejects the **Old Testament** and conventional views of the **Trinity**.

JESUS MOVEMENT

This term covers a number of **evangelical** groups that arose during the 1960s. These groups stress a literal interpretation of the **Bible** and the compassionate teachings of **Jesus**.

NEW AGE MOVEMENT

The term "new age" is used for various movements loosely connected with religion. Disciplines as diverse as the green movement, alternative medicine, astrology, and **occultism**, as well as many Eastern religions, are included. These people believe that the world is entering a "new age" of spiritual evolution, emphasize healing (of body, mind, and spirit), and seek to develop a personal experience of the sacred to realize their inner potential.

STONE CIRCLES CREATED IN AN "ENERGY" SPOT IN ARIZONA

TRANSCENDENTAL MEDITATION CAN INCLUDE "YOGIC FLYING," WHERE PEOPLE LEAP IN THE AIR AFTER MEDITATING.

TRANSCENDENTAL MEDITATION

This technique for achieving deep relaxation and pure consciousness was developed by Maharishi Mahesh Yogi and became well known during the 1960s. It is claimed to help people move beyond everyday consciousness to a more creative state.

SCIENTOLOGY

Developed during the 1950s, this movement blends ideas derived from Christianity with those of its founder, the American writer L. Ron Hubbard. Hubbard taught that people develop guilt feelings that build up over many reincarnations. Through a system of counseling, Scientology aims to remove this guilt by releasing the "Thetan" (spirit), thereby making a person more fulfilled. Scientology has courted controversy because of its recruitment methods, but still has a widespread following.

KRISHNA CONSCIOUSNESS

The International Society of Krishna Consciousness was founded in 1965 by Bhaktivedanta Swami Prabhupada. It is widely known as the Hare Krishna movement, after the **mantra** that followers repeat. One of the most popular new religions with Eastern roots, Krishna Consciousness seeks to raise awareness of God through the ancient **Vedic** scriptures of India. Members of the movement are recognizable by their saffron-colored robes. They are vegetarians, avoid intoxicating drink and drugs, and do not permit gambling.

FOLLOWERS OF BHAGWAN SHREE RAJNEESH

RAJNEESHISM

Followers of Bhagwan Shree Rajneesh use **yoga** and meditation to resolve problems and to become aware of their inner energy or "life force." Members wear orange clothing and take new names.

SOKA GAKKAI

Founded on the ideas of **Nichiren** Buddhism, this Japanese sect differs from mainstream Buddhism in seeking to help people achieve happiness and fulfillment. It teaches that everyone can reach Buddhahood, through reciting specific **mantras**.

HAILE SELASSIE

RASTAFARIANISM

Originating in Jamaica during the 1930s, Rastafarianism holds that black people are the true Jews of the **Old Testament**. Leaders such as Marcus Garvey campaigned for black people to return to Africa, which was promoted as a promised land for disaffected black youth. In 1930, Prince Ras Tafari was crowned emperor of Ethiopia with the title Haile Selassie. He was thought to be the new **messiah**. Rastafarians have developed their own lifestyle and appearance, including the wearing of dreadlocks and the smoking of marijuana as an aid to achieving mystical experiences.

CAO DAI PRIESTS

CAO DAI

Founded in southern Vietnam during the 1920s, Cao Dai combines the teachings of many different faiths, including Christianity, Buddhism, Taoism, and Confucianism. Followers seek spiritual growth and salvation through strict ascetic practices.

MEMBER OF AN OCCULT SECT

OCCULTISM

Occult ("hidden") beliefs draw on a host of traditions – the ancient religions of the Celts and Egyptians, astrology, magic, and modern versions of **witchcraft**. Some elements of **new age movements** use occult practices. Such beliefs often attract disapproval from orthodox religions.

THE MOONIES

Members of the Unification Church are known as Moonies, after their Korean founder, Sun Myung Moon. Moon's teachings are summed up in his book, *Divine Principle*. One key idea is that redemption can be achieved through marriage, the children of which will be born in a state of innocence. The church performs mass weddings.

General Terms

ABSTINENCE The act of going without something, or refraining from doing something. In religious terms, this usually involves doing without some luxury, contact with the opposite sex, or avoiding alcohol, meat, or rich foods.

AFTERLIFE The continuation of life after physical death, for example in heaven, hell, or the underworld.

AGNOSTICISM The belief that it is impossible to be absolutely certain whether or not God exists.

ALMS Charitable gifts given to the poor or needy.

ALTAR Table or platformlike structure, used for the performance of certain rituals, such as offerings to the gods, sacrifices, or the Christian Mass or Communion.

ANGEL An attendant, or a messenger, from God.

ANTISEMITISM Discrimination against, or persecution of, the Jews.

APOSTASY The abandonment of one's religious faith.

ASCETIC A person who gives up comforts and pleasures for religious reasons.

ATHEISM Disbelief in the existence of a God or gods.

BEATIFICATION In the Roman Catholic Church, a formal announcement that a dead person has shown outstanding holiness in his or her life, and is therefore blessed; a first step toward becoming a saint.

BLASPHEME To speak in a way that shows disrespect for God.

BLESSING A call for a divine favor or protection; a short prayer before a meal.

CANON The accepted body of sacred writings belonging to a particular faith.

CANONIZE To declare that a person has been made a saint, or to place a piece of writing or text within a canon.

CELIBATE To refrain from sexual relations, or to remain unmarried, especially for religious reasons.

CHANTING Method of singing in which several consecutive syllables or words are assigned to the same note.

CHARITY The act of helping those in need, specifically by giving alms; love for one's fellow human beings.

CIRCUMCISION The surgical removal of a male's foreskin, performed for religious reasons in faiths such as Judaism and Islam.

CONFLICT Struggle or disagreement between opposing forces, ideas, or faiths.

CONVERSION Adopting, or encouraging others to adopt, a new belief or religion.

COSMOLOGY View or theory of the structure of the universe (cosmos). This may include beliefs about the existence and position of heaven, hell, or other supernatural realms.

COVENANT An agreement or promise; specifically, God's promise to the Israelites in the Hebrew Bible, and their agreement to worship him alone.

CREATION The making of the universe, and the accounts of this that occur in most religions.

CULT Beliefs or rituals linked to a particular group of gods or spirits, often forming part of a wider religion; a body of believers.

DEMON An evil spirit or devil.

DIVINITY The state of being godly or divine, or the academic study of theology.

DOCTRINE The official teachings and beliefs of a particular faith.

DOGMA A set of beliefs or teachings, or a doctrine, laid down as being authoritative by a church.

DRUID Priests in ancient Celtic religion; a member of a modern faith based on the revival of the old Celtic religion.

ECSTASY A state of heightened joy or overwhelming feeling.

ECUMENISM Promotion of unity among the world's Christian churches.

ENLIGHTENMENT In Buddhism, the realization of the ultimate truth experienced by the Buddha; release from the cycle of death and rebirth that may be experienced by the Buddha's followers.

EXORCISM The removal of an evil spirit or ghost by means of a religious ceremony.

FAITH A strong belief that is not based on proof, or belief in a doctrine or teachings of a religion.

FANATICISM Extreme devotion to a religion or god.

FESTIVAL A time of celebration, ceremonies, and feasting to mark an event of particular significance to a religion

FUNDAMENTALISM Strict adherence to the basic beliefs of a religious faith; the belief that sacred texts are inspired by God, and are therefore literally true

GOD The supreme force and creator of the universe, or controller of some aspect of the universe. A supernatural being, usually seen as responsible for a certain area of human affairs

HEAVEN The dwelling place of God or the gods; often the place where the souls of the faithful live after death; frequently seen as a place in the sky or on a mountain, or as a state of bliss

HELL The place where devils, evil spirits, and the souls of those who have not gone to heaven are thought to live; often seen as a place underground or as a state in which God is absent.

HERESY Beliefs or opinions opposed to the orthodox views held by a religion.

ICON Image or statue; especially, in Orthodox Christianity, an image of a sacred being itself regarded as holy.

IDOL An object, such as a statue, worshiped as a god. A term once used in Christianity and Judaism to refer to the religious images of other faiths.

IMMORTAL Having everlasting life.

INCARNATION The human or bodily form taken by a god.

LAYPERSON An individual who is not a member of the clergy or priesthood.

MARTYR A person who dies for his or her religious beliefs.

MEDITATION Mental exercise that may be performed by contemplation (for example, thinking about a god, or a sacred object), or by emptying the mind to help the person achieve a higher mental or spiritual state.

MESSIAH An awaited savior, liberator, or ruler sent by God. In Judaism, this is seen as being the long-awaited King of the Jews, who will be sent by God. In Christianity, Jesus is described as the Messiah.

MONASTERY Religious community, usually either all male or all female, living under vows such as poverty, chastity, and obedience.

MONK A male member of a monastery.

MONOTHEISM Belief in one God as creator and ruler of the universe.

MYSTIC A person who achieves or seeks direct personal experience of the divine, often by means of meditation or an ascetic lifestyle.

NIRVANA In Buddhism, a state involving liberation from desire and release from the cycle of death and rebirth.

NUN A female member of a monastery.

ORACLE In ancient Greek religion, a shrine at which it was possible to consult the gods and ask them questions; prophecies received from the gods at such a shrine.

ORDINATION In Christianity, the ritual by which people are admitted to the priesthood. In Buddhism, admission to the sangha.

PANTHEISM The belief that the entire cosmos (universe) is god, and that god is in everything.

PANTHEON A collection of deities worshiped by a particular people or group.

PARABLE A story told to teach a moral or spiritual lesson.

PATRIARCH In Judaism, one of the founders of the Jewish people, especially Abraham, Isaac, and Jacob. In Orthodox Christianity, a bishop of one of the principal cathedral towns. In Roman Catholicism, a bishop holding a rank immediately below that of the Pope.

PENANCE A confession of sin, or a punishment imposed to bring about atonement for a sin.

PERSECUTION Ill-treatment, harassment, or discrimination of a group of people for religious or other reasons.

PILGRIMAGE A sacred journey undertaken to a holy place, as part of the obligations of a religion, as a penance, or as an act of worship and celebration.

POLYTHEISM Belief in many gods.

PRAYER An act of communication with God or gods, usually as an act of worship, or to make a request.

PRIEST An official or minister of a religion authorized to lead worship and other rituals and therefore to act as mediator between the worshipers and the deity.

PROPHET A person who speaks, writes, or teaches under divine inspiration. In Islam, "the Prophet" refers to Muhammad

REINCARNATION Rebirth; the idea, especially prevalent in Indian religions, that after death, a person's soul is reborn into another body.

RELICS The physical remains of a saint or other holy person, preserved and venerated.

RITE A religious ceremony, part of a ceremony, or a collection of such ceremonies.

RITUAL A formal religious ceremony involving specific words, movements, and actions.

SACRED A term describing anything dedicated to a deity or its worship, or made holy by its links with a deity.

SACRIFICE Something killed or offered as part of the worship of a deity.

SAINT A person whose holiness has brought him or her devotion by other believers and special recognition by the church.

SANCTUARY A place regarded as especially sacred. In Christianity, the easternmost part of a church, where the high altar is placed.

SCRIPTURES Sacred writings that are especially important to a religious community, or believed to be divinely inspired.

SECT A specific group within a religion, whose members have beliefs slightly different from orthodox or established doctrines.

SECULARIZATION The tendency for society to be unconcerned with religious values.

SHRINE A place of worship, or similar structure, that has an association with a specific deity or holy person; a box containing relics of a holy person.

SIN To act against a divine law; in Christianity, rebellion against God, a state which began with Adam's expulsion from Eden.

SOUL The spiritual part of a person, said in many religions to survive after the death of the physical body.

SPIRITUALITY A person's concern with religion and other matters of the spirit.

SYNCRETISM The combining of more than one religious tradition to make a new movement, thereby preserving some aspects of the original faiths.

TEMPLE A building used for a place of worship, especially in Hinduism, Sikhism, and Buddhism.

VOCATION The feeling that a person is called by a deity to a career, especially as a priest or member of a religious order.

VOWS Solemn promises made to a deity or saint, for example, those made at baptism, marriage, or before a person becomes a monk or nun.

WORSHIP An act of devotion or homage to a deity usually performed by means of rituals that may incorporate prayer, offerings, singing, or chanting.

INDEX

FURTHER READING

Alexander, Pat and Dowley, Tim, (editors), *A Lion Handbook: The History of Christianity*, Lion Publishing, 1998

Brown, Alan, Rankin, John, and Wood, Angela, *Religions*, Longman, 1988

Ching, J., *Chinese Religions*, 1993

Dundas, P, *The Jains*, 1992

Esposito, J., *Islam: The Straight Path*, Oxford University Press, 1991

Gordon, Matthew S., *Islam, Facts on File*, 1991

Greuber, H.A, *The Myths of Greece and Rome*, 1990

Hamilton, Malcolm, *Sociology and the World's Religions*, Routledge, 1999

Hartz, Paula R., *Taoism, Facts on File*, 1993

Hoobler, Thomas and Dorothy, *Confucianism, Facts on File*, 1993

Kinsley, David, *Hinduism*, Princeton University Press, 1982

Knott, Kim, *Hinduism: A Very Short Introduction*, Oxford University Press, 1998

de Lange, Nicholas, *Judaism*, Oxford University Press, 1986

Momen, M., *A Short Introduction to the Baha'i Faith*, One World, 1998

Oldfield, K., *Jainism, The Path of Purity and Peace*, Derby CEM, 1989

Owen-Cole, W. and Sambhi, P.S., *The Sikhs: Their Religious Beliefs and Practices*, 1995

Rahula, Ralpola, *What the Buddha Taught*, Gordon Frazer, 1978

Reader, I., *Religion in Contemporary Japan*, 1991

Shah, N., *Jainism, The World of Conquerors, Volumes 1 and 2*, Brighton, Sussex Academic Press, 1998

Skilton, Andrew, *A Concise History of Buddhism*, Windhorse, 1997

Smart, Ninian, *The World's Religions*, Cambridge University Press, 1991

Smith, Huston, *The World's Religions*, Harper Collins, 1991

Wilson, Bryan and Cresswell, Jamie (editors), *New Religious Movements*, Routledge, 1999

A Lion Handbook: *The World's Religions*, 1992

ACKNOWLEDGMENTS

The author would like to thank:
The team at PAGEOne for their painstaking work in planning, designing and editing this book; David Hill and the other consultants at the Roehampton Institute for their guidance and checking; and Zoe Brooks for all her support.

PAGEOne would like to thank:
Sarah Watson for her initial editorial work; Connie Robinson and the consultants in the United States for their patient checking; the consultants at the Roehampton Institute for their expert guidance; and our author Phil Wilkinson for his patience and hard work.

Photography by:
Peter Anderson, Geoff Dann, Andreas von Einsiedel, Lynton Gardiner, Christi Graham, Peter Hayman, Alan Hills, Ellen Howden, Colin Keates, Nick Nicholls, James Stevenson

Illustrations by:
Anthony Duke; map artworks by John Woodcock